THE
BAKERY
RESTAURANT
COOKBOOK

THE
BAKERY
RESTAURANT
COOKBOOK

 LOUIS
SZATHMÁRY

CBI

CBI Publishing Company, Inc.
286 Congress Street
Boston, Mass. 02210

Library of Congress Cataloging in Publication Data

Szathmáry, Louis.
  The bakery restaurant cookbook.

  Includes index.
  1. Cookery.   I. Title.
TX715.S9865   641.5   80-36675
ISBN 0-8436-2195-8

Production Editor: Deborah Flynn
Text Designer: DeNee Reiton
Compositor: Williams Graphic Service, Inc.
Illustrator: Mimi Turner

Printed in the United States of America

Printing (*last digit*): 9 8 7 6 5 4

TO SADA
with love

CONTENTS

4. POULTRY 111

5. FISH & SHELLFISH 127

6. VEGETABLES 149

7. CHEESE, PASTA, & RICE   167

8. SALADS   187

9. SAUCES 199

10. BREADS 227

11. DESSERTS 237

APPENDIXES 299

INDEX 313

FOREWORD

by Anthony Athanas

Writing the foreword to THE BAKERY RESTAURANT COOK-BOOK, authored by my long-time friend Chef Louis of Chicago's famous restaurant *The Bakery,* is an honor that I deeply appreciate.

This book firmly secures Chef Louis' position as a leader in the world of culinary art. Its recipes welcome you to a voluminous series of delightful adventures in fine cosmopolitan cooking—with practical instructions that readily explain how to prepare them.

Many of the Chef's Secrets outlined with the recipes are of great value to the professional in this field and, of course, all the more so, to those who are looking for elegant at-home cooking.

Anthony Athanas
ANTHONY'S PIER 4
Boston, Massachusetts

INTRODUCTION

It is always a great thrill to send a new book on its way, but sending a cookbook out into the kitchens of homes all over this continent-sized country of ours involves a great responsibility—and a bit of anguish.

As long as you, dear reader, do no more than read this book, we have what you might call a literary relationship. But as soon as you start to cook from it, and you put on the table a dish you have prepared from this book, then our relationship changes to one of partnership. You become an essential part of my success or failure. Those who dine at your table, tasting your interpretation of my recipe, will know me as a chef through you. The relationship will be somewhat like that between a composer, the performing artist, and the audience. It all sounds a bit complicated, but it's true.

This, my fourth cookbook in the past ten years, was written to meet the demands of all those friends who have dined at our little *Bakery Restaurant* during almost two decades and who want the recipes for what they have enjoyed. Some of these recipes have already appeared in my *Chef's Secret Cook Book* and in my *Chef's New Secret Cookbook*—but not all. It's happened frequently that people buy one book because they want the recipe for a particular dish from *The Bakery,* and when they look for recipes for other dishes from the same meal, they find that they are in the other volume.

Now here in THE BAKERY RESTAURANT COOKBOOK are recipes for all the food we serve, in one book, in a form that is easy to follow. Every recipe in this book was cooked from beginning to end at least six times before it was ready to be sent to the publisher. Let me explain why.

In my collection of more than 18,000 cookbooks, some of the very best books are useless for the homemaker because they are extremely difficult to follow, or because the author has assumed that the degree of knowledge and experience needed to prepare a recipe is shared by everyone who opens the book. Years ago I found that this just isn't so. Because I know something, I cannot assume that everyone else does. So when I prepare the recipes for my cookbooks, I try to assume nothing. After I cook a dish and my assistant carefully writes down the ingredients and the method, I cook it again according to what she has written. Then she cooks the dish and we compare notes. We then give the recipe to someone on our staff who repeats the preparation while we watch and make notes. After this fourth cooking and rewriting of the recipe, we give it to a friend or acquaintance whom we know is not necessarily an accomplished cook. We ask this person to cook the dish at home and let us check the results. Again, a correction or two. Finally the recipe is ready for the editor—but when the final text is prepared, the dish is cooked once more by a non-professional. Cumbersome, slow, and difficult? Perhaps, but the success of my previous books proves that the process is worthwhile and that the reader is the great beneficiary.

Professional chefs, restaurant cooks, food managers, cooking school demonstrators, and other culinarians who use this book will find no difficulty adapting it for their own purposes. While the recipes are not intended for large gatherings, the matter of adding to the recipes in proportion will not be a problem for the skilled chef.

This book is an important part of my life, just as *The Bakery* is. Writing this introduction, after the whole book is finished, I feel I am about to share a part of my life with those of you who will read it and cook from it. I wish I could also share with you the feeling of owning and operating a restaurant, the joy of preparing the kind of food that allows me to walk proudly among my tables during dinner, greeting my guests and thanking them for their patronage—and sometimes getting into the most fascinating conversations with them. To be the owner and chef of a restaurant is a little bit like being on stage all the time.

I hope you will share some of this excitement that goes with the creation of good food for people who you love. I am sure that when your guests praise your Clear Tomato Soup, or your Deep-fried Ham Crepes with Mushroom Sauce, or your Brownie Bottom Bourbon Pie, you will accept their applause graciously and drop a hint that, "This is the way it's done at *The Bakery Restaurant!*"

THE
BAKERY
RESTAURANT
COOKBOOK

1
APPETIZERS

How many times have you heard, or seen on menus: "Not to fill you up, but to whet your appetite." And how many times did you get filled up eating appetizers?

Not only does legend have it, but historical proof can testify that it all started with those wealthy Russians who moved to western Europe, especially to Paris, but also to Rome, Madrid, and London. In Paris, at the demands of Russian emigres, appetizers became a meal in themselves, an institution. A whole trade developed just to cater to that first course.

It's not that people hadn't eaten artichokes, baked green peppers, galantines, potted duck, or Quiche Lorraine. They certainly had, but not as appetizers. It was the Russian nobleman, who felt homesick in Paris and longed to recreate homeland customs, who wanted twenty-two kinds of herring dishes with his vodka, just a bite of each, but so mouthwatering, fragrant, and delicate, or robust and strong, and so different from one another!

The French chef, who was king in his domain, refused to fix this type of food on demand. So, the hotel owner, who sorely wanted the business of those Russians, brought it in from the outside and marked on the menu hors d'oeuvres ("brought in from the outside"). They are still called hors d'oeuvres today, even though they have not been brought in from the outside for a long, long time (although lately some restaurants seem to be "ordering out" again).

At *The Bakery Restaurant* we don't smoke salmon and we don't salt sturgeon roe to make caviar. But we do make pate maison fresh every day according to the recipe you will find in this section, and for eighteen years this has almost always been the only appetizer we offer. On some festive occasions we offer a second appetizer with it or as an alternative selection. And sometimes we prepare special appetizers for cherished guests who we know love something that we prepare very much our way.

As a rule we offer bite-sized hors d'oeuvres in our waiting room on Saturday evenings. Most of the other appetizers are served by special request, ordered by guests, or served at parties, banquets, or special occasion dinners when a cocktail hour or champagne reception precedes the dinner.

For the homemaker, my only advice is to avoid last-minute preparation and not to serve too many appetizers, especially heavy ones, before an elaborate meal.

ARTICHOKES
Serves 8

8 medium to large fresh artichokes
2 tablespoons salt
water to cover
2 lemons, halved
4 tablespoons red wine vinegar

½ teaspoon salt
¼ teaspoon dry mustard
8 tablespoons olive oil
freshly ground black pepper
½ tablespoon minced shallots

Break off the stem of each artichoke by bending it until it snaps. Pull off the small leaves at the base. Trim the base with a knife to flatten it so it will stand. Slice about 1 inch off the top of each artichoke and trim off the sharp points of the leaves with a kitchen scissors.

Bring to a rapid boil enough salted water to completely cover the artichokes. Plunge the trimmed artichokes into the water. Squeeze the juice of the lemon halves into the boiling water, then drop in the pieces of lemon. Cook, uncovered, at a slow boil for 30 or 40 minutes, depending on size. Remove the artichokes from the water and turn upside down. Run cold water over them until they are cooled. Drain. Cover with ice cubes. When the ice has melted, drain the water.

With your fingers, pull out the purple center and reserve. Scrape the choke (hairy center) with a spoon until all the fibers are removed from the bottom. Discard fibers. Replace the purple center by inverting it into the hollow cavity.

In a small bowl, blend the wine vinegar, salt, and dry mustard. Slowly add the oil, stirring constantly. Stir in the pepper and shallots.

Place the artichokes in a deep-sided serving dish and pour the dressing over them. Marinate in the refrigerator until ready to serve.

 CHEF'S SECRET   While cooking the artichokes, weigh them down with a plate so they are fully immersed. The artichokes are cooked when a fork will easily pierce the bottom and when the long lower leaves can be pulled out with little effort.

If you wish to serve artichokes the Italian, rather than the French way, select artichokes with a stem at least 3 to 3½ inches. Cut the top of the stem on the diagonal. Do not cut off the stems, just peel them. Discard the purple middle and put the artichokes upside down in the marinade. Serve with the stems standing up on an angle. If you wish, add 1 or 2 chopped cloves of garlic to the marinade. Remove and discard the garlic before serving.

ARTICHOKE LEAVES WITH RED CAVIAR
20 to 30 hors d'oeuvres

2 large globe artichokes	salt and freshly ground pepper
2 tablespoons salt	to taste
½ lemon	2 cups sour cream
1 quart water	1 jar red caviar

Wash and trim the artichokes. Put them in a saucepan and cover with cold water. Add salt and the juice of the ½ lemon (keep the squeezed lemon for later use). Cook the artichokes until they are tender; 30 to 45 minutes, depending on their age and size.

Discard the cooking liquid and rinse the artichokes two or three times in cold water, or until they are cool enough to handle.

Cut the squeezed ½ lemon into three or four pieces and put these into 1 quart of cold water. Beginning at the outside, remove the artichoke leaves one by one and drop them into the cold water. (See illustration.) When you get to the "choker" discard it and remove the fine hair from the inside of the bottom, or heart, of the artichoke. Save the hearts of the artichokes. Lay the leaves on absorbent paper and let them dry.

Chop the artichoke hearts very fine and season with a little salt and freshly ground pepper. Fold them into the sour cream.

Divide this mixture by the number of leaves you have and put dabs on the stem end of the leaves. Top each dab with a few dots of red caviar. Arrange the leaves on a serving platter and serve them chilled.

CHEF'S SECRET   Before boiling the artichokes, cut off the sharp tips of the outside leaves with a sharp scissors and discard them. This will save a lot of trouble in preparing them.

Empty the red caviar into a sieve and dip the sieve in and out of lukewarm water until the water has washed off all the gluey substance covering the caviar. Cold water will not do this, and hot water turns the liquid around the fish eggs into shreds like egg whites, which are ugly and hard to remove. So be sure that the water is lukewarm.

The artichoke hearts will turn blue after they are chopped and will make a nice color combination with the white sour cream and red caviar.

BAKED GREEN PEPPERS
Serves 8

8 cubinella peppers, or 16 sweet banana peppers or light green peppers (Sorry, for this dish bell peppers won't do.)
1 cup oil

¼ cup vinegar mixed with ¾ cup water
1 tablespoon sugar
1 teaspoon salt
1 clove garlic

Preheat oven to 400°. Wash and wipe dry the peppers. Dip one or two fingers in the oil and gently coat the peppers. Place them in a large pan or on a cookie sheet and bake. Turn every 2 or 3 minutes until the peppers turn limp and brownish with pale bubbles. It will take 20 to 30 minutes for light green peppers or cubinellas, somewhat less with sweet banana peppers.

Remove from the oven, cool, peel, and slit up the side about a third of the way from the stem toward the tip. Carefully remove the seeds and the core, leaving on the stem and leaving the peppers whole.

In a small saucepan boil the vinegar and water, sugar, and salt. When the mixture comes to a rapid boil, pour it gently over the peppers.

In a small bowl, mash the garlic with a few drops of the oil, then slowly add the remaining oil and stir until all the garlic is mashed. Place the peppers in a shallow dish, strain the garlic-oil through a fine sieve over them, and let them cool to room temperature. Cover the dish and chill the peppers overnight. Serve one pepper to a person with a thick slice of crusty bread. These peppers are excellent with cocktails or with Slivovitz or Barack on the rocks.

CHEF'S SECRET   In Transylvania this is a favorite first course for festive dinners. It is usually made on the top of a wood stove, and the smoke coming through the cracks at the top of the range gives a special delicate flavor to the peppers. In the summer, if you roast the peppers in an aluminum foil pan on an outdoor grill before the fire dies, you will have the same smoky tang.

If you wish, add a few drops of Tabasco to the vinegar, or slice in a hot pepper or just a part of it. Don't ever use hot peppers for the recipe proper, because you won't be able to control the "heat."

This dish may be kept 2 or 3 weeks in the refrigerator as long as it is covered with oil.

Sweet, ripe red peppers are also delicious prepared this way.

BEEF TARTAR
Serves 8

8 ounces lean round or sirloin, free of fat
8 ounces lean tenderloin tip
1 egg, coddled
2 tablespoons finely minced onion
1 tablespoon rinsed capers, chopped
1 teaspoon Chef's Salt (see appendix)

generous grinding of fresh black pepper
½ ounce Kirschwasser, vodka, or bourbon
German type rye bread, pumpernickel, or cocktail rye, thinly sliced
unsalted butter
chopped onion or cleaned scallions

To make Beef Tartar is almost a religious ceremony. The classic way is to have the beef ground twice. Pile it up in the middle of a large platter, put an indentation in the top, and surround it with small containers (saucers from demitasse cups, for example, or other tiny dishes).

On one container place the coddled egg (to coddle an egg, you slowly submerge it in boiling water for about 30 seconds, then remove and cool by placing it for a minute or so in cold water). On another small plate place the finely minced onion. (No, you cannot chop the onion the day before or even a few hours ahead; it must be chopped just before serving.) On other plates put the capers, the Chef's Salt, and finally the freshly ground pepper. Have ready in a small glass the spirits of your choice.

Break the egg into the indentation in the middle of the meat, sprinkle on the Chef's Salt and the pepper, and gently stir the spices into the egg with a fork. Add the onion, the capers, and the spirits. Work through the mixture with two forks until all the ingredients are well blended and the Beef Tartar is in the form of a ball in the middle of the large plate.

Remove the small plates used for the ingredients and surround the beef with the bread. Place the fresh butter next to it as well as generous amounts of chopped onion or cleaned scallions.

 CHEF'S SECRET   If possible, grind the beef for this dish yourself, first cutting both meats into 2-inch-long and ½-inch-thick strips. Use a grinding plate with the largest holes, but grind it two or three times.

If tenderloin is not available, use all round or sirloin, but be sure it has no fat, not even marbling (that's the fatty tissue inside of the muscle that runs crisscross in the meat). As pleasant as the raw meat tastes if it is lean, that's how unpleasant it can taste if it is fat. The raw fat sticks to the roof of your mouth and coats it.

EGGPLANT APPETIZER
Serves 8

2 eggplants, 1½
    to 2 pounds total weight
1 teaspoon Chef's Salt
    (see appendix)
½ teaspoon freshly ground
    black pepper
¼ cup oil
1 teaspoon finely minced
    garlic, or ¼ teaspoon
    garlic salt
3 to 4 tablespoons vinegar
    (to taste)

½ teaspoon sugar
½ cup finely minced
    onion, or ½ cup minus 2
    tablespoons grated onion
Greek-style black olives, bell
    peppers, and cherry
    tomatoes, for decoration
Greek bread and unsalted butter,
    or toasted, buttered bread
    triangles

Preheat oven to 350°. Split eggplants in half lengthwise, sprinkle the cut surfaces with Chef's Salt and black pepper, and rub with some of the oil. Bake 75 to 90 minutes. Remove and let cool on the baking sheet until cool enough to handle.

Peel the purple skin and discard it. With a stainless steel knife, first cube the eggplant into 1-inch cubes on a chopping board. Then chop fine with the stainless steel knife. Place in the bowl of an electric mixer, add remaining oil, garlic or garlic salt, vinegar, sugar, and minced onion. Beat first on slow, then on medium speed until smooth. Let the mixture stand overnight in the refrigerator. Cover the bowl securely with plastic wrap.

Before serving, stir gently with a spoon or spatula, taste, and add a little more vinegar and salt if it is too bland or a small pinch of sugar if it is too tart. Transfer to a glass or silver bowl. Grind fresh black pepper on top and decorate with slices or rings of green pepper, black olives, and cherry tomatoes.

Serve with flat bread (Greek, Lebanese, Turkish, etc.) and unsalted butter, or with lightly toasted, buttered bread triangles.

 CHEF'S SECRET   Use about a teaspoon of oil to rub on each half of the eggplant to protect the surface from evaporation. Eggplant contains a large amount of water, and if you don't protect the cut surface with oil, as soon as the temperature of the eggplant reaches the boiling point for water it will start to evaporate. The evaporation point of oil is much higher, so even a very thin layer of oil will protect the eggplant and will keep the moisture inside, making it smoother and tastier.

Eggplant turns black and blue from a carbon steel knife. That's why we emphasize the stainless steel knife. In the Mediterranean, where this dish is a favorite, wooden knives are used to chop the eggplant.

EGGS A LA RUSSE
Serves 8

2 cups boiled potatoes cut
    into ½-inch or smaller cubes
1 cup cooked carrots cut
    into ½-inch or smaller cubes
1 cup cooked green peas
    (fresh, canned, or frozen)
10 hard-boiled medium eggs
salt and pepper to taste

juice of 1 large lemon
2 cups mayonnaise (see
    appendix)
6 tablespoons sour cream
2 tablespoons butter
1 tablespoon anchovy paste
fresh parsley for decoration

Combine the potatoes, carrots, green peas, and chopped whites of two eggs. (Save the two yolks for later use.) Sprinkle with salt and pepper to taste and add the lemon juice.

Gently fold together the mayonnaise and sour cream, then fold one-third of this mixture into the vegetables. Let stand at room temperature.

Split the remaining eggs lengthwise and remove the yolks. Press the yolks through a sieve. Add soft butter, anchovy paste, and 2 tablespoons of the mayonnaise-sour cream mixture. Beat with an electric beater until fluffy. Using a pastry bag with a star tube, pipe the egg yolk mixture into the sixteen egg halves. You will have about 1 teaspoon for each. Arrange the egg halves and the vegetable-mayonnaise mixture on a serving platter.

Gently mash the two remaining egg yolks through a coarse sieve with a blunt knife or small spatula. Sprinkle some over the top of each egg half.

Decorate the platter with green parsley. Serve chilled, with the remaining mayonnaise mixture in a side dish.

 CHEF'S SECRET   The eggs must be absolutely fresh, and the best method of cooking eggs seems to be the old-fashioned one. Place room-temperature eggs in a stainless steel or enamel (not aluminum) pot. Put in enough cold water so that the water level is about 1 inch above the top of the eggs. Add 1 teaspoon salt and bring the eggs to a slow boil. Let them boil for 10 minutes, then discard the boiling water and rinse the eggs under running cold water until they are cool. Cover the pot after discarding the cold water. Hold the lid on with both hands and gently shake the pot to break the eggshells. Now fill the pot again with cold water and peel the eggs under water. This is the fastest, cleanest way.

To split the eggs in half, use the thinnest knife you have, or cut them with a thread.

EGGS FROU-FROU
Serves 6

¾ cup frozen peas
¾ cup frozen asparagus tips
¾ cup frozen whole string
   beans, diced
1 envelope unflavored gelatin
2 cups canned chicken broth,
   undiluted, at room temperature
yellow food coloring
6 poached eggs

6 slices Canadian bacon
   (optional)
1½ cups mayonnaise
   (see appendix), cold
3 hard-boiled egg yolks,
   pressed through a sieve
salt and pepper to taste
black olives or truffles
parsley sprigs for decoration

Cook the three vegetables, separately, according to package directions. Drain and refrigerate.

Make an aspic by mixing the gelatin with the chicken broth. Bring the mixture to a boil, stir, then remove from the heat. Color a pale yellow with the food coloring.

Place ice cubes in a bowl and add cold water. Place the pan of aspic in the ice water and stir until it begins to gel but remains a liquid. Remove from the water.

Place the cold poached eggs on the slices of Canadian bacon, then place each on a cake rack and set the rack in a shallow pan.

Measure out ½ cup aspic and stir it into 1 cup of the cold mayonnaise. Add the sieved egg yolks and salt and pepper to taste. Spoon this mixture over the eggs until they are completely coated. Keep the coating even and do not let little holes or bubbles form. Coat the eggs 2 or 3 times, refrigerating after each coat. Collect the drips from the pan and reheat over low heat, then cool by stirring over the ice water, to use again.

Place a slice of black olive or truffle on each egg. Glaze each egg with the aspic until a thin, shiny coat adheres to it. Refrigerate.

Add the remaining mayonnaise, including the unused portion used to coat the eggs, to the cold vegetables. Stir in ¼ cup of the syrupy aspic. Place in a decorative mold and refrigerate.

Pour the remaining aspic in a small flat pan and place in the refrigerator to gel.

When the vegetables with the mayonnaise have gelled, unmold onto a serving platter. Dice the aspic into small cubes, using a sharp knife. Surround the vegetable mold with the cubed aspic. Place the eggs on the diced aspic. Decorate with parsley sprigs.

CHEF'S SECRET   This is a beautiful dish and well worth the little work involved.

You may add 1 teaspoon sugar and a little salt to the liquid in which you cook the aspic. It will make the aspic's flavor much more pungent.

The French word "aspic" scares many homemakers. They think it is something very complicated, although it is nothing but a gelatin dish without sugar or fruit flavor.

If you like, remove 3 to 4 tablespoons of the broth and substitute a small amount of white wine or lemon juice for added flavor.

It is best to stir the gelling aspic with your finger. The aspic is ready to work with when you feel the temperature become cooler than your body temperature, or when your fingers feel sticky if you press them together and then pull them apart. It is advisable to have some hot water on hand in case you overchill the aspic in the ice water bath. You can immediately place the pan into the hot water, remelt, then repeat.

To poach the eggs, place 1 quart of water and ¼ cup white vinegar in a saucepan and bring to a simmering point over low heat. Break each egg into a cup. Slip the egg from the cup onto the surface of the water. Wait until it sets before you add another. Poach each egg until the white is solidly white and no longer transparent; the yolk must remain runny. It will take about 2½ to 3 minutes. Keep the water simmering. Remove each egg with a slotted spoon. Drain on paper toweling.

After poaching the eggs, for a "professional" look, trim the edges of the white with a kitchen scissors. If you are using the Canadian bacon, trim it together with the egg.

ELEGANT CANAPES
Serves 12

½ loaf fine, firm-textured
    white bread, such as
    Pepperidge Farm, sliced
½ loaf sliced dark bread
8 ounces butter, whipped
    with electric beater
prepared mustard (optional)
anchovy paste (optional)
1 envelope unflavored gelatin
¼ cup cold water
⅔ cup boiling water
1 teaspoon vinegar or
    2 teaspoons lemon juice

salt to taste
light sprinkling of sugar
4 ounces thinly sliced ham
1 can small sardines
fresh parsley sprigs for decoration
4 ounces braunschweiger
1 teaspoon prepared mustard
⅛ teaspoon cinnamon
4 hard-boiled eggs
4 ounces sliced Muenster
    cheese
sliced carrot for decoration
black olives for decoration

Trim the bread and spread all the slices evenly with whipped butter. If you wish, divide the butter into two parts and mix some prepared mustard or anchovy paste into one of the parts, according to your taste. Cover buttered bread slices with a damp towel.

Soften the gelatin in the cold water. To the boiling water, add vinegar or lemon juice, salt to taste, and a light sprinkling of sugar. Dissolve the softened gelatin in this mixture, then let it stand at room temperature until it becomes syrupy.

Lay out the ham slices side by side, brush them one at a time with the gelatin mixture, and roll them up jelly-roll fashion. When all are rolled, place them in the refrigerator with the lapped edges on the bottom.

Carefully remove the sardines from the container. Set them side by side on waxed paper or aluminum foil and gently brush them two or three times with thin coats of gelatin mixture. Before the gelatin sets, put a single parsley leaf at the top of the sardine where the head is cut off. Refrigerate.

In a small bowl or coffee cup, mash the braunschweiger with a fork and add the mustard and cinnamon. Now add 1 tablespoon of gelatin mixture. Stir vigorously. Using a pastry bag with a star tube, press ½- to ¾-inch stars onto aluminum foil. Refrigerate.

Slice the eggs with an egg slicer. Carefully lay out on aluminum foil the pretty middle slices with the yolk and white intact. Brush gently with gelatin mixture. Refrigerate.

Separate the yolk from the white of the remaining pieces of egg. Chop each very fine.

After you have come this far, remove from the refrigerator all the ingredients you have been chilling. Uncover the buttered bread slices and place the Muenster cheese, trimmed, on some of the slices of dark bread.

From this point on, everything is up to your taste and imagination. The bread slices may be divided into thirds or halves, depending on the size of canapes desired. The ham rolls may be sliced into 1-inch or smaller pieces. The number of possible combinations is larger than you think. You may combine sardines with eggs, ham, cheese, and so on. Decorate the canapes so that the colors of the decorations contrast or match. For example, blanch the carrot slices and, with a small cookie cutter or aspic cutter, cut them into stars or flowers and place these on the egg yolk. Make small discs from the blanched carrot slices, egg white, and black olives, by using the cap from a fountain or ball-point pen, and apply them as decorations.

CHEF'S SECRET   Your work will be much easier if you cut out of strong cardboard a perfect square that fits onto a slice of bread, so you can trim off all the crust by cutting along the cardboard. The slices will then be exactly alike.

If you prepare everything ahead of time and assemble the canapes at the last minute they will be prettier and look much more professional than if you do all the work haphazardly just before serving.

Some people make the mistake of brushing the whole canape with gelatin. It is not necessary for the bread to be soaked with gelatin; if it is, the canapes will taste rubbery.

GALANTINE
Serves 20

1 frying chicken,
    3½ to 4 pounds
2 tablespoons salt
3 envelopes unflavored
    gelatin
1 cup coarsely chopped onion
1 tablespoon coarsely chopped
    garlic
10 to 12 black peppercorns,
    crushed
10 to 12 white peppercorns,
    crushed
1 cup lukewarm water
1 pound ham steak
1 pound lean ground veal
1 pound ground pork shoulder
1 pound ground smoked
    picnic ham

1 cup finely chopped onion
    sauteed in 3 tablespoons
    shortening
3 eggs
salt and finely ground black
    pepper to taste
½ cup shelled and cleaned
    pistachio nuts
2 carrots (about 4 ounces)
1 parsley root or parsnip
2 ribs celery
1 small onion, unpeeled
2 cloves garlic, unpeeled
1 teaspoon whole black
    peppercorns
1 whole clove
10½ ounce can chicken broth,
    undiluted

With a sharp knife, cut through the back of the fryer from the neck down to the tail, or ask the butcher to do so. Remove the bones from the opened fryer, leaving only the wing bones. Make a surface with a double layer of aluminum foil at least 18 inches wide and 2½ feet long. Lay the boned fryer, skin side down, on the aluminum foil. Sprinkle the flesh with salt and 1 envelope of dry gelatin.

In a small glass or plastic container, mix the coarsely chopped raw onion, chopped garlic, crushed peppercorns, and about ½ to 1 tablespoon salt (depending on how salty the smoked picnic ham is; it varies from brand to brand) and pour the cup of lukewarm water over this mixture. Let stand at room temperature for at least 1 hour, stirring occasionally.

Cut the ham steak into equal-sized cubes and then run the trimmings, ends, and fat parts through a blender. Add the blended ham pieces to the other ground meats. Add the sauteed onion, including the shortening, and the raw eggs. Add ½ to 1 tablespoon salt and 1 envelope of dry gelatin. Through a strainer, add to the meat mixture the lukewarm water in which the onions, garlic, and crushed peppers have soaked. Work the mixture together using both hands. Taste and add salt and black pepper if needed.

Puree the meat mixture, bit by bit, in an electric blender. Do not overfill the blender because this will only delay the work. Collect the blended meat in a large mixing bowl. Spread half the meat mixture over the inside of the fryer. Gently press the ham cubes into the center of the meat mixture inside the fryer, distributing them evenly. Do the same with the pistachio nuts. Spread the second half of the meat mixture on top.

Bring the two sides of the skin of the chicken together in the middle. With a strong white thread, sew it from the tail to the neck, overlapping the skin. The fryer will then look as it did before being split and boned, the filling being completely enclosed. Sprinkle the third envelope of gelatin evenly over the skin and fold the aluminum foil over the fryer from all sides, securing it on the back.

Preheat oven to 400°

Coarsely chop the carrots, parsley root, and celery. Slice the small onion and garlic cloves, leaving the skin on. Place the vegetables in a large roasting pan along with the whole black peppercorns and the clove. Lay the foil-wrapped fryer, breast down, on top of the vegetables. Put the bones, gizzard, heart, and liver into the pan. Add the chicken broth and enough water to cover the fowl completely. Cover and bake 2½ hours.

Remove the galantine from the oven and place it on a tray. Strain the liquid and reserve it, discarding the bones and vegetables. Prepare a surface of double aluminum foil the same size as before. Carefully open the foil covering the fryer and let the liquid run from it onto a tray.

Let the galantine cool at room temperature just enough so that you can handle it comfortably. Place it on the fresh double aluminum foil and mold the foil firmly around it. Place the galantine back in the roasting pan and pour the strained cooking liquid over it. Let this cool to room temperature and then refrigerate overnight.

Remove the galantine from the foil and, with a very sharp knife, slice it into ¼-inch slices. Arrange the slices on a large serving platter. Chop up some of the natural gelatin (or aspic) that the liquid has turned into while being refrigerated. Decorate the platter with chopped aspic and serve with Oxford Sauce (see page 204) or Sauce Louis (see page 206).

CHEF'S SECRET   The big secret here is the use of three envelopes of gelatin. The first, sprinkled on the surface of the fryer's flesh, is activated as the chicken cooks and causes the ground meat to adhere to the flesh. The second package, mixed into the meat, gives a firmness to the filling and makes it possible to slice it nicely. The third, sprinkled on the skin, catches and absorbs the juices oozing from the chicken during cooking. Eventually, a great part of this gelatin is dissolved into the cooking liquid and turns into a lovely aspic.

JAMBON PERSILLE
Serves 6

1½ envelopes unflavored
    gelatin
2½ cups beef or chicken stock
½ cup Madeira wine

1 cup freshly chopped parsley
3 cups cooked smoked ham,
    cut in ½-inch cubes

Dissolve the gelatin in ½ cup of warmed stock. Add this to the remaining stock and the wine. Heat the mixture slowly almost to boiling. Remove from heat and cool to room temperature. Add chopped parsley.

Place ham in a 2-quart mold or bowl; pour the gelatin mixture over it. All pieces of ham should be covered. Cover the surface with plastic wrap and chill several hours or overnight.

Run hot tap water around the sides and bottom of the mold and turn it over onto a platter. Cut in ¼-inch slices with a very sharp knife. Serve cold.

CHEF'S SECRET   The cooling time of the aspic can be reduced by placing it in a light aluminum pan or in a bowl in an ice water bath and stirring it constantly. Chill the mold or bowl in the refrigerator, then pour in some room-temperature gelatin and move it quickly in all directions before adding the ham mixture. This will coat the bottom and walls of the mold with gelatin.

Before running the hot water around the outside of the mold, remove the plastic wrap and ease away the edges of the gelatin with a warm thin knife. Cover the mold again with the plastic wrap; then run the hot water around the mold. Remove wrap and place the platter over the mold; then invert onto the serving platter. Turn the two together so that the platter is on the bottom and the mold is on the platter. If the aspic still will not move, dip a towel in very hot water, wring it dry, and place it over the mold. By leaving the plastic wrap on when running the hot water around the outside of the mold, you will prevent any water from getting into the mold.

STOCK YARD INN MARINATED BEEF
Serves 8

1 pound boiled, broiled,
     or roasted beef, cut into
     julienne strips
1 large onion, cut the same
     as the beef
juice of 1 lemon
salt to taste
1½ tablespoons prepared
     mustard
2 tablespoons sugar

¼ teaspoon freshly ground
     black pepper
2 teaspoons (or more)
     curry powder
2 cups sour cream
½ cup white vinegar
salt to taste
lettuce leaves for decoration
sprinkling of paprika
sprinkling of chopped parsley for
     decoration

In a large bowl, mix together the beef and onion. Sprinkle with lemon juice and salt. Let stand at room temperature for 20 minutes.

In another bowl, mix the mustard, sugar, pepper, and curry powder until it forms a paste. Gently fold the sour cream and vinegar into the spice mixture. Fold this sauce into the beef and onions. Let it marinate in the refrigerator for at least 4 hours.

Taste for salt; add more if necessary. Serve on beds of lettuce, sprinkle with paprika and parsley.

CHEF'S SECRET   This recipe originated in Chicago at the famous Stock Yard Inn. Its secret is really in the quality of the meat used. Do not use any fat; use only the lean or marbled beef. If you feel the quality of the meat you have is not the best, cut the julienne strips very small—no bigger than matchsticks—and avoid cutting along the grain.

Marinating the beef and onions in the lemon juice and salt gives a very good taste to the beef, which will not be overpowered by the lemon. If you were to do the marinating with vinegar, the taste would be impaired.

You can make the same dish with yogurt instead of sour cream, but while folding in the vinegar be very careful not to destroy the texture of the yogurt.

PATE DU CAMPAGNE

For liquid spice mixture:

½ cup finely minced onion
   (1 medium onion)
1½ teaspoons minced garlic
   (2 to 3 large cloves)
1 tablespoon salt
1 teaspoon freshly ground
   black pepper

1 teaspoon crushed juniper
   berries
1 teaspoon Parisian Spice
   (see appendix)
4 to 5 bay leaves, crushed fine

Combine all ingredients with 1 cup hot water and let stand at room temperature for several hours or overnight. Stir occasionally.

For pate:

½ pound loin pork chops
   (about 2 chops with bone in)
2 cups water
2 pounds ground pork (ground
   on the largest holes of your
   meat grinder)

2 eggs
spice mixture (recipe above)
1 envelope unflavored gelatin
4 tablespoons cognac or brandy
3 or 4 tablespoons lard
3 bay leaves

Cut the pork chops into ½-inch cubes, including fat parts. Discard bones.
   Bring the water to a vigorous boil. Add the cubed pork, boil again, and stir. When the water boils vigorously, remove from heat, strain, and rinse meat with cold water until completely cooled. Drain well and let stand at room temperature.

Place the ground pork in a 2-quart bowl and add the eggs. Stir the spice mixture and drain 1 cup of liquid through a fine sieve into a bowl. Spoon remaining spice mixture into a wet kitchen towel, form it into a ball, and squeeze remaining juices into the bowl. Discard the spices and fibers. With your hands, work the liquid and eggs into the ground pork. Add gelatin dissolved in cognac. Mix well, then distribute the cubed pork evenly throughout the ground meat.

Preheat the oven to 350°. Brush a loaf pan (9 × 5 × 3½) or similar ovenproof dish with shortening, preferably a tablespoon or so of lard. Transfer the meat mixture to the pan, pat it in, and strike the bottom of the pan on the table to remove air pockets. Place 3 whole bay leaves on top of the pate, then baste with 2 to 3 tablespoons melted lard.

Set the pan in a larger pan of hot water and bake about 2 hours, or until the internal temperature of pate registers 160 to 165 degrees. Remove from the oven, cool briefly, and pour off liquid and fat from the pan.

For aspic:

1 envelope unflavored gelatin	few drops of lemon juice
½ cup cold water	(optional)
10¾ ounce can chicken broth,	2 to 3 tablespoons cognac or
undiluted	brandy
pinch of salt	

Dissolve the gelatin in cold water until it swells. Bring the chicken broth to a boil, stir in gelatin mixture, and add salt and lemon juice if you wish. Remove from heat, cool a few minutes, add cognac, and pour over pate in pan.

Cut a piece of cardboard somewhat smaller than the bottom of pan. Wrap the cardboard in foil, place it on top of the pate, press down gently, and weight it to keep the pate submerged in aspic. Chill overnight.

To serve, briefly dip the pan in warm water or surround it with a hot wet kitchen towel, turn it out on a serving platter, and slice. Garnish with tiny sour gherkins or baby dill pickles or assorted olives. If you wish, serve with Oxford Sauce (see page 204).

CHEF'S SECRET   If you wish to keep the color of this country pate vivid pink, add a pinch of saltpeter to it. Be careful—don't overdo it. The suggested ratio of saltpeter for large amounts is around 2 ounces for 25 to 30 pounds total weight of ingredients, so for a small amount a little pinch really will do the trick.

The word "campagne," spelled without an "h," means *country,* and it is used in this case to indicate a rougher textured and less elaborate spicing than a haute cuisine pate. It is another pate from the Champagne region that is called Pate du Champagne, with a "Ch."

If you once master the liquid spice mix, you will never put dry spices into any kind of pate, especially if you plan to prepare it several days ahead and keep it refrigerated, or for some weeks ahead for the freezer. Ground spices keep "growing" in the freezer, and the pate that tastes perfect when it is made, can taste really overspiced after being kept in the freezer for a few weeks. Incidentally, if you plan to prepare some of these pates for the freezer, I suggest you freeze them raw, then defrost them for baking, rather than freezing them after they are baked.

PATE DE FOIE EN BRIOCHE
Serves 8

1 long round or triangular can of pate imported from France, or a good quality smoked liver sausage (braunschweiger)
1 loaf fine, firm-textured, sliced white bread

1 cup canned chicken broth, undiluted
1 envelope unflavored gelatin
3 tablespoons warm water
1 tablespoon lemon juice
½ teaspoon sugar

Slice the pate to the same thickness as the bread slices. Trying this recipe many times we have found that breads such as Pepperidge Farm, Brown-berry Ovens, a good milkbread, or plain coffeebread from your local baker are the best choices.

With a cookie cutter the size of the pate (or with the empty pate can), carefully cut a hole in the middle of each slice of bread (see illustration). Lay the sliced bread on cookie sheets or aluminum foil and ease a slice of the pate or liverwurst into the hole you have cut. Refrigerate 3 to 4 hours.

Bring the chicken broth to a boil. Dissolve the gelatin in the warm water, add to the chicken broth, and stir until it comes to a boil. Remove from heat. Add lemon juice and sugar. Keep the mixture in the saucepan in which it was cooked and place the pan in ice water. Gently stir until the mixture becomes syrupy.

With a pastry brush, carefully coat the pate in each bread slice with gelatin so that some of the gelatin trickles down the edges of the pate and adheres to the bread. Chill the slices again in the refrigerator, then remove them from the cookie sheet or aluminum foil with the help of a spatula. Reassemble the loaf and serve.

CHEF'S SECRET   The whole recipe itself is a secret—not mine but that of a clever young man who is chef at the world-famous Pyramide Restaurant in Vienne, near Lyons, France. The original owner, Chef Point, who died some years ago, took to the grave the secret of a brioche filled with goose liver or just plain liver pate. He had taught his staff how to prepare all the dishes that made the Pyramide famous—except this one. Because the guests demanded it, the new young chef, who did not know how to make the dish, invented a perfect substitute.

How do I know this? More than twenty years ago, on my honeymoon, I went with my wife to the Pyramide. We had the pate-filled brioche as a first course. It was excellent. On close examination I discovered a visible aspic ring around the pate in the brioche slices. I thought this to be a brilliant idea, so I wandered into the kitchen by a deliberate "mistake" on my way from the men's washroom to the dining room. Sure enough, a young kitchen worker was standing by a table, cutting out round discs from the middle of brioche slices and inserting the canned pate into the holes.

I thought (and think today) that the inventor of this method was a genius. People don't eat methods, they eat results. A Francophile couple, the Hesses, in their book *The Taste of America* crucified me for my discovery, but when on a CBS radio show I offered a free first-class trip to France and $10,000 for their favorite charity if the Hesses would take me to the Pyramide at *my* expense and the Pyramide would produce the dish in any other way than described above, the Hesses declined my offer. Madame Point never sued me. I still think Pate de Foie en Brioche is a great culinary invention.

PATE EN CROUTE
Serves 12

2 eggs
½ cup milk
3 to 4 tablespoons good
    brandy or cognac
1 tablespoon salt
¼ teaspoon garlic salt
½ teaspoon freshly ground
    black pepper
1 teaspoon Parisian Spice
    (see appendix)
½ pound ground beef
½ pound ground veal
½ pound ground lean pork
1 cup finely minced onion

3 tablespoons shortening,
    preferably lard or bacon
    drippings
4-ounce slab of bacon cut
    into ½-ounce cubes, or
    4 ounces ham from a thick
    slice cut into ½-ounce cubes
3 envelopes unflavored gelatin
2 whole bay leaves
1 package pie dough mix
1 egg yolk, beaten with a
    sprinkling of sugar and
    1 tablespoon warm water

Preheat oven to 400°.

Beat eggs, milk, and brandy with a fork, adding salt, garlic salt, pepper, and Parisian Spice. Let mixture stand at room temperature.

In a large mixing bowl, combine ground meats.

Saute the onion in the shortening.

If you use bacon, blanch the bacon cubes. Drop them into a small pan filled with cold water and bring to a boil. After 3 minutes, pour off the boiling water and cool the blanched bacon cubes immediately under cold running water.

Add the cooled sauteed onions to ground meats. Spreading your hands over the surface, make holes in the meat mixture by pressing all of your fingers into the meat. Beat the egg-spice mixture again with a fork and pour it evenly over the meat so that it runs into the holes. Knead the meat as you would a bread dough until you feel that the mixture is very even. Then sprinkle 2 envelopes of the dry gelatin over the meat and work the gelatin into the mixture vigorously and thoroughly.

Brush a loaf pan with shortening and dust it with flour. Press half the meat mixture into the loaf pan. Distribute the bacon or ham cubes evenly over the middle of the loaf. Place the remaining meat mixture on top, pressing it down gently. Set the loaf pan in a larger pan containing 2 inches of boiling water. Place bay leaves on top of the meat and bake about 2 hours.

Remove the loaf from the oven and pour off excess fat. Let it stand 10 to 15 minutes, then remove it from the pan, turning it upside down on a rack or tray. If you use a tray, put two or three layers of paper towel under the loaf so that it will absorb the fat oozing out. Let the loaf cool overnight in the refrigerator.

Meanwhile, prepare the pie dough according to package directions. Chill it for several hours or overnight in the refrigerator.

Next day, preheat the oven to 400°. Roll out the pie dough on a slightly floured surface into an oblong shape about ¼ inch thick and large enough to enclose the pate loaf completely. Rinse the pate loaf under hot water for about 1 minute, then sprinkle the third envelope of gelatin evenly over its surface. Place the rinsed, sprinkled loaf on one end of the pie dough. Fold the rest of the dough over, seal the edges, and trim the excess.

Loosen the bottom with a spatula and lift the pastry-enclosed loaf onto a lightly greased cookie sheet. With a round cookie cutter or a plastic pill container, cut two or three holes ½ inch in diameter in the top of the pate. Mix the three cut-out pieces with the other dough trimmings and make simple decorations for the top. Brush the entire surface of the dough with the beaten egg yolk, then bake the loaf for 10 minutes. Remove from the oven, brush the top a second time with the egg yolk mixture, and bake another 15 to 20 minutes. Remove from oven, cool to room temperature, and refrigerate overnight. Serve with Oxford Sauce (see page 204).

CHEF'S SECRET   It used to be a great art to make a pate en croute; the best chefs worked many years to learn the secret of making it without having the dough burn while the meat cooked. Problems included the undercrust and side crusts being half raw, gummy, and loaded with aspic. With my method, any cook can make a perfect pate without special skill or training. Of course, you can use the same method with any other type of pate mixture.

The loaf must be rinsed with hot water before the gelatin is sprinkled over it. Any ground meat oozes fat when it is cooked, and in this case the fat is undesirable; gelatin will not adhere to fat.

PATE MAISON
2 pounds

1 cup finely minced onion
8 tablespoons lard, or chicken or duck fat
8 ounces chicken or duck livers
2 cups (approximately ¾ pounds) cooked meat
6 tablespoons unsalted butter at room temperature

4 tablespoons lard, or chicken or duck fat (no other shortening will do)
2 to 3 tablespoons brandy or cognac
2 teaspoons Parisian Spice (see appendix)

Saute onion in 8 tablespoons lard until very limp, but do not brown. Add livers, raise heat, and cook until the last trace of pink disappears from the thickest part of the thickest liver. Cool.

Grind the cooked meat three times, using the medium holes in the meat grinder. (Any roasted, broiled, boiled, baked, braised, or fried meat is good, especially chicken with skin, duck, turkey, pork, veal, or beef, but do not use lamb or mutton.)

Grind the livers and onion three times.

Beat the butter and 4 tablespoons lard together in an electric mixer; then, continuing to beat at low speed, blend in the ground liver and meat. Beat until fluffy, then add brandy or cognac and Parisian Spice. Correct seasoning if necessary by adding more salt or Parisian Spice. Chill and serve with pickles and crusty bread.

 CHEF'S SECRET   In this recipe the method is really more important than the ingredients. As you can see, you have a choice of lard, chicken fat ("schmaltz"), or duck fat. You have an option of chicken livers or duck livers or a mixture of the two. As for the cooked meat, it can be several different kinds. But please do not try to change the procedure. Do not combine the steps.

When you mix the butter with the lard or chicken or duck fat, note that I say, "No other shortening will do." Most any natural shortening will give the pate its necessary fluffiness. Oil will not work, and man-made shortening will give the pate a taste of tallow.

The amount of cognac or brandy may be adjusted somewhat, but if you do not wish to use any alcohol in the pate, you must add 2 to 3 tablespoons of some other liquid such as chicken broth or beef broth for proper consistency.

Liver gets tough if salted before cooking so don't add salt to it in this or any other recipe. If salt is needed, salt it after cooking.

POTTED DUCK
About 24 slices

1 duckling, 4½ to 5 pounds
1 tablespoon plus 2 teaspoons
    Chef's Salt (see appendix)
8 ounces lean veal
8 ounces pork shoulder
1 small carrot
1 small onion (the size of
    an egg)

2 large cloves garlic
8 to 10 whole peppercorns,
    bruised
1 bay leaf
½ teaspoon dried tarragon
1 quart water
4 envelopes unflavored gelatin
1 ounce cognac or brandy

Preheat oven to 400°.

If you use a frozen duck, remove it from the freezer, submerge it in a large container of tap water for 2 hours, wipe it dry, and refrigerate it for at least 12 but not more than 24 hours. To defrost it to refrigerated temperature without first submerging it in tap water, allow at least 24 to 36 hours in the refrigerator.

Remove the bag containing the neck, liver, heart, and gizzard from the cavity. (Be careful, sometimes the liver alone is in an extra small bag inside the neck cavity.) Wipe the duck dry with a towel and rub the surface inside and outside with 1 tablespoon Chef's Salt. Let it stand.

Rub the surface of the veal with 1 teaspoon Chef's Salt and rub the pork with the other teaspoon of Chef's Salt.

Slice the carrot and onion and quarter the cloves of garlic. Distribute on the bottom of a roasting pan with a tight-fitting lid. Add the peppercorns, bay leaf, and tarragon. Pour into the pan 1 quart water. Place the duck, breast side down, and the pork and veal in the roasting pan. Sprinkle 2 envelopes of gelatin on the back of the duck and 1 envelope each on top of the veal and pork. Cover and place in the oven. Be sure the lid fits tightly; if not, cover the roasting pan with aluminum foil and then put the lid on.

Roast 1 hour. Remove the roasting pan from the oven and lift the lid carefully so that the hot steam will escape toward the rear of the pan without burning your arm or face. Turn the duck breast side up, and turn the pork and veal. Tilt the roasting pan and baste all the meats. Replace cover and roast for another 30 minutes.

Remove the duck, pork, and veal and place on a wire rack or a baking sheet. Strain the pan juices through a sieve into a tall, narrow container. Let it stand an hour at room temperature, then place it in the freezer so the duck fat that comes to the top will be easy to remove. Discard the carrots and peppercorns; retain the bay leaf, onion, and garlic.

When the duck is cool enough to handle, gently remove the skin from the whole duck. Then remove the two breast halves by hand.

Press the breasts flat between the bottoms of two plates and refrigerate. Debone the duck and discard bones. Cut up the gizzard and liver and debone the neck. Check the veal and pork and discard any bones. Grind duck skin, meat, veal, and pork with the onions and garlic twice through the disc with the largest holes. Do not grind the bay leaf; you will use it later.

Prepare an oval-shaped tureen (about 2 quarts) or a round glass casserole by gently brushing the inside with some of the duck fat you removed from the top of the cooking liquid.

Press half the ground meat firmly and evenly into the bottom of the dish. Cut the breasts lengthwise into finger-thick strips, and lay the strips parallel so that they are evenly distributed over the ground meat.

Press the second half of the ground meat over the strips of breast.

Warm the pan juices to lukewarm; add cognac or brandy and slowly, spoon by spoon, ladle it over the ground meat, waiting until the liquid seeps down.

Place the casserole on the bottom shelf of the freezer. Leave the duck fat at room temperature, and after one hour remove the duck from the freezer and spoon enough duck fat on top to cover. Place the bay leaf in the middle and chill for at least 24 hours before serving.

 CHEF'S SECRET   Perhaps this recipe sounds very different from other recipes for similar dishes. Please trust me.

Sprinkling the gelatin onto the meat before baking is not customary, but through hundreds of experiments I have convinced myself that even if the method is unconventional, the results are classic.

If you dissolve the gelatin in cold water and then mix it with the hot roasting liquid before pouring it over the duck, you will always have a gelatin taste whatever you do. Sprinkling the gelatin will give you the same taste cooks obtained a hundred years ago by extracting the gelatin from calves' feet and pork rinds. The pork and veal will absorb most of the juices oozing out of the duck, and the only flavor will be that of the duck.

When you cut the potted duck, always cut with a warm, very sharp knife, and wipe the knife with a wet cloth after each slice. If your guests are not embarrassed to admit that they don't know how to eat and enjoy it, don't hesitate to explain that the best way to eat potted duck is to spread a little of the top layer of duck fat on a bit of warm toast and then cut a small piece from the potted duck and put it into your mouth with the toast. Chew it slowly, and swallow it only after it is well warmed by chewing. Many people hurry through a meal, swallowing everything before the taste, aroma, and fragrance of the food have a chance to develop from the warmth of the tongue and palate.

Serve very tart, crisp gherkins or pickled onions with the potted duck. A well-chilled white wine goes well with it, too.

RADISHES, BUTTER, AND BLACK BREAD
Serves 8

1 bunch (about 2 dozen) small,
    firm, fresh red radishes
    with the leaves on
16 butter balls or butter patties,
    unsalted, ½ ounce each

8 slices dark German-type
    rye bread, unsliced
coarse salt (kosher salt)

Place the radishes with their leaves on in a colander and wash under cold running water, then shake or swing them dry in an absorbent kitchen towel.

Remove the leaves one by one, but leave the middle core with one or two tiny tender leaves.

Remove all but ¼ inch of the root of each radish. Cut through this ¼ inch of root two-thirds into the radish toward the remaining leaves. Turn the radish and make a second cut, forming an "X." Be sure not to cut into the remaining leaf core (see illustration).

Place the prepared radishes in a plastic container, fill the container with enough water to cover the radishes, add four to six ice cubes, and refrigerate for 1 hour or more.

Keep the butter and bread at room temperature.

To serve, arrange the radishes on a small silver or glass plate. Serve butter and bread to accompany.

CHEF'S SECRET   Americans traveling in Europe wonder why this appetizer always appears on menus in the finest restaurants and is ordered by so many gourmets. The chef's secret lies not in the ingredients or in the preparation, but in explaining to your guests how to eat it. Four ordinary ingredients— bread, butter, salt, and radishes—become a gourmet delight if they are eaten properly. First, spread some unsalted fresh butter on a bite-sized piece of fresh bread that has a crust. The bread and butter should be chewed slowly. The radish must be sprinkled with a little coarse salt, then placed in the mouth

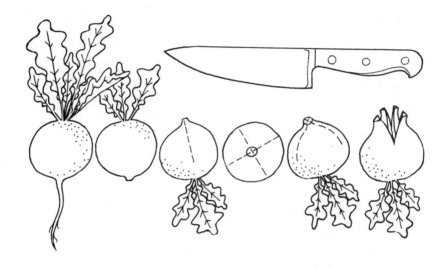

along with the green leaf core, and should be chewed slowly and thoroughly together with the bread and butter. If you start with the radish, the effect will be entirely different, as it will be if you proceed by swallowing a bite of bread before taking a bite of radish.

If your guests do not already know how to eat this appetizer, and you cannot tactfully explain the method to them, spread the butter on the bread and slice the radishes wafer thin, omitting the crosscuts. Place the tiny green leaves and stems on the buttered bread and cover them with a ½-inch-thick layer of sliced radishes. Serve, offering the salt at the last minute.

SHRIMP TREE

styrofoam cone
thin florist wire, or toothpicks
    and florists' green
    selfsticking tape

fresh parsley
boiled and deveined shrimp
cherry tomatoes

Buy a styrofoam cone in a dime store, department store, florist shop, or florist supply store. Secure the styrofoam cone in any container you choose.

With a sharp tool such as an ice pick, make holes in the cone. Insert in each hole a very small bunch of parsley sprigs tied together firmly with green florist wire, or insert a toothpick into the small bunch of parsley and tape it firmly to the toothpick.

Sprinkle the whole tree liberally with ice-cold water and cover it with a water-dipped kitchen towel. The tree will stay surprisingly fresh this way in the refrigerator for as long as three or four days.

Using toothpicks, place on the tree boiled shrimp, cherry tomatoes, and other bite-sized tidbits.

CHEF'S SECRET   To make the little bunches of parsley, cut the stems of the sprigs at an angle so that after you wrap them with florist wire they will form a point and stick into the foam without breaking.

Keep the parsley fresh by soaking the bunches in ice water as you make them, then place them on the tree.

TRUFFLED PORK TENDERLOIN
Serves 8

1 pork tenderloin, cleaned
    and trimmed (about 20 to
    24 ounces trimmed weight)
1 small can black truffles
1 tablespoon Chef's Salt
    (see appendix)
4 teaspoons unflavored gelatin
½ cup carrots, coarsely
    chopped
½ cup celery tops, coarsely
    chopped

½ cup onions with skins,
    coarsely chopped
1 quart water
salt to taste
¼ teaspoon white pepper
2 tablespoons fresh lemon juice
4 drops yellow food coloring
    (optional)

Preheat oven to 350°. Cut the tail end of the pork tenderloin so that it is about the same thickness from end to end. With the point of a sharp knife, carefully cut a hole from each end of the tenderloin toward the middle, being careful to make the hole meet at the center. Insert your forefingers into each end to open the hole and to make sure it goes completely through.

Slice truffles into ¼-inch by ¼-inch sticks, laying them the length of the tenderloin to make sure there will be enough for stuffing. Again, insert the forefinger of your left hand into one end of the tenderloin so that it goes approximately to the middle of the loin. Working from the opposite end, insert the pieces of truffle so that the first one touches the forefinger of the left hand, the next touches the first piece, and so on. After one end is filled, repeat from the opposite end.

Rub the tenderloin's outer surface with ½ tablespoon Chef's Salt and sprinkle with about ½ teaspoon of gelatin. Roll the tenderloin tightly in a piece of aluminum foil about 18 inches square.

Place carrots, celery tops, and onions in the bottom of a small roasting pan. Add water and sprinkle remaining Chef's Salt in the water. Lay foil-wrapped tenderloin on the vegetables, cover, and roast 45 minutes, turning tenderloin once after 20 to 25 minutes. Remove from the oven and let cool 15 or 20 minutes, then open the foil and return the tenderloin to the oven for an additional 25 minutes.

Remove the tenderloin from the foil and set aside to cool for a few minutes. With a wet kitchen towel, straighten the piece of baking foil, sprinkle it with ½ teaspoon gelatin, and reroll the tenderloin in the foil. Be sure to roll it tightly and evenly, gently pressing it as you wrap. Chill for at least 4 hours before you slice it.

Strain pan juices through a sieve and skim fat from the surface. Place two or three ice cubes in the center of a wet kitchen towel, gathering the towel together and twisting it to secure the ice cubes in a ball; gently move it over the surface of the liquid, submerging it slightly. The fat will firm up and adhere to the ice in the wet cloth. Strain the juice again through a wet cloth; it should be very clear.

Correct the seasoning of the juices by adding some salt, white pepper, and lemon juice. For each cup of clear liquid you have (about 3 cups), dilute 1 teaspoon gelatin in 2 tablespoons water. Let stand for a couple of minutes, then stir into strained pan juices. Simmer the mixture over low heat for 15 to 20 minutes, being careful that it doesn't boil.

Remove and cool to room temperature. Add yellow food coloring if you wish. Pour into a flat container and chill.

To serve, carefully hand slice the truffled cold pork tenderloin and arrange it in a row in the middle of a small silver platter. Remove the firm aspic to a cutting board and chop finely. Put the chopped aspic in a pastry bag with a plain ⅓-inch pastry tube and pipe it around the slices of truffled tenderloin. Serve with very thin dry toast, fresh butter, and tart, tiny pickles.

 CHEF'S SECRET   As the tenderloin is cooked, it will shrink and may even change shape a bit. That's why I suggest that after it cools you straighten out the foil, sprinkle some gelatin on the foil, and roll up the tenderloin again. This second packaging will straighten the tenderloin so that after the final cooling it will be an even tubular shape with a gelatin coating already on it.

If you wish, you may add some applejack or French apple brandy (Calvados) to the liquid from which you make the aspic.

If you have some leftover truffle, wrap it in aluminum foil with the liquid from the can and place it in the freezer. The liquid will make an excellent addition to a sauce, and the leftover truffle can be used in many ways. The best way to keep it for more than a few days is to put it into a small plastic container such as the kind a pharmacist uses for pills. Pour in the canned liquid and fill it up with enough port wine or sherry to cover. The alcohol won't freeze solid, but it will protect the very expensive truffle.

CREPES
8 to 12 crepes

4 eggs
1 cup flour
½ teaspoon salt
1⅓ cups milk

½ cup club soda
½ cup butter
½ cup oil

Break the eggs into a bowl, add the flour and salt, and vigorously mix with a wire whip until the mixture is smooth. Slowly add the milk and stir until all has been added. Let stand in a covered bowl at room temperature for at least 30 minutes. Add club soda and stir.

In a small pan, over medium heat, heat together the butter and oil.

Place an empty 8-inch, heavy aluminum frying pan (the bottom will be 6 inches in diameter) over medium heat. When it is hot, pour in the whole amount of melted shortening and heat it over medium heat for about 5 minutes or more. Pour shortening back into the small pan.

Heat the heavy aluminum pan for another 2 or 3 minutes and then start to make the crepes as follows: Place a scant tablespoon of shortening in the pan and swirl pan with a circular motion. Holding the pan in the air, with one hand, pour into it a scant ¼ cup of the batter, swirling it until the batter covers the entire bottom.

Place the pan over medium heat and cook until the batter firms up and the edges start to look done. Dip the edge of a metal spatula into the hot shortening and loosen the edges all around. With a wiggling motion, ease the spatula under the crepe and turn it over. Finish cooking. The crepe should be creamy yellow, with very light brown areas on it. Holding the handle of the pan, shake it with a back-and-forth motion and if the crepe moves, lift it out to a plate covered with absorbent paper.

Repeat until all the batter is used. This recipe will make at least 12; under ideal conditions it will make 13 to 14 crepes.

CHEF'S SECRET   This is really a dish in which the most important part is the cook's skill and not the ingredients.

In mixing the crepe batter, don't hesitate to make small adjustments in the amounts of flour or liquid used to compensate for the fact that flour is not as consistent as salt, sugar, or shortening.

For frying crepes, a mixture of lard and oil is, in my opinion, the very best. If you keep the shortening hot and maintain a very hot, even pan temperature throughout the preparation, you will need very little shortening, and the crepes won't be greasy.

DEEP-FRIED HAM CREPES WITH MUSHROOM SAUCE
Serves 8

8 unsweetened crepes
   (see page 35)

Ham filling:

4 to 6 ounces ham, ground twice
1 egg
½ cup sour cream

¼ teaspoon freshly ground
   black pepper
1 teaspoon sifted breadcrumbs
salt to taste

Breading:

1½ to 2 cups sifted breadcrumbs
   (see appendix)
2 eggs beaten with 2 tablespoons
   cold water until frothy

shortening for frying

Mushroom sauce:

5 to 6 ounces firm, small,
   white button mushrooms
1 tablespoon flour
1 quart water
4 tablespoons butter
2 tablespoons finely
   chopped parsley
½ teaspoon salt
¼ teaspoon freshly
   ground black pepper

2 tablespoons flour
2 tablespoons cornstarch
2 cups milk
1 cup chicken broth or
   ½ chicken bouillon cube
   dissolved in 1 cup warm
   water
½ cup sour cream or heavy cream
   (optional)
fresh parsley for decoration

Prepare crepes and keep warm.
   In a bowl, combine ground ham, egg, sour cream, pepper, and 1 teaspooon breadcrumbs. Mix gently until well blended. Taste and add salt if needed (this will depend on the saltiness of the ham). Divide filling into 8 portions and place a portion on each crepe (see illustration).

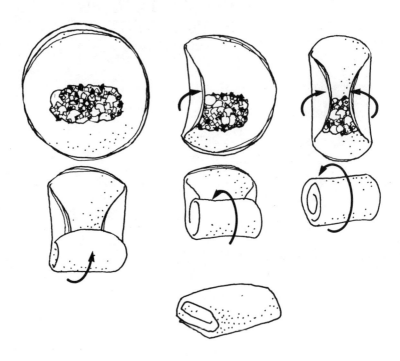

Fold the part of the crepe closest to you over the filling. Fold up first the left then the right sides, covering the filling. Then roll the crepe away from you so that after rolling it twice the edge farthest from you will be the bottom of the roll. Gently press so it turns into a flat rectangle. Chill 1 hour.

Spread the 1½ to 2 cups breadcrumbs in a pie tin and pour the beaten eggs with the water into another pie tin. Roll the crepe gently in the breadcrumbs, then dip in the egg mixture and roll in the bread-crumbs again.

When all crepes are breaded, heat the shortening—preferably half lard, half oil—until a breadcrumb dropped into it immediately jumps to the surface and bubbles. Fry the crepes, not more than 2 or 3 at a time, until both sides are golden brown, turning just once. You may have to keep adjusting the heat as you do this in order to make the crepes come out perfectly. Place the crepes on absorbent paper towels and keep warm.

To make the sauce: Cut off and discard stem ends of the mushrooms. To wash the mushrooms, sprinkle a tablespoon of flour on top of 1 quart of water, plunge in the mushrooms 4 or 5 at a time, and gently, quickly wash them. Lift out and pat dry immediately. Don't allow the mushrooms to remain in the water for more than a minute.

Slice mushrooms. In a saute pan over moderate heat, melt the butter and add the parsley, mushrooms, salt, and pepper. Cook 5 minutes, stirring occasionally. Mix the flour and cornstarch with the milk and chicken broth. Add to saute pan, stir, lower the heat, and cover. Bring gently to a boil, which will take not more than 2 or 3 minutes. Uncover, stir for a minute or so, then remove from heat and let stand for at least 1 hour.

Reheat immediately before serving. If you wish, stir in ½ cup sour cream or heavy cream.

Serve the crepes on a platter decorated with fresh parsley, with the sauce in a small bowl on the side.

CHEF'S SECRET   This dish may seem complicated, but it is not. You can easily make the crepes a day ahead of time, filling them with the ham mixture and leaving the breading for the day you serve them. You can also make the sauce a day ahead, mixing in the cream just after reheating and just before serving.

Don't try to add cold sour cream or heavy cream at once. Warm it first by stirring in some of the hot sauce, then stir the cream into the rest of the sauce.

Many cookbooks will tell you never to wash mushrooms. I strongly disagree. Mushrooms are dirty and should be washed. The important thing is that they be washed properly and quickly. Sprinkling flour on the surface of the water before plunging in the mushrooms seems to help carry off the dirt and perhaps also coats the mushrooms so that they don't get water-soaked.

If you like a tangy mushroom sauce, add a good squeezing of lemon juice when you start to saute the mushrooms.

FISH EN CROUTE
Serves 10 to 12

pie dough for a double-crust pie
1 pound lake trout filets or
    any other skinless, boneless,
    mild fish
salt and pepper to taste
½ pound medium-sized fresh
    mushrooms
2 tablespoons oil or shortening
2 tablespoons butter

4 ounces chopped or cubed ham
3 tablespoons flour
1 cup white wine
1 cup half-and-half or cream
1 egg
sugar and salt to taste
fresh parsley for decoration
lemon slices for garnish

Prepare the pie dough and chill.

Cut the trout filets into 2 × 2-inch pieces. Season them with salt and pepper.

Remove the stems from 10 to 12 nice mushrooms, one for each serving you desire. Chop up the stems and the remaining mushrooms and saute all the mushrooms in the oil and butter for 3 minutes. Set aside the nice mushroom caps to use later as a garnish.

Add the chopped ham to the pan and sprinkle the ham and mushrooms with the flour. Stir for 2 to 3 more minutes over low heat. Add the white wine and the pieces of trout. Simmer 3 to 4 minutes. Add the half-and-half or cream. Stir until the mixture reaches a slow boil.

Remove from heat. Place a strainer over a saucepan, empty the mixture into the strainer, and let it drip through into the saucepan.

Swirl the saute pan clean with some white wine and pour this over the mixture in the other pan.

Roll out the pie dough to a rectangle 11 by 10 inches. Beat the egg and brush the entire surface of the dough with it.

Preheat the oven to 350°.

Carefully spoon the fish, ham, and mushroom mixture, without any sauce, onto the side of the dough near you, leaving 1 to 2 inches at the ends empty.

Starting at the edge near you, roll the dough over the filling and keep rolling it until you have reached the far side. Form the left end into the shape of a fish head and the right end into the shape of a fish tail. Make an eye out of a small piece of dough. Gently lift the whole fish roll onto a well-greased baking sheet. Brush it with the remainder of the egg. Take a scissors and cut scales in the dough.

Bake the fish at 350° to 375° for 5 minutes. Brush with egg again and bake another 10 to 14 minutes, according to the size of the fish and the temperature of your oven.

If necessary, reduce the sauce by simmering, or thicken it with a mixture of butter and flour. Correct the seasoning with sugar and salt if necessary.

Serve the fish decorated with green parsley and lemon slices, and pour the sauce over each serving. Place one of the mushroom caps on each serving.

 CHEF'S SECRET   Any kind of smoked pork or ham cooked together with seafood improves the flavor. Chinese chefs consider this one of the secrets of their success with fish and shellfish. Their fish dishes are so popular because they always put pork bones or ham in Court Bouillon.

It is easier to make the scales if you dip the tip of the scissors in flour before snipping the little pieces. If you hold the scissors at about a 45-degree angle, the tips of the scales will turn up, and since the dough is thin, they will brown faster than the other parts and will make the fish very attractive.

The dough expands somewhat in the first 5 minutes of baking and in so doing absorbs a part of the egg wash. Therefore a second brushing on the already hot surface will immediately bake onto it and keep the fish shiny.

SAUCISSON EN CROUTE
Serves 12

3 cups sifted flour

1 cup butter

8 ounces cream cheese

1 pound sausage, not too dry
    (for example, thin, "ring"
    bologna, or "German"
    bologna, Polish sausage
    ready to cook or cooked, or
    not-too-dry Hungarian
    sausage)

1 egg

1 tablespoon water

In a large cold bowl, mix the flour, butter, and cream cheese, working very quickly with your fingertips until the mixture looks like coarse cornmeal. Press into a ball, then divide into two portions. Wrap each portion in plastic and refrigerate at least 3 to 4 hours.

Remove the casing or skin of the sausage. Roll out enough dough to encase the sausage. If you use one large sausage, combine the two pieces of chilled dough. If you use two sausages, roll out each piece of dough and encase the sausages separately.

Beat the egg with water. Preheat the oven to 425°.

Lightly grease a cookie sheet. Brush the top of the dough-wrapped sausage with the egg wash and bake 15 to 25 minutes, according to the size of the sausage. Let the sausage stand at room temperature for a few minutes before slicing. Serve warm but not hot.

 CHEF'S SECRET   This dough is highly versatile and can be used for a hundred different dishes once you have mastered its preparation.

You must mix it with your hands, and you must be sure they are not warm. Have ready some ice water in a tightly closed plastic bag, and chill your hands on its surface. Be sure they do not get wet.

When you drop the sticks of butter and slab of cream cheese into the flour, cover their entire surfaces with flour before you touch them. Then break the sticks of butter in two and dip the broken surfaces into the flour. Break the pieces of butter again and dip again in flour. Then start breaking the cream cheese, dipping in flour. Keep repeating this procedure, never touching the same piece of butter or cream cheese twice in succession. When all the pieces are the size of an almond, put both hands at the bottom of the mixing bowl and turn the whole mixture over.

From then on, press the mixture together with your fingertips, working quickly and running your thumbs from the little finger to the index finger in a circular motion. After two or three tries, you will master this dough, and you will find that you can roll it and fold it once, twice, or three times as you would the famous puff paste. This dough, however, is much quicker, easier, and more economical, and does not require as much skill in preparation.

HOME-ROASTED NUTS
2 pounds

1 pound shelled almonds
4 ounces shelled hazelnuts
4 ounces shelled English walnuts
4 ounces shelled cashews
1 tablespoon corn oil

1 tablespoon butter at room
    temperature
1 egg white
3 to 4 tablespoons coarse salt,
    to taste

Wipe dry an enamel-coated or iron skillet large enough to hold the nuts when spread out. Coat the pan evenly with the oil.

Add the nuts and place the pan over medium heat. After 2 or 3 minutes, gently shake the pan until you notice a warm nut smell. Then increase the heat and with a metal spatula or large spoon, turn the nuts gently. If they brown too quickly, reduce the heat; if they brown too slowly, increase it.

When the nuts are roasted to your liking, remove them from the heat and cool to lukewarm, adding the butter and turning the nuts so they all will be buttered.

Beat the egg white into a light froth and add the salt. Transfer the nuts to a mixing bowl with the egg white and gently shake the bowl until all the nuts are evenly coated. Spread the nuts out on aluminum foil, and sprinkle more coarse salt on them if you wish.

CHEF'S SECRET   Store-bought nuts will never taste as good as the ones you roast at home the morning of the party or the day before. The coating of the egg white dries evenly on the nuts and keeps the salt on them.

If you can, buy kosher salt in the specialty section of your supermarket. Its consistency is entirely different from that of regular kitchen salt.

LUMBERJACK PIE
24 to 36 pieces

1 package pie dough mix
3 tablespoons finely chopped
    onions
2 strips bacon, finely
    chopped, or 2 tablespoons
    bacon drippings
½ cup finely chopped ham,
    leftover roast pork, or any
    other leftover meat

½ cup boiled potatoes cut
    into ¼-inch cubes
freshly ground black pepper
salt to taste
1 egg
1 tablespoon cold water

Prepare the pie dough according to package directions and place it in the refrigerator to chill.

Saute the onions in the bacon fat or with the finely chopped bacon. When the onions start to brown, add the chopped meat and stir. Add the potatoes and cook the mixture until the potatoes heat through and absorb some of the fat. Remove from heat and add freshly ground black pepper and salt to taste. Let cool to room temperature.

Roll out half of the pie dough to form a square approximately 12 by 12 inches. Gently press a ruler into the dough and divide it into twelve or sixteen equal-sized pieces. Beat the egg with the cold water and lightly brush the surface of the dough with this egg wash. Repeat with the other half of the dough.

Preheat the oven to 375°.

Place a small dab of the filling on each section of the dough. Cut the dough along the marks into individual pieces and fold over half of each piece so that the filling is completely covered. Gently press the edges together. Bake on a lightly greased cookie sheet 12 to 15 minutes, the time depending on the size of the pieces. Serve hot.

CHEF'S SECRET   Many people have difficulty measuring equal-sized pieces of dough, even with a ruler, especially if the dough is not rolled to a near-perfect square. The best method is this: Cut a piece of waxed paper exactly the size of the dough and carefully fold it to give you equal-sized sections. For example, for twelve equal sections you would fold the waxed paper first in thirds in one direction, then in fourths in the other direction. Then place the waxed paper over the dough and mark along the folds.

If you do not have boiled potatoes on hand, you can cook potatoes very quickly if you cut them uniformly as follows: Peel a potato and cut it with a thin-bladed knife into even slices but only to 1 inch away from one end, so that the slices do not fall apart. Turn the potato and cut crosswise, being careful that the knife does not run through the whole potato. Then slice in the third direction, and you will have even small cubes that will cook quickly.

PEPPERONI PINWHEELS
About 40 pieces

1 package pie dough mix
11- to 12-inch pepperoni or
    similar thin, dry sausage if
    pepperoni is not available
1 small egg
1 cup ketchup

1 teaspoon finely crushed
    oregano
2 tablespoons grated Parmesan
    cheese
shortening

Prepare the pie dough according to package directions and roll it out to form an oblong shape as long as the pepperoni plus 1 inch.

Beat the egg and mix it with the ketchup, oregano, and cheese. Spread the mixture over the pie dough, leaving ½ inch of space on three sides and 1 inch on the edge farthest from you. Place the pepperoni on the dough and roll it jelly-roll fashion to the edge farthest from you. Place the roll on a sheet of aluminum foil, being sure that the outside edge of the foil is on the bottom of the roll. Wrap the roll. Chill overnight or freeze 4 to 5 hours.

Cover a cookie sheet with aluminum foil. Brush lightly with shortening. Preheat oven to 400°.

With a very sharp knife, cut the roll into slices ¼ to ⅜ inch thick. Lay these on the aluminum foil lining the cookie sheet. After the slices reach room temperature, bake 10 to 12 minutes. Serve hot or cold.

 CHEF'S SECRET   The beaten egg in the ketchup thickens the mixture and keeps it from running.

If you place two or three thin-bladed sharp knives in hot water and change them after each two or three slices, you can slice the roll while it is still frozen, making even and straight-surfaced slices.

QUICHE LORRAINE
Two 9-inch quiches

pie dough for a double-crust pie
¼ cup butter
½ pound Cheddar cheese
½ pound Swiss cheese
2 tablespoons grated Parmesan
    cheese
4 tablespoons flour
sprinkling of nutmeg

8 large eggs
1 teaspoon salt
4 cups half-and-half
1 cup minced ham or
    other smoked or cured
    meat (optional)
sliced mushrooms (optional)

Divide the pie dough in half, roll out, and line two 9-inch pie dishes. Preheat oven to 375°.

Heat the butter until it is dark brown. Let it cool to lukewarm.

Grate the Cheddar and Swiss cheese coarsely. Mix them with the grated Parmesan, 1 tablespoon of the flour, and a sprinkling of nutmeg. Divide this mixture evenly and place in the two pies.

Beat the eggs with the salt and 1 tablespoon of flour. Add the half-and-half and the remaining 3 tablespoons of flour. Strain this mixture through a fine sieve into another bowl. (This is a very important step.) Beating vigorously, add the browned lukewarm butter. Divide this mixture between the two pies.

Place the pie dishes on a cookie sheet and bake 10 minutes. Add the minced ham or sliced mushrooms and bake 20 minutes longer. Lower the heat to 350° and bake an additional 15 to 20 minutes.

Cut in wedges, small diamonds, or triangles. Serve lukewarm.

 CHEF'S SECRET   This Quiche Lorraine freezes extremely well and can be easily reheated in aluminum foil. If you bake it in an aluminum foil pie pan, you can freeze it in the pan. Add finely chopped luncheon meat, instead of ham, to this Quiche Lorraine if you desire.

You can also bake the quiche in square pans. Then, of course, the oven temperature should be a little lower, beginning at 350°, and the baking time should be shorter because the filling will be thinner.

With this basic Quiche Lorraine recipe, your imagination is the only limit in developing your own hors d'oeuvres.

At *The Bakery Restaurant* we use ham, Westphalian ham, chopped Hungarian sausage, all kinds of smoked fish, shrimp, and lobster for quiche—but it seems that the plain version is the most popular.

STUFFED CHICKEN LEGS AND WINGS
12 pieces

8 chicken wings
4 chicken livers
4 chicken legs,
    about 8 ounces each
4 breakfast link sausages
lard or oil for deep-frying

flour
salt and pepper to taste
4 eggs, beaten
3 cups Italian breadcrumbs
    (see appendix)

Using a sharp knife, loosen the skin and flesh around the base of the second wing joint, toward the tip. When it loosens, grip the bones in your right hand and the meat in your left, then gently pull out the two bones.

Cut the chicken livers into small pieces, and stuff the pieces into the pocket of each wing.

Starting at the tip end of the thigh, remove the bone from the leg without cutting into the meat. Cut into the joint where the thigh and drumstick meet. Cut the tendons, cutting toward the bone gently but firmly from the outside of the flesh until you have cut them all around just under the top end of the drumstick bone. Scratch back the meat from the bone using a paring knife, and with one fast movement you can then remove the drumstick so that the chicken leg is turned inside out.

Place a sausage in the place where the bone was, and turn the flesh back into the original position.

Place the fat in a heavy frying pan and heat it slowly over medium heat. Preheat oven to 350°.

Season the flour with salt and pepper. Dredge the stuffed wings and legs in the flour, dip them in the beaten eggs, then roll in the bread-crumbs.

Deep-fry the legs in hot fat until golden brown. Place on a sheet pan and finish cooking for 15 to 20 minutes in the oven. Deep-fry the wings while the legs are baking.

CHEF'S SECRET   In order to place the breakfast sausages easily in the chicken legs, first freeze the sausages briefly.

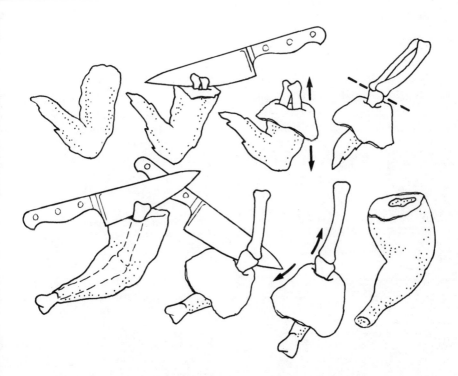

2
SOUPS

The truck driver who has removed our refuse for many years dines at *The Bakery* on his birthday, on his wife's birthday, and on his wedding anniversary. He is no fool. He tells the waiter and my brother, who is our general manager and host, that what impresses him the most about a restaurant is if he finds meaty bones, bigger than his fist (and you should see his fist), and piles of chicken backs and necks in the trash, rather than empty cans and boxes. And bones are what he finds at *The Bakery*.

Since we opened we have never yet cooked soup from water. We always make our soup from stock; the 30-gallon stainless steel kettle is a part of our kitchen we could not do without. Then why do many of the recipes in this book use canned consomme, canned chicken broth, or even bouillon cubes? Because, being a realist, I know that it is simply impossible for a homemaker to always start with a large pot of bones and vegetables to make 2 cups of stock for a sauce, or 4 cups for soup. The so-called purists just kid themselves and chase busy people away from the kitchen. Soup extracts and commercial canned soups have an important role to play in both commercial and private kitchens. But if the time and the know-how are there, my first choice will always be the stockpot.

The favorite soup through almost two decades is our clear tomato soup, but our cream of asparagus, cream of cauliflower, and many other soups also have partisans. We change our soups with the season, serving legumes (such as split peas, lentils, and navy beans) in the winter, and offering soups you hardly ever get in other places, such as cream of kohlrabi or corn chowder, when they are in season.

OLD-FASHIONED BEEF SOUP
Serves 8 generously

1 pound soup bones
1 pound lean beef,
    preferably marbled
½ pound fat beef
1 onion, unpeeled
1 whole clove
2 medium carrots, peeled and
    split in two
1 parsnip or parsley root
2 ribs celery or a piece of
    celery root

1 small turnip or slice of a
    larger one
2 cloves garlic, unpeeled
1 teaspoon black peppercorns,
    slightly bruised
1 whole bay leaf
3 tablespoons salt
3 quarts water

Place all the ingredients in a large soup pot in the order listed, the 3 quarts water last. Cover, place over medium heat, and bring to a boil. Immediately reduce the heat to low, and simmer the soup for 2 hours or more.

One hour before serving, remove from the heat and strain through a large colander into another pot. Place the meat and vegetables on a tray and cool until you can handle them. Discard all spices and bones.

Peel the onion and discard the peeling. Cut the onion into small pieces. Cut up the carrot, parsnip or parsley root, celery, and turnip. Cut up the lean meat into ½-inch cubes. Trim the fat meat, discard the fat, and cut the edible parts into cubes.

Place all the meat and vegetables in a large soup tureen. Remove the fat from the soup. About 10 minutes before serving time, cover and heat the soup over medium heat until it begins to boil. Pour it over the warm vegetables and meat and serve it at once.

CHEF'S SECRET   The best way to handle the clove is to make a cross-cut at the root end of the onion with a sharp knife and press the clove into the onion. The skin of the onion adds a dark hue to the beef soup. Without it, the soup will be light yellow, like chicken soup.

If you have only a large onion and want to use just half of it, cut it crosswise, dividing the root end from the leaf end. Lightly brush the cut surface of the onion with shortening and press it to the hot surface of the stove top for 30 seconds. Or, in a small frying pan, heat a little shortening until it is smoking and press the cut surface of the onion into it. With this method, the natural sugar in the onion will caramelize and darken the color of the soup.

If you skim the fat from the soup and want to remove the last particles, dip a towel into cold water, wring it dry, place three to four ice cubes in the towel, and, holding the ice cubes tightly, dip the towel about ½ inch into the soup and move it slowly. All the fat particles will adhere to the surface of the towel, and you can remove them at once.

REAL DOUBLE CONSOMME
Serves 8

2½ quarts beef stock (see
    appendix) or 4 cans beef
    consomme (10½ ounces each)
    with 4 cans cold water
2 egg whites
1 pound lean ground beef

2-inch carrot, finely grated
1 tablespoon unsalted butter
1 teaspoon cornstarch
1 cup cold water
dry sherry or Marsala wine,
    to taste

Pour beef stock into a large pot.

Beat egg whites until frothy and mix thoroughly with the ground beef. Add this mixture, spoonful by spoonful, to the beef stock, stirring after each addition so that the meat particles separate.

Saute the grated carrot in the unsalted butter. Drain off any remaining fat and add carrot to the meat mixture.

Mix the cornstarch with cold water. Bring the soup to a boil over medium heat, stirring with a wire whip every 4 or 5 minutes. Slowly add

\xture, stirring constantly. Bring the soup to a boil again,
\, and let it bubble slowly 1 hour. Remove from heat, cover
\d let it stand for at least another hour.

\im off as much fat as possible and, without stirring, pour the
\m soup into another pot through a wet kitchen towel or several layers
of cheesecloth. Do not try to pour the bottom part with the meat in it.

When ready to serve, reheat the soup, but be careful not to bring it
to a boil. Add a few tablespoons of the wine.

CHEF'S SECRET   Having been served various misrepresen-
tations of this soup by overworked personnel in understaffed
hotel kitchens, people often have a wrong idea about this most
delightful of all soups. Once you discover how simple it is to
prepare, you will want to serve it often to your guests and
family. The cornstarch gives the delightful syrupy texture, and
the grated carrot heated in the butter adds the beautiful deep
golden color.

The beef adds the extra beefy flavor, and the egg whites
capture all the particles that would otherwise make the soup
cloudy or mar its brilliant transparency.

The ground beef mixed with the egg white makes an
excellent meat pudding. Combine it with the yolks of 2 eggs, 4
slices of white bread soaked in milk and pressed, plus salt,
pepper, and freshly chopped parsley. Steam in a shallow dish in
a waterbath.

CHICKEN CONSOMME
WITH MOUSSELINES
Serves 8

4 ounces raw chicken breast,
    skinless and boneless
1 pinch nutmeg
¼ teaspoon salt, or more to taste
2 egg whites
1 cup heavy cream or whipping
    cream

1 quart water, lightly salted
4 cans chicken broth, 10½ ounces
    each, diluted according to
    directions, or 2 quarts good
    chicken stock

Cut the chicken breasts into ¼ inch cubes. To an electric blender, add the nutmeg, salt, half the egg whites, and half the cream. Add half the chicken and puree the mixture until it turns into a frothy, pale substance. Add the remaining egg whites, chicken, and cream. Blend on highest speed until the mixture resembles overwhipped heavy cream. Chill the mixture in the coldest part of your refrigerator for at least 30 minutes.

In a shallow pan, bring to a gentle boil approximately 1 quart of lightly salted water. Dip a tablespoon into the boiling water, and use it to take from the mousseline preparation an amount about the size of an unshelled almond. Gently slide it into the water. Repeat until you have eight to ten mousselines.

Increase the heat slightly until the mousselines begin to puff. They will grow to double their original size. Remove from water, drain, and repeat until all batter is used.

Just before serving, divide the mousselines among soup bowls and pour hot chicken broth or stock over them. Serve immediately.

CHEF'S SECRET   It is advisable to cook one mousseline and then taste it for saltiness before cooking more. You can then correct the seasoning by adding more salt if needed. If you want to make the mousselines beforehand, they must be kept sub-merged in warm water at approximately 160° to 170° until serving time. Do not try to keep them in the stock, because they will lose their beautiful snow-white color. For a variation, add thin slivers of tender ham to the mousseline preparation before poaching.

OLD-FASHIONED CHICKEN SOUP
Serves 8

1 stewing hen, 3½ to 4 pounds,
    halved or quartered
2 cups coarsely chopped carrots
4 celery ribs, cut up
1 small onion, unpeeled, studded
    with 1 clove in the
    root end
1 parsley root or parsnip
1 piece celery root or turnip
    (white or yellow)
1 clove garlic
1 tablespoon salt
12 black peppercorns,
    slightly bruised

1 pinch mace
1 pinch nutmeg
1 or 2 blades saffron (optional)
1½ to 2 pounds beef or veal bones
1 gallon water
1 tablespoon chopped parsley
1 piece chicken belly fat
    from the cavity of the hen
1 tablespoon sugar
1 tablespoon butter
1 tablespoon finely grated carrot

Place all the ingredients except the last five (parsley, chicken fat, grated carrot, butter, and sugar) in a large soup pot. Bring to a boil over medium heat. Reduce the heat and simmer at least 4 hours. Remove from the heat and let the soup stand 30 minutes. Skim off the fat and pour the soup carefully through a sieve into another pot. Let the meat and vegetables cool on a cookie sheet.

Saute the chopped parsley for 1 to 2 minutes in the chicken fat. Then add the cooked carrots, celery, and parsnip or parsley root. Cover, reduce the heat to very low, and cook 10 minutes.

In a small frying pan, heat the sugar slowly until it starts to turn brown. Add the butter and the grated carrot. Stir this mixture 10 to 15 seconds, then remove from heat and dilute with ½ cup chicken soup. Bring it to a rapid boil and then strain it through a fine sieve into the soup. This will give color to the soup.

Remove the chicken skin and bones; cut the meat into chunks. Put the meat and the vegetables sauteed with the parsley into a serving dish. Pour the soup over them and serve at once.

CHEF'S SECRET   The belly fat of the chicken is at the end of the breast and around the upper part of the thigh. The parsley sauteed with this fat will give an intense chicken flavor that people look for in vain in most modern chicken soups. The vegetables sauteed with this parsley will taste as vegetables should.

The carotene, released from the grated carrot by the heat, combined with the browned sugar, gives the color that Grandma's chicken soup used to have.

Although the soup is called chicken soup, do not try to make it with a young chicken. Only a stewing hen will give you the taste you want.

TURKEY CHOWDER
Serves 8

1 bunch green parsley
1 bay leaf
1 rib celery
4 pounds turkey wings
4 tablespoons shortening
1 cup celery, diced to the
     size of a kernel of corn
½ cup green pepper, diced to
     the size of a kernel of corn
1 cup onion, diced to the
     size of a kernel of corn

2 tablespoons salt
½ teaspoon freshly ground
     black pepper
2 quarts water
20-ounce can creamed corn
20-ounce can whole kernel corn
2 to 3 egg yolks
1 cup cream or half-and-half

Tie the parsley, the bay leaf, and the celery together.

Wash the turkey wings, cover with water, and bring to a boil. Boil 3 to 4 minutes, then pour off the water.

In a large soup pot, melt the shortening and add the celery, green pepper, onion, and half the salt. Cook over high heat, stirring, until the vegetables start to brown. Reduce the heat, add the turkey wings, the remaining salt, the black pepper, and the parsley bouquet. Add 2 quarts water, cover, and simmer 2 to 2½ hours. If the water evaporates too much through simmering, adjust to the original water level in the pot by adding a little water.

Remove the meat and let it cool. Remove the parsley bouquet and discard. Remove the flesh from the bones and discard the bones. Return the meat to the chowder and add both cans of corn. Simmer 15 more minutes.

Mix 2 to 3 egg yolks with the cream or half-and-half and place in the bottom of a large soup tureen. Stirring constantly, add a few tablespoonfuls of the hot chowder to the egg yolk-cream mixture; add more hot liquid, then pour in all the chowder and serve.

 CHEF'S SECRET   The few minutes' preboiling of the turkey wings will improve the taste of the chowder and will remove a considerable amount of the turkey fat under the skin.

This soup would be thick enough to eat without adding the egg yolk-cream mixture, because of the creamed corn and the thoroughly cooked vegetables, but of course it would not taste the same.

If fresh corn or frozen corn is available, by all means use it instead of the canned kernels, but do *not* substitute for the canned creamed corn.

CAULIFLOWER SOUP
Serves 8

2 tablespoons shortening,
    preferably lard
½ cup chopped onion
1 small carrot, scraped
1 cup chopped celery
1 tablespoon sugar
1 head firm white cauliflower,
    cut into small flowerets
    (about 1 quart)
2 tablespoons chopped fresh
    parsley
2 quarts veal stock or
    chicken stock, or enough
    canned chicken broth,
    diluted, to make 2 quarts

½ teaspoon peppercorns,
    ½ bay leaf, and 1 teaspoon
    dried tarragon tied in a
    cheesecloth bag
1 tablespoon salt
4 tablespoons butter
6 tablespoons flour
2 cups milk
1 cup half-and-half
1 cup sour cream at room
    temperature

In a large soup pot, melt the 2 tablespoons of shortening. Add the chopped onion and cook, stirring constantly, over medium heat until the onion starts to turn yellow. Add carrot and celery and cook another 2 minutes, continuing to stir. Add sugar, cauliflower, and 1 tablespoon of the chopped parsley. Cover and cook over very low heat, stirring occasionally. Be sure the ingredients do not stick to the bottom of the pot. After 15 minutes, add the stock of your choice, the cheesecloth bag of herbs, and half the salt.

Bring the soup to a boil over medium heat. Reduce the heat and simmer.

In a small saucepan, melt the butter. Mix the flour into the milk with a wire whip, and slowly, stirring constantly with the wire whip, add the flour-milk mixture to the butter. If you add it slowly enough, it will thicken immediately, and when you finish you will have a white sauce of medium consistency. Remove from heat and dilute with the half-and-half. Pour this mixture into the simmering soup. Stir gently with a wooden spoon and let it simmer another 15 to 20 minutes. Check for seasoning and add a little more salt if necessary. (The amount will depend on the saltiness of the stock used.)

Just before serving, place the sour cream in the soup tureen. Mix in the remaining chopped fresh parsley. Put two to three ladles of hot soup into the tureen and stir it into the sour cream. Remove the cheesecloth bag from the soup, pour all of the soup into the tureen, and serve immediately.

CHEF'S SECRET   If you make your own veal or chicken stock for cauliflower soup, be sure that the green leaves, white stalks, and hard white core of the cauliflower are all cooked with the soup bones. The stock itself will then have a cauliflower flavor. (For kohlrabi soup, use the peelings of the kohlrabi heads only, don't use the leaves.)

If you use canned chicken broth, chop the cauliflower trimmings and boil them in the water which you use to dilute the canned broth.

Sauteing the celery, onion, carrot, and cauliflower over low heat, without adding any water, intensifies and blends the aromas.

If you wish, you many remove a cupful of the cauliflowerets from the soup, puree them in a blender, and add this puree to the soup. This will also intensify the cauliflower taste.

Following this recipe exactly, but substituting the cauliflower with the same amount of peeled, cubed (¼-inch to ½-inch cubes) kohlrabi will make an excellent kohlrabi soup.

CLEAR TOMATO SOUP
Serves 12

2 pounds veal bones
1 coarsely chopped carrot
1 chopped parsley root or
    parsnip
1 cut-up celery rib
½ onion, unpeeled
5 to 6 black peppercorns
1 tablespoon salt
1 bay leaf
1 clove garlic
3 quarts water
3 tablespoons sugar
1 teaspoon butter

6-ounce can tomato paste
46-ounce can tomato juice
2 tablespoons dried tarragon
2 tablespoons dried dill weed
6 tablespoons cornstarch
fresh dill weed, if available
fresh lemon juice, sugar,
    and salt to taste
liquid from 2 ripe tomatoes,
    chopped and run through a
    blender
lemon slices for garnish

In a large soup pot, place the veal bones, carrot, parsley root or parsnip, celery, onion, peppercorns, salt, bay leaf, and garlic. Add about 3 quarts of water. Cover and cook slowly at least 4 hours. The amount of stock should then be approximately 2 quarts. Strain the stock into another pot and skim the top if necessary.

Dissolve the sugar in the butter, heating until it starts to caramelize. Pour 1 quart of stock over the butter-sugar mixture. Add the tomato paste and tomato juice. Bring to a boil, reduce heat, and simmer.

Meanwhile, cool 2 cups of stock and bring another 2 cups to a boil. Sprinkle into the boiling stock the tarragon and dried dill weed. Boil 2 minutes. Strain this stock, removing the herbs, into the simmering tomato soup.

Stir the cornstarch into the remaining cool stock and slowly pour the mixture into the simmering soup. This will make the soup syrupy-thick and clear.

Add chopped dill weed if you have fresh dill. Correct the seasoning of the soup with lemon juice, sugar, and salt. Pour the liquid from the ripe tomatoes into the soup tureen and ladle the hot soup over it. Serve immediately, garnished with lemon slices.

CHEF'S SECRET   Adding sugar to the tomato juice and tomato paste brings out a fresh tomato flavor and reduces some of the acidity.

The addition of fresh lemon juice before serving adds a tang, and using cornstarch instead of flour as a thickening agent makes a translucent and syrupy soup that is very different from other tomato soups.

If you cannot buy really ripe fresh tomatoes, keep the two tomatoes in a brown paper bag at room temperature overnight, then place them in a warm, if possible sunny, place for a few hours. Cut them crosswise and remove all seeds before blending. If they are not fully ripe, adding 1 extra tablespoon of sugar to them will improve their flavor.

CORN CHOWDER
Serves 8

2 pounds raw turkey wings
1 cup carrots, peeled and cut
    into ½-inch cubes
2 tablespoons minced onion
1 small turnip, peeled and cut
    into ½-inch cubes
½ cup chopped celery
2 small potatoes, peeled and cut
    into ½-inch cubes
1 tablespoon chopped parsley
2 tablespoons butter

1 tablespoon Chef's Salt
    (see appendix)
pinch of sugar
1 tablespoon finely grated carrot
½ teaspoon Hungarian paprika
10 cups water
2 ears fresh or frozen corn on
    the cob
2 tablespoons flour
2 cups milk or half-and-half

Cut the turkey wings crosswise into pieces 1½ to 2 inches long, leaving the bones in, or ask your butcher to do it on the electric saw.

Combine the chopped carrots, onion, turnip, celery, potatoes, parsley, butter, and Chef's Salt in a large soup pot. Place over medium to high heat to brown the vegetables, stirring frequently. When the edges of the vegetables start to brown, add the turkey. Add a light sprinkling of sugar to improve the caramelization, and add the tablespoon of grated carrot. Add paprika. Keep stirring, and when the bits on the bottom of the pot start to turn brown, add the water. Continue to stir until all the small bits are loosened from the bottom of the pot. Cover, reduce the heat to low, and simmer 1 hour.

Cut each ear of corn in half crosswise, split each half lengthwise, cutting through the cob, and then cut crosswise again into approximately one-inch pieces. Add to the soup and continue to simmer for another hour.

Remove soup from heat. Remove the pieces of turkey and let them cool; then remove and discard the bones and, if you wish, remove the skin. Return the pieces of meat to the soup.

About 1 hour before serving, adjust the liquid so that you have 2½ to 3 quarts, place over medium heat, and bring to a boil again. Mix the flour into the milk or half-and-half, then stir the mixture into the soup. Simmer over low heat for approximately 20 minutes. Remove and keep warm until serving time.

CHEF'S SECRET   If you make this chowder on a day when you serve roast turkey, the raw, cut-up second wing joints and wing tips of the turkey, along with the neck, will be enough for a chowder for 8. In this case, add to the chowder those juices from the roasting pan that you did not need for the giblet gravy.

The recipe says, "Adjust the liquid so that you have 2½ to 3 quarts." How do you do this? Very simple. When you start with 10 cups water, just measure with the handle of a wooden spoon how far the water level is from the top of the soup pot. Then, when you get to the point where you want to adjust the liquid back to the original level, place the same wooden spoon into the pot and slowly pour water until it reaches the mark on the spoon handle.

When you read about "cubing" of vegetables, it doesn't mean that you have to keep only the perfect ½ × ½ × ½-inch cubes and discard the rest. What it means is that you should try to cut the carrots, potatoes, or whatever so that most of the pieces will be cubes, but don't throw out the rest. This applies also to meat cubing.

CREAM OF POTATO SOUP
Serves 8

4 tablespoons shortening, preferably lard, bacon drippings, or a mixture of lard and oil
4 cups potatoes, peeled and cut into ½-inch cubes
½ cup chopped flat-leaf parsley
1 cup finely minced onion
1 bay leaf
1½ teaspoons salt
½ teaspoon freshly ground black pepper
5 cups chicken stock, chicken broth, or water
2 cups light cream or half-and-half
4 tablespoons flour
1 cup sour cream
additional chopped parsley for decoration

In a large soup pot, melt the shortening and saute the potatoes with the parsley, onion, bay leaf, salt, and pepper over medium heat for 10 minutes, stirring occasionally. Cover and cook over low heat 15 to 20 minutes. Add the stock (or water or broth) and continue cooking.

Mix the light cream with the flour and stir into it some of the soup, then pour the warmed up mixture into the soup. Keep stirring while pouring so that no lumps form. Simmer the soup at least 30 minutes.

Serve with additional cream (or egg yolk and cream mixture, as in other cream soups) or, just before serving, stir in sour cream. Sprinkle the top with additional chopped parsley or with chopped chives.

CHEF'S SECRET   This soup is the basic form of a large family of soups you can create by adding different ingredients. In some parts of my native Hungary, dried marjoram is added to the soup, in other parts a few bruised caraway seeds are sauteed together with the onion. During Lent it is made with oil, and for each person a whole egg is broken into the soup— carefully, so that the yolk doesn't break—5 or 6 minutes before serving. Or try this: Break the eggs one by one into a cup. Have the soup just below boiling point. Carefully plunge the eggs, one by one, into the soup, stirring gently while you do it.

Polish or Hungarian sausage may be added to the soup, or the soup may be started by boiling a ham hock and using the stock from it instead of the chicken broth (omit the salt in this case).

FRESH ASPARAGUS SOUP
Serves 8

1½ to 2 pounds fresh asparagus
2 tablespoons shortening
⅓ cup chopped onions
1 small carrot, scraped and
    chopped
1 cup chopped celery

tie securely in a piece of
    cheesecloth or gauze:
    ½ teaspoon black
    peppercorns; 1 very small
    clove garlic; 2 to 3 sprigs
    fresh parsley; 1 teaspoon
    dried tarragon

2 quarts veal or chicken stock,
    or enough canned chicken
    broth diluted to make
    2 quarts
salt, as needed (about
    1 tablespoon altogether)
4 tablespoons butter
8 tablespoons flour
2 cups milk
1 cup half-and-half
1 cup sour cream at room
    temperature
2 tablespoons chopped fresh
    parsley

Wash the asparagus and cut off approximately ¼-inch from the bottom end and discard. Lay 6 to 8 pieces of asparagus so that the heads or tips are all together. Cut off the tips. Set them aside and cut off a 1-inch length just below each tip. Make a separate batch of these pieces. Now cut the rest of the asparagus into small discs down to the white part. Keep the hard bottom part, giving you 4 separate batches. Repeat these steps with all of the asparagus.

In a large soup pot, melt the shortening. Add the onions and cook over medium heat, stirring constantly, until the onions start to turn yellow. Add carrot and celery and cook for another 2 minutes, continuing to stir. Add the third batch of asparagus (the one next to the hard bottom parts). Cover the soup pot, adjust the heat to very low, and simmer.

In another pot, add the bottom parts of the asparagus, the cheese-cloth bag with the spices, and the veal or chicken stock. Add salt as needed (this will depend on the saltiness of the stock used). Bring to a boil, then simmer.

In a small saucepan, melt the butter. Mix the flour into the milk with a wire whip. Slowly, stirring constantly with a wire whip, add the flour-milk mixture to the hot butter and keep stirring. If you add it slowly enough, it will thicken immediately. When you finish, it will be just like a white sauce of medium consistency. Remove it from the heat and stir in the half-and-half.

Strain the broth, in which the hard parts of the asparagus have simmered, through a fine sieve into the pot with the onion, carrot, celery, and asparagus. Discard spice bag and hard stalks. Add the white sauce, stir, and simmer over low heat.

Put the second batch of asparagus (from just below the tips) into an electric blender and blend until liquefied. Set aside.

Add the first batch, the asparagus tips, to the soup and gently simmer over low heat 10 minutes. Taste and add salt if needed.

In a soup tureen, stir together the liquefied asparagus and the sour cream. Add to it one ladle of the hot soup, then a second one. When the asparagus-sour cream mixture heats through, add it to the soup, garnish with parsley, and serve.

 CHEF'S SECRET   On first reading this sounds very complicated and involved, but if you read the recipe a second time
before you start to prepare it, you will realize it is a simple soup

to fix. The uncooked asparagus juice and the barely cooked tips will give such an intense flavor as to make this incomparable with any other asparagus soup.

To further intensify the asparagus taste, add a teaspoon of sugar when you saute the onions, carrots, celery, and asparagus discs.

LENTIL SOUP WITH FRANKS
Serves 8

1 clove garlic
1 teaspoon salt
4 tablespoons bacon drippings
    or lard
1 large onion, finely chopped
    (about ¾ cup)
1 cup dried lentils
1 bay leaf
salt and coarsely ground black
    pepper to taste
1 ham bone, or some small
    pork ribs or neck bones, or
    1 or 2 smoked pork shanks

1 small carrot cut into
    1-inch cubes
3 quarts cold water
2 cups potatoes cut into
    1-inch cubes
salt to taste
1 frankfurter per person
1 cup yogurt or sour cream
some vinegar at the table
    (optional)

Mash the garlic with the 1 teaspoon salt. Melt the lard or bacon drippings in a large soup pot and saute the onion until glossy. Add lentils, mashed garlic, bay leaf, and salt and a generous amount of coarsely ground black pepper to taste. Stir with a wooden spoon until the onion turns yellow and the frying lentils begin to make a noise.

Add the ham bone, carrot, and cold water. Bring to a gentle boil, cover, and cook about 30 minutes, keeping the soup just at boiling point.

Add the potatoes and stir. Add more salt if necessary and more water if too much evaporates.

Just before serving, add the franks, sliced or whole. When serving, offer yogurt or sour cream to be stirred into the soup by your guests. Also serve vinegar in a small jar if you wish.

 CHEF'S SECRET   The potatoes are the thickening agent for this old German soup, and the vinegar offered at the table counterbalances the heaviness of the soup.

The color of the lentils will change according to the type of cooking pot used. An enamel-coated or cast iron pot is best. Lentils will have a completely different color if cooked in heavy aluminum. Discoloration does not mean any change in quality; nevertheless, if possible, do not use an aluminum pot.

REAL BEAN SOUP
Serves 8

2 cups dry white navy beans
    or other small white beans,
    soaked overnight in 1 quart
    of cold water in a 2-quart
    pan
2 carrots, scraped and split
1 parsley root or parsnip,
    scraped and split
½ pound smoked ham shank,
    or 1 pound smoked neck
    bones or a ham bone

2 quarts water
1 to 1½ tablespoons salt,
    depending on saltiness of
    the ham
1 whole bay leaf
2 tablespoons shortening
1 small clove garlic
1 small onion, finely minced
2 cups milk mixed with 4
    tablespoons all-purpose flour

Rinse the soaked beans and discard the water. Place the carrot, parsley root, and smoked shank in a soup pot. Add the beans, water, salt, and bay leaf. Cover and bring to a gentle boil.

When beans are tender, melt the shortening in a skillet. Add garlic and onion and cook over medium heat, stirring constantly, until onions are golden. Remove garlic, increase the heat, and stir in the milk-flour mixture. Keep stirring, using a wire whip, until the mixture comes to a boil.

Remove from the heat and stir in two to three ladles of the soup. Stir until completely smooth. Remove the carrot, parsnip or parsley root, and bay leaf from the soup. Pour the milk-flour mixture into the bean soup and continue cooking over low heat for 30 minutes. Serve at once.

 CHEF'S SECRET   To test the beans for doneness, remove a few with a slotted spoon and blow on the beans. When the skin pops on the beans and turns away from the air, the beans are done.

WAX BEAN SOUP
Serves 8

½ a medium-sized onion,
    finely minced
2 tablespoons chopped flat-leaf
    parsley
3 tablespoons butter
1 pound fresh wax beans,
    cleaned and cut up
½ teaspoon white pepper
1 clove garlic crushed with
    ¼ teaspoon salt

1 bay leaf
2 cups chicken stock or canned
    chicken broth
4 cups water
2 cups milk
2 tablespoons flour
1 tablespoon cornstarch
parsley and sour cream for garnish
½ cup vinegar (optional)

In a heavy pot, saute onion and parsley in butter until onion turns transparent. Add wax beans, white pepper, garlic-salt mixture, bay leaf, chicken stock, and water. Cover and cook until beans are tender, about 45 minutes.

Thicken soup with a mixture of milk, flour, and cornstarch, stirring constantly while adding it to the soup. Serve garnish with fresh chopped parsley and sour cream. You may add ½ cup vinegar for a tangy soup.

CHEF'S SECRET   A cold, thick soup can be made from this recipe by using an extra tablespoon each of flour and cornstarch. When the soup is ready, let it cool, stir in the sour cream, chill, and serve it on a hot day with a half-lemon per serving to squeeze into it.

If you cut the beans, cut them on a diagonal. It is even better simply to break them by hand if the beans are fresh and snap when you break them. Of course, you can substitute fresh green beans for the wax beans, but the taste is somewhat different.

3

MEATS

Every year—or at least every other year—another food substance is found to be cancer-causing. Gourmet gurus announce, with about the same frequency, that Beef Wellington is out, nobody likes it anymore.

When I hear this I always panic, because since we opened the only dish we have never removed from our menu for even a single day is individual portions of filet of Beef Wellington. More than half (52.5 percent to be exact) of our customers order Beef Wellington year in, year out, month after month, week after week, day after day.

In this book the longest recipe is the one for Beef Wellington. We never wish to be accused of omitting something from it. We have mailed several thousand copies of it in the past two decades; it has been published in the bible of the American hotel and restaurant industry, the Cornell University *Hotel Quarterly*, and has been reprinted perhaps more often than any other article from that august publication. In our files we have more than a thousand warm thank-you notes from people who have successfully cooked the recipe at home.

Beef Wellington is not the most complicated of the meat dishes in this book, but it may be the most unlikely dish for a homemaker. To produce a few Wellingtons you have to set up, start, run, stop, and dismantle many different "production lines." So the recipe is designed to be easily doubled or tripled. In a good home freezer, the uncooked Wellingtons will keep safely for 2 to 3 months, ready for baking. I advise you to spend a good long afternoon making 24 Wellingtons, and freeze what you don't use immediately. It is worth the effort.

While Beef Wellington has remained consistently popular through the sixties and seventies, dining tastes seem to be perpetually changing. When we first opened we could hardly sell a few portions of veal a night, and even in the mid-seventies it was difficult to convince people that veal is not a tea room ladies' luncheon dish. Today the situation is different: as a rule we can now sell as much veal as we prepare. Although meat consumption in general has declined somewhat as poultry and fish have grown in popularity, meat dishes remain the choice of the majority of people.

BEEF STROGANOFF
Serves 8

2 tablespoons finely minced
    onion
1 tablespoon butter
1 tablespoon oil
1 cup beef consomme
2 tablespoons flour
1 teaspoon tomato puree, or
    1 tablespoon tomato juice
2 teaspoons Chef's Salt
    (see appendix)
½ teaspoon freshly ground
    black pepper

1 bay leaf, washed (optional)
1½ pounds thinly sliced beef
    tenderloin
2 tablespoons lard
½ cup red wine or beef
    consomme
1 to 1½ cups thinly
    sliced mushrooms
1 tablespoon butter
2 cups sour cream
8 firm white mushrooms caps,
    roughly equal size

Saute onions in 1 tablespoon butter and 1 tablespoon oil over medium heat until the onions turn limp and translucent, about 3 minutes. Add ½ cup of the consomme, stir, and continue cooking for another 3 minutes.

Meanwhile, mix the flour, tomato puree or tomato juice, 1 teaspoon Chef's Salt, and black pepper into the remaining ½ cup of consomme. Stir until smooth and pour over the onions. If you wish, add the bay leaf. Simmer the sauce over low heat for at least 15 minutes, stirring occasionally to prevent scorching. Remove the bay leaf after 10 to 15 minutes.

Sprinkle the meat with 1 teaspoon Chef's Salt and divide it into three even portions. Place 1 tablespoon lard in a large heavy skillet. When it heats to the smoking point, add ⅓ of the meat and saute for a minute or so, turning constantly. Remove to a serving platter. Repeat with the second tablespoon of lard and the second portion of meat, then with the third. With the third portion, you won't need to add more lard.

After cooking the meat, pour the ½ cup red wine or consomme into the pan and, with a spatula, loosen the bits and pieces stuck to the bottom of the pan. Strain the liquid into the sauce. If you wish, saute the thinly sliced mushrooms in the same pan with 1 tablespoon butter, or simply saute them with the last part of the meat. If you like the sliced tenderloin medium or medium well, cook it longer.

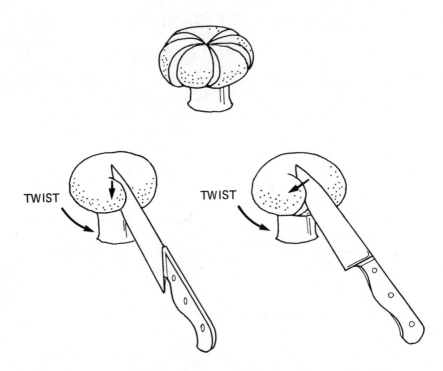

Dilute the sour cream with 2 tablespoons of the hot sauce, then add the sour cream to the rest of the sauce. This method prevents the sauce from curdling. Ladle the hot sauce over the meat.

If you wish, cut the 8 mushroom caps (see illustration), and saute them in a very small amount of fat in a hot pan, stems up. This way the surface of the mushrooms will brown but the carved design will remain white. Place the decorated mushroom caps on top of the sauce and serve the Stroganoff with Alsatian noodles, plain noodles, or rice.

CHEF'S SECRET   It is best to make the Stroganoff from tenderloin tails or tenderloin tips. Buy them already trimmed or trim them yourself. Roll each piece tightly, wrap in aluminum foil, and place in the freezer for an hour or so. Then cut on a diagonal into very thin slices, preferably less than ¼ inch thick.

If you prefer to make "medallions of Stroganoff," cut ½-inch thick medallions from the tenderloin and saute them over low heat 2 to 2½ minutes on each side. Arrange them just as you would tomato slices, halfway overlapping, placing on each portion one mushroom cap.

The bay leaf, which is optional, gives an authentic taste to the Stroganoff sauce, but if you don't remove it after 10 to 15 minutes of simmering it will overpower the sauce. I suggest you wash the bay leaf before you add it. Its taste and fragrance will be much better if you wash it in tepid water, rubbing the surfaces with your fingers.

Suggestions for carving the mushroom caps: Classic French cuisine uses the term "turning" to describe the preparation of the mushroom caps. It is done by pressing a small, very sharp paring knife at an angle to the top of the mushroom and guiding it with the thumb while turning the mushroom. If you follow the illustrations and try it a few times, the mushrooms will look very pretty.

BEEF WELLINGTON
Serves 8

5-to-6 pound trimmed beef
    tenderloin
4 cups flour
1 teaspoon salt
10 tablespoons butter, chilled
10 tablespoons lard, chilled
1 egg yolk
10 tablespoons cold water
1 pound (approximate) ground
    beef from the edible
    tenderloin trimmings

½ pound Pate Maison
    (see page 27)
1 to 1½ teaspoons Parisian
    Spice (see appendix)
pinch of salt
pinch of freshly ground black
    pepper
Chef's Salt (see appendix)
¼ cup corn oil
1 egg mixed with 1 tablespoon
    cold water

Remove the fat surrounding the tenderloin, then remove the tough silvery surface which is called the "silverskin." The best way to do this is to loosen the skin at the tail end with the point of a sharp knife. Pulling and cutting toward the "head end," remove the skin in strips. Place the cleaned tenderloin on a sheet of freezer or plastic wrap and, holding it firmly with one hand, push the tail end in toward the head end to form a cylinder. Wrap tightly and place in the freezer to chill. It need not be completely frozen, but it should be chilled to at least 26 to 28 degrees.

From the trimmings, remove every bit of edible meat and cut it into half-inch cubes for grinding. Put aside all the fat to use as you like. Reserve the non-edible trimmings for the Red Wine Sauce "Cumberland" (see page 221).

Prepare the dough. Sift together 4 cups flour and 1 teaspoon salt. Cut in the chilled butter and chilled lard (no other shortening will do), working quickly. Then work in 1 egg yolk and the cold water. Form the mixture into a ball, wrap in plastic, and chill several hours before using. You must work quickly and with a light hand to combine the ingredients without overworking the dough. (A good grade of commercial piecrust mix prepared according to package directions will also give satisfactory results.)

Once the whole tenderloin has chilled, cut it with a sharp knife into equal portions. From the average steer tenderloin you can cut eight 5-ounce steaks. (Use the ends for Beef Stroganoff—see page 73.) After cutting, place the steaks back in the freezer.

Grind the edible trimmings from the tenderloin twice through the medium or large hole of a meat grinder. You should have approximately 1 pound ground meat. To this add the Pate Maison, Parisian Spice, a pinch of salt, and a pinch of freshly ground black pepper. Mix thoroughly. Refrigerate.

Heat a large, heavy skillet to the point where a drop of oil will immediately smoke and burn. Remove the steaks from the freezer (they should be at the freezing point or below), sprinkle them lightly with Chef's Salt and brush each with a thin coat of corn oil. Quickly sear the steaks in the hot skillet, a few at a time, for 3 or 4 seconds on each side; then immediately return to the freezer and rechill.

Remove the steaks from freezer. Divide the pate mixture into eight equal portions, about 3 ounces each. Place one portion on each of the seared steaks and round the top with your palm. Return the steaks to freezer.

Roll out the dough to ⅛-inch thickness on a lightly floured pastry board. Beat the egg with cold water and brush the surface of the dough with the eggwash. Cut the dough into triangles about 9 × 5 inches. Place a steak close to the narrow corner, so that the bottom is completely on the dough, and pull the long end over the steak, completely covering it and pressing the dough firmly together to form a seal around the bottom rim. Your first Wellington may look clumsy and hopeless, but don't give up.

With a knife, trim the pastry to about ¾ inch from the base of the steak. Pick up the pastry-covered steak in one hand, and with the other make a pinched rim around the base, as you would edge a pie.

From the leftover dough, cut eight triangles, ¾ × 1½ inches, pinch together the short end of each triangle so that it looks like a leaf, and then score veins into the leaf with a knife. Brush the Wellingtons with the eggwash again, place the leaves on top, and return them to the freezer. At this point the Wellingtons are best kept on a well-floured tray, but if they will be stored overnight or longer, they must be tightly covered.

To finish for serving, preheat the oven to 475°. Bake the prepared Wellingtons on a cookie sheet until a meat thermometer registers 115° for rare, 120° for medium rare, 130° for medium, or 140° for medium well. After 5 minutes baking time, brush each Wellington again with eggwash and continue to brush every 5 minutes.

CHEF'S SECRET   If your butcher can supply a fully trimmed tenderloin, 2½ to 2¾ pounds, approximately 11 to 12 inches in length, and 2½ to 3 inches in diameter, plus 1 pound of ground beef for the pate and another pound of scraps or ground meat for the sauce, you can begin the preparation by wrapping the trimmed tenderloin in the aluminum foil to chill.

Don't skip the eggwash basting every 5 minutes while baking, because it has a much more important purpose than simply beautifying the Wellingtons. The cold eggwash cools off the pastry while the meat keeps cooking. This way, even if you like the beef done to medium well (which we really don't recommend), the pastry won't burn or dry out.

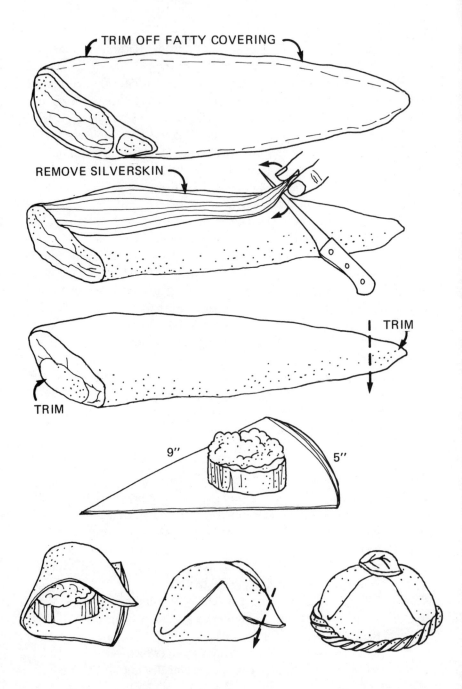

Not knowing your oven and how correct its temperature is, I am reluctant to give specific baking times for the Wellingtons. Our experience shows that in a preheated, accurate 475° oven, eight Wellingtons on a cookie sheet bake to rare in 12 to 13 minutes; to medium rare in 15 minutes; to medium in 18 minutes; and to medium well in about 20 minutes at most.

Meat is so expensive that I feel you should invest in a good professional meat thermometer that is a scientific instrument rather than a gadget. (See note on page 84.)

FRENCH PROVINCIAL PEPPER STEAK
Serves 8

For the sauce:

1 teaspoon sugar

2 slices bacon cut into
½-inch pieces

1 cup chopped onions (½-inch squares)

1 medium green pepper, cored, cut into ½-inch squares

1 medium red bell pepper, or 1 small can (about 2 ounces) whole pimientos, cut into ½ inch squares

1 tomato, not too ripe, peeled and seeds removed, cut into ½-inch pieces

1 cup Burgundy or similar red wine

10½ ounce can beef consomme, undiluted

1 tablespoon flour and 1 tablespoon cornstarch mixed with 4 tablespoons cold water

8 ounces small fresh mushrooms

salt and pepper to taste

In a saucepan wiped completely dry, brown the sugar over high heat. As it starts to brown, add the bacon cut into ½-inch pieces. As the fat from the bacon is rendered, add onions and saute quickly, then add green pepper, red pepper, and tomatoes, and set the heat to low. (If you use canned pimiento, don't add it until after you add the mushrooms because it will fall apart.)

In a small saucepan, bring to a boil the wine and consomme. When it boils, stir in the flour-cornstarch-water mixture. Let it come to a boil again and then simmer.

Wipe mushrooms with a damp cloth and cut each into 2 to 3 pieces, depending on size. Add to the onion-bell pepper mixture. Saute the mixture 8 to 10 minutes, then add it to the sauce and simmer another 10 to 15 minutes. Correct seasoning. The amount of salt you have to add will depend on the saltiness of the consomme used.

For the steak:

8 boneless strip sirloin steaks,
    12 ounces each, closely
    trimmed on the fat side
4 tablespoons Kitchen Bouquet
2 tablespoons Chef's Salt
    (see appendix)

8 tablespoons whole black
    peppercorns, gently bruised
1½ cups corn oil

Brush steaks with Kitchen Bouquet. Mix Chef's Salt with crushed peppercorns. Press this mixture gently but firmly into the surface of the steaks. Place the steaks in a shallow dish and pour the oil over them. Refrigerate at least 4 hours.

Remove half the oil from the steaks and pour it into a heavy skillet over moderately high heat. When the oil starts to smoke, place 4 of the steaks in the pan. Remove after about 30 seconds. Let the oil heat up again and when it starts to smoke, return the steaks to the pan on the uncooked sides. Cook about 2 minutes, then turn and cook on the other side for the same time. Remove to a warm place.

Add the remaining oil to the pan and repeat as above with the remaining steaks.

Let the steaks stand on a warm platter for not longer than 10 minutes, then reheat the pan and finish pan-frying—3 minutes per side for rare, 5 minutes per side for medium rare, or 6 minutes per side for medium.

Have the sauce ready at serving temperature. Arrange the steaks on a hot serving platter with sauce to cover about ⅓ of each. Serve the rest of the sauce in a boat.

CHEF'S SECRET   I am sure you have often seen, in restaurants and homes, steaks that are beautiful on one side and pale on the other. This happens regardless of how the steaks are prepared—on the grill over charcoal, or pan-fried, or even under the broiler. The reason is that cooks do not realize that after the steak touches the surface of whatever utensil you use, a tremendous amount of heat is lost. If you remove the steak after a few seconds and wait until the utensil recovers the heat, the other side of the meat will also brown quickly. This is why it is so important to follow the instructions here closely.

Steaks as we know them are American in origin. For hundreds of years they were never prepared in any other way than pan-fried. That is why I feel that pan-frying is the ideal way to prepare a good steak. I am convinced that after you try this method you will never again prepare a good steak any other way.

HUNGARIAN GOULASH OR PAPRIKASH
Serves 6

2 pounds beef chuck, cut
    into 1-inch cubes
Chef's Salt (see appendix)
freshly ground black pepper,
    to taste
½ cup lard or chicken fat
2½ to 3 cups onions, peeled and
    finely chopped

2 tablespoons sweet Hungarian
    paprika
2 tablespoons flour
3 cups water or beef stock
2 tablespoons tomato paste
1 teaspoon caraway seed,
    slightly bruised
2 cups sour cream (if served
    as "Paprikash")

Season meat with Chef's Salt and additional black pepper.

In a large heavy saucepan, heat the lard to the smoking point. Brown the meat in the lard, turning with a spatula so that it browns on all sides. Add onions and cook until they become limp. Sprinkle the paprika and flour over the meat and onions. Cook for 2 minutes on low heat, stirring to keep the mixture from sticking.

Add the water or beef stock, tomato paste, and caraway seed. Stir. Simmer, covered, over low heat for 1½ hours, or until meat is tender. Check occasionally to see if there is enough liquid; if necessary, add more.

Serve from a large casserole. If it is served as "Paprikash," serve it with the sour cream on the side in a sauceboat.

 CHEF'S SECRET   Whenever available, add ½ bell pepper cut into strips, or 1 whole Hungarian pepper together with the liquid and tomato paste. If possible use imported Hungarian or Spanish paprika; they will give the real flavor. But if you can't get either, add ¼ teaspoon sugar to the paprika you are using.

If you double this recipe, by all means buy a piece of shank, with the marrow bone in it if possible, and add this to the goulash. It will greatly improve the taste. Some of the goulash may be frozen for later use.

Few dishes are as misunderstood and abused as this fine dish. The word *goulash* means "cowboy" or "herdsman," and the Hungarian name of the dish, *gulyás—hús,* means "herds-man's meat."

If you add sour cream to a "goulash" it turns into "Papri-kash." Chicken, veal, lamb, and pork, like beef, can be made into goulash by cooking them with the same ingredients, by the same method—but as soon as the sour cream is added, the dish can no longer be called goulash.

ROAST BEEF
Serves 8

4 tablespoons Kitchen Bouquet
4 tablespoons corn oil
1 U.S. Choice 4-rib roast or
   standing rib roast,
   7 to 8 pounds
1 small clove garlic
⅓ cup Chef's Salt
   (see appendix)

1 large onion, skin on, and
   coarsely chopped
1 carrot, scraped and
   coarsely chopped
1 rib celery, chopped

Preheat the oven to 375°. Mix the Kitchen Bouquet with the corn oil and rub the whole surface of the roast, especially the two cut ends and the surface of the bony part, with the mixture. Score the fat on top if you wish.

Crush the garlic to a pulp with some of the Chef's Salt, then mix it with the remaining Chef's Salt. Rub the meat with this mixture, covering completely.

Pour water to a depth of 1 inch in the bottom of a roasting pan, and add the coarsely chopped onion, carrot, and celery. Place the meat on top of the vegetables, fat side up. Roast uncovered 30 minutes. Cover and continue roasting 1½ to 2 hours until a meat thermometer registers the temperature you wish: 100° for rare, 115° for medium rare, or 140° for medium. Remove the roast from the oven and let it stand on a board for at least 1 hour.

Ten minutes before serving, bring the oven temperature as high as the control allows. Put the roast on a cookie sheet and place it in the oven for 10 minutes. If you like a dark crusty surface, heat 4 to 6 tablespoons shortening to the smoking point and pour this hot fat over the beef before putting it back into the oven. Be careful: the hot fat splatters. Cover your arms to protect them.

CHEF'S SECRET   The beef will not be salty. The salt will not penetrate the meat and it will not "draw" the juices as some people believe. In fact, the British cover their roast beef completely with salt and bake it in a crust. It is never salty.

Rubbing the surface with the Kitchen Bouquet and oil will close the pores and give a caramelized color. This may also be achieved through searing, but searing is very cumbersome in a household kitchen, takes a lot of time, is wasteful, and demands considerable skill. Kitchen Bouquet gives the same results in a few seconds.

Be sure to invest in a good food thermometer which registers from 0 to 200 degrees—one that you don't leave in the meat like ordinary meat thermometers but just insert for registering temperature, then remove. These are expensive in comparison with ordinary thermometers, but if properly used they save their price at least twenty times in the first year.

If you are unable to find such a thermometer, you may write me for an order form and price list:

Chef Louis
Thermometer
2218 North Lincoln Avenue
Chicago, Illinois 60614

ROAST A LA HOTEL ADLON
Serves 8

8- to 10-pound boned prime rib
    roast, or a 5- to 6-pound rib
    eye covered with a
    thin coating of beef fat
8 ounces Westphalian ham or
    country ham, raw,
    in one piece
3 tablespoons Chef's Salt
    (see appendix)
2 envelopes unflavored gelatin

1 cup chopped carrots
1 cup chopped onions
½ cup chopped celery
½ cup chopped turnip, parsnip,
    or parsley root (only one
    of the three)
2 to 3 sprigs parsley
1 tablespoon rinsed capers
1 clove garlic
2 cups dry white wine

For the sauce:

1 quart pan juices
1 tablespoon cornstarch and
    1 tablespoon flour diluted in
    1 cup dry white wine or
    fruity, not sweet, white wine
1 teaspoon rinsed capers,
    chopped

1 black truffle, chopped fine,
    or 4 to 5 pitted black olives
    brought to a boil in ½ cup
    of white wine, cooled,
    rinsed, and chopped
1 ounce cognac, brandy, or
    strong whiskey
1 tablespoon rinsed whole capers

Ask the butcher to debone the prime ribs and cut the coat of fat from the top. Or if you buy rib eye, ask for half of a rib eye, lip off, covered with a square piece of surface fat from the sirloin or rib.

Cut the ham into 2-inch-long pieces as thick as a matchstick. Lay the pieces on a piece of aluminum foil and freeze.

Sharpen the end of a wooden kitchen spoon and pierce the outside of the rib eye approximately 2 to 2½ inches deep, aiming toward the center of the beef. Make about 6 holes around one circumference, and about 7 of these rows along the length of the beef. You should end up with about 42 holes and as many matchstick pieces of ham.

After you have made the holes, remove the ham from the freezer and stick the pieces into the holes.

Chop the remaining ham, if any, and save it for the sauce. Preheat the oven to 375°.

Rub the surface of the roast with the Chef's Salt mixed with the gelatin. Roll the whole roast into the blanket of fat and tie with butcher's string. The ties should be an inch apart from one another. Make a knot and cut the string each time you go around, or run the string spirally from one end to the other and then back.

Place the carrots, onions, celery, turnip, parsley, capers, and garlic in a roasting pan with a good cover. Mix the wine with enough water to almost cover the vegetables. Place the roast on top of the vegetables, cover the pan, and roast about 2 hours for medium rare. Remove the roast, cut off the string, and discard the fat blanket. Let the meat stand for 30 to 45 minutes in a warm place before carving.

For the sauce, drain the pan juices into a dish, add a handful of ice cubes, stir, and skim the fat that accumulates on the top. Bring the juices to a boil, add the mixture of cornstarch, flour, and wine, and cook until it comes to a boil. Simmer a few minutes. Add the chopped ham and rinsed and chopped capers and continue to simmer.

Place the finely chopped black truffle or the chopped olives in a small pan over high heat. Pour on the cognac and ignite it with a match. Pour the truffle or olives with the flaming brandy into the sauce, add the rinsed whole capers, and correct seasoning by adding perhaps a small sprinkling of sugar or a few more spoonfuls of white wine.

Slice the beef into even, medium-thick slices. Pour some of the sauce over it and offer the rest in a sauceboat.

 CHEF'S SECRET   This dish was created by Auguste Escoffier, the famous French chef who worked for a while in Berlin at the legendary Hotel Adlon. To my knowledge this is one of the few beef dishes prepared and served with white wine. Germany excels in white wine but has not much to show in reds. That's why Escoffier developed a great beef dish with a white wine sauce.

As a rule, Beef Adlon is served with pan-fried or hashed brown potatoes or with a very finely mashed potato or creamed pureed potato. You can also serve it with rice or noodles.

If you have leftover chopped ham after inserting all the pieces in the beef, stir it into the sauce at the last minute. But be careful: if the ham you use is too salty, you may have to adjust the amount of salt in the sauce.

The gelatin mixed with the Chef's Salt will help the beef coagulate as it cools and will prevent the juices from oozing out.

Don't worry if the holes you make in the beef are larger than the ham pieces. The meat has a natural gelatinous substance that will surround the ham pieces as they cook and hold them tight so that they won't fall out and so that no juice will run from the meat.

ROAST TENDERLOIN
Serves 8

5- to 6-pound untrimmed tenderloin, or 3 to 3½ pound trimmed tenderloin
½ teaspoon sugar
1 tablespoon Chef's Salt (see appendix)
1 teaspoon coarse black pepper or ½ teaspoon fine black pepper

2 to 3 tablespoons Kitchen Bouquet
½ cup corn oil
1 cup red wine or consomme
1 cup lard, bacon drippings, shortening, or oil

Rub the whole surface of the tenderloin with the sugar, Chef's Salt, and pepper. Mix the Kitchen Bouquet with the ½ cup corn oil, pour the mixture onto the beef, and massage it in. Let stand at room temperature.

Preheat the broiler. Line the broiling pan with aluminum foil. Place the tenderloin on it and bring it as close to the source of heat as possible.

Turn it every 2 to 3 minutes until the whole surface is seared. Let the tenderloin cool at room temperature.

Wrap the tenderloin in heavy-duty aluminum foil, pouring the wine or consomme over the meat before closing the foil on top. Roast the foil-wrapped tenderloin at 350° for 35 to 40 minutes. Remove and cool to room temperature. This can be done in the morning, and the meat can stay at room temperature all day long (except on hot summer days, when you would refrigerate it if it were to stand longer than 2 hours at room temperature).

Half an hour before serving, heat the 1 cup of shortening in a small saucepan until it reaches the smoking point. Place the tenderloin on a cookie sheet covered with aluminum foil. Pour the smoking hot fat over the surface of the meat and roast, uncovered, at 450 to 500 degrees for 10 to 15 minutes. Let it stand 10 minutes before slicing.

 CHEF'S SECRET   I have been called "crazy" and "a nut" for this method by just about every "expert" in the country — until they try it once. After you try it, you will find that it is not as complicated as it sounds when you first read it. It takes very little work, and it will produce the greatest yield, with pink, juicy, tasty roast tenderloin throughout.

Tenderloin is the most expensive cut of beef, so it is worthwhile to take very good care of it. Rubbing the sugar into the surface with the salt and pepper will not make the beef sweet at all but, together with the Kitchen Bouquet and oil, will give a very desirable surface that will never burn or overcook.

The Kitchen Bouquet and oil should be rubbed or massaged into the surface by hand. No brush would give the necessary pressure to penetrate the surface.

The wine or consomme used in the first 40 minutes of roasting, mixed with the natural juices oozing out of the beef, will serve as an excellent *au jus*, or it can be used as the stock for any sauce you plan to serve with the roast tenderloin. If used as *au jus*, add some Worcestershire sauce to it.

Exactly the same method may be used for roasting boneless, well-trimmed sirloin strip or whole rib eye. Of course, the moist-roasting time is longer for a 6-pound (completely trimmed) sirloin strip. In this case, 1½ hours would be required for a medium rare roast; about the same time would be needed for a rib eye of the same weight.

If you let the completely finished meat cool to room temperature and then refrigerate it overnight, you will have the world's best-tasting and best-looking cold beef. With a good knife, a roast tenderloin which would serve 8 people as a hot main course can be sliced into 24 to 30 beautiful cold slices, depending on your skill.

STEAKS
Serves 4

4 strip steaks, or equivalent,   1 tablespoon Kitchen Bouquet
   12 to 16 ounces each   Chef's Salt to taste
2 to 3 tablespoons corn oil   (see appendix)

Broiling:

Set the oven control to broil. Brush the steaks with oil and Kitchen Bouquet and sprinkle with Chef's Salt. As soon as the broiler is ready, place the steaks very close to the source of heat for a few seconds. As soon as the surface starts to brown, turn and repeat.

After the second side is slightly browned, move the steaks 5 to 6 inches away from the heat and continue broiling, turning once or twice, until an inserted meat thermometer registers the desired doneness.

Pan-Frying:

Place a large skillet over medium heat and melt a small amount of shortening. (A combination of two shortenings—lard, butter, or oil—is preferable.) Increase the heat until the shortening reaches the smoking point. Brush the steaks with corn oil and Kitchen Bouquet and sprinkle with Chef's Salt. Gently lower the steaks into the fat in the skillet.

After 10 to 15 seconds, turn the steaks. Lower the heat to medium and fry the steaks 2 to 3 minutes, shaking the pan occasionally. Turn them again and continue frying, shaking the pan, until the steaks reach the required doneness.

CHEF'S SECRET   The greatest part of success in preparing steak is the shopping. Buy only in a reliable store, and select U.S. Government-graded, cherry red, well-marbled, evenly cut steaks with a firm white fat cover.

If the steaks are refrigerated, have them at room temperature for broiling or frying. If the steaks are frozen, do not defrost. Rub the frozen steak surface with oil and spices and proceed according to directions, using either method, but increase the cooking time.

Don't serve the steaks immediately after they are done. Start the preparation in advance so the steaks can rest in a warm place, after being broiled or pan-fried, 10 to 15 minutes before serving.

RAGOUT OF VENISON
Serves 8

4 pounds boneless venison, cut into 1-inch cubes
½ pound very lean slab bacon
2 to 3 cups water
⅔ cup finely minced shallots (or white parts of scallions)
½ cup lard
2½ teaspoons Chef's Salt (see appendix)

4 tablespoons flour
1 small clove garlic, crushed
1 cup red wine
1 teaspoon brown sugar
½ cup tomato juice
1 cup stock or water
2 teaspoons Kitchen Bouquet
1 tablespoon cornstarch
1 cup sliced mushrooms
2 tablespoons butter

Wash the venison cubes and leave them in water for about 1 hour. Remove, dry on a towel, and let stand at room temperature.

Cut the bacon into ½-inch cubes. In a small saucepan, boil the bacon in 2 to 3 cups water 15 minutes, then drain. Save the water for use in the ragout. Set the boiled bacon aside.

In a large pot, saute shallots in shortening.

Combine 2 teaspoons Chef's Salt, 2 tablespoons flour, and crushed garlic, and rub the mixture into the venison. Increase heat and add the meat to shallots in small amounts so that the heat in the pot won't decrease. Keep turning the few pieces of meat before you add more, and keep scraping the bottom with a metal spatula. When all the meat is in the pot, add ½ cup of the red wine, ½ teaspoon Chef's Salt, brown sugar, and tomato juice. Reduce heat to very low, cover, and cook, stirring occasionally, about 30 minutes. Add stock or water and increase heat to medium. Add Kitchen Bouquet and preboiled bacon cubes.

Mix 2 tablespoons flour and the tablespoon of cornstarch into the second ½ cup of wine and stir into the pot until smooth. Simmer 1 hour.

Saute mushrooms in butter. Add to meat 5 minutes before serving. Serve with noodles, rice, or potatoes.

CHEF'S SECRET   Soaking the meat will extract some of the "wild" taste, and having it at room temperature will help to make it more tender.

If you wish to add more vegetables than the mushrooms, mix 1 cup carrot slices and 1 cup frozen green peas (without defrosting) into the pot at the same time you add the cornstarch mixture.

CASSOULET
Serves 8

Each village in France has its own recipe for cassoulet. How to decide which is more authentic than the other? After eating cassoulet in a dozen restaurants in France, all famous for their cassoulets, we simply decided which recipe we liked the most, and this is what we serve at *The Bakery Restaurant*. Our guests like it very much; we hope you will like it too.

1 pound small white dried
    beans
1 tablespoon salt
1 pound assorted French- or
    German-type sausages, such
    as French garlic sausage,
    blood sausage, knockwurst,
    frankfurters, ring bologna,
    or Polish sausage
1 jar or tin potted goose or
    goose confiture (or homemade
    potted goose, see page 28)

2 cloves garlic
1 small onion, finely minced
1 pound lamb front, cubed
2 cups water
1 teaspoon mixed dried
    tarragon, chervil, marjoram,
    and parsley flakes, to taste
20-ounce can tomato sauce
1 cup breadcrumbs
2 cups tomato juice
1 tablespoon sugar

Soak the beans in lukewarm water overnight. Discard the water and add new water to cover, plus the salt. Over low heat, gently cook the beans until tender. Remove from heat and place the whole sausages in the cooked beans. Let stand until cool.

Remove some of the fat from the potted goose and, in a skillet, saute the garlic cloves in the fat until they start to turn brown. Discard garlic or set aside for use in the sauce.

Add the onion to the skillet and, stirring, saute until limp. Add the lamb cubes, increase the heat, and, stirring constantly, sear the surface of the cubes. Pour about 2 cups water over the lamb and add the dried herbs. Cover and simmer about 30 minutes, or until the lamb cubes are tender.

Pour off the cooking liquid from the lamb and combine the liquid with the tomato sauce.

Preheat the oven to 300°. In a heavy casserole, make an even layer of beans, using ⅓ of them. Skin the sausages and then slice them and distribute half over the beans. Add the lamb cubes and ladle on some of the sauce. Add another layer of beans, distribute the potted goose over it, add the rest of the sausage, and cover with the remaining beans. Pour the remaining sauce evenly over the top. Sprinkle the top with breadcrumbs. Cover and bake at least 2 hours. During the last 15 minutes of cooking, add the tomato juice with the sugar.

 CHEF'S SECRET   If you like a very moist cassoulet, add an extra 1 to 1½ cups water to the cooking liquid from the lamb when you mix it with the tomato sauce.

The best way to test the beans for doneness is to remove about 1 tablespoon from the pot and gently blow on them. If the skins break and start to curl back, the beans are done.

If you like a good garlicky taste, don't throw away the cooked garlic. Mash it and mix it into the tomato sauce.

ROAST LEG OF LAMB
Serves 8

5- to 6-pound leg of lamb
Chef's Salt (see appendix)
3 cloves garlic
2 cups carrots, coarsely
    chopped
2 cups onions, coarsely
    chopped

3 to 4 ribs celery, cut in
    1-inch pieces
4 tablespoons shortening
2 teaspoons tarragon
stuffing (optional, recipe
    follows)

Ask the butcher to remove the bones from the leg, or remove them yourself by proceeding as follows (see illustration). Lay the leg in front of you with the slightly rounded outside part on the cutting board and the

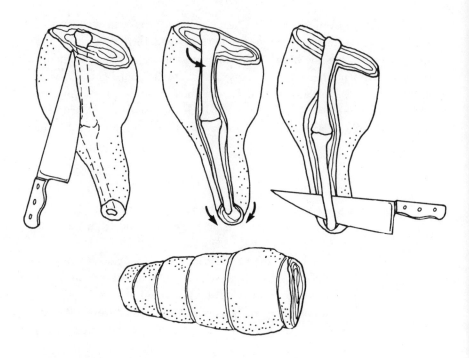

inside part upward. You will see the round head of the joint where the leg was attached to the hip or, probably, part of the back bone with the joint casing of the hip still on. In either case, cut with a sharp knife from the hip joint toward the shank, cutting right along the bone. The ideal way to do it is to let the point of the knife on the bone. Do this until you get to another big rounded joint. Then, again starting at the hip end, repeat the cut on the other side of the bone. Loosen all the flesh under the bone until you are able to move the freed leg bone in the knee joint. Cut the skin on both sides of the knee joint, then the whole bone will come out easily. Save the bones.

Preheat the oven to 350°. Sprinkle the inside surface generously with Chef's Salt and rub the flesh with 1 clove of the garlic, crushed. If you wish to serve in the French way, fill with a stuffing.

Reshape the leg and tie with a string. Then rub the outside surface with Chef's Salt.

Split the remaining 2 cloves of garlic crosswise, two-thirds of the way down. Over the bottom of a roasting pan, evenly distribute the carrots, onions, celery, garlic, and just enough water to almost cover the vegetables. Place the leg of lamb on the vegetables. Put in the bones you removed.

Heat the shortening to the smoking point and pour it over the surface of the leg of lamb. Cover and roast 1 hour. Remove cover, turn the leg so the bottom side is up, sprinkle with 1 teaspoon of the tarragon, and return to the oven uncovered for about 30 minutes. Then turn the leg over again and sprinkle the top with the remaining tarragon. Cover and finish cooking to the desired degree of doneness. A thermometer, when inserted in the thickest part, should register 125 degrees for medium rare, 135 to 140 degrees for medium, and 165 to 170 degrees for well done.

For the stuffing:

5 ounces fresh mushrooms
1 tablespoon coarsely
    chopped green parsley
2 tablespoons shortening
salt and pepper to taste

½ cup cream
1 egg
1 cup firmly packed soft
    breadcrumbs

Quickly wash the mushrooms under cold running water, then dry. Chop them coarsely and saute them with the parsley in the shortening. Sprinkle with salt and pepper.

Beat the cream and the egg together. Place the soft breadcrumbs in a mixing bowl and pour the cream-egg mixture over them. Add the lightly sauteed mushrooms and parsley. Mix gently. Stuff the leg where the bones were removed.

ROAST RACK OF LAMB
Serves 6

1 whole or "double" rack
  of lamb
2 cloves garlic
1 tablespoon Chef's Salt
  (see appendix)

2 to 3 tablespoons tarragon, to taste
2 to 3 tablespoons soft
  butter

Ask the butcher to prepare a rack of lamb, figuring about 2 to 3 rib widths as a serving per person.

Preheat the oven at 475°. Rub the surface of the lamb with a mixture of the garlic crushed with the Chef's Salt. Then rub it with dried tarragon, to taste, combined with the soft butter.

Roast uncovered 15 minutes. Baste with its own drippings, tilting the pan and adding a few tablespoons of hot water if necessary. Reduce the heat to 375° and roast the lamb for 20 to 25 additional minutes, or until a meat thermometer inserted into the thickest part registers 110 to 120 degrees.

It is a sin to carve a rack of lamb, prepared like this, crosswise, so that it resembles lamb or pork chops. The proper way to carve this is in ribbon-like slices. First, cut down from the top of the backbone to the beginning of the ribs, then slice on a 90-degree angle from the first cut into long thin ribbons (see illustration).

CHEF'S SECRET   Lamb should be eaten pink or not at all. If you don't have a meat thermometer you can test the doneness by sticking a long needle into the lamb. If a pink liquid starts to run through the hole, the lamb is just about right. Before it is cooked, nothing will come out; if overdone, the liquid will be colorless.

It is probably more important for a leg of lamb or a rack of lamb to stand before being carved than for any other type of meat. Find a warm place where the lamb can stand (the leg

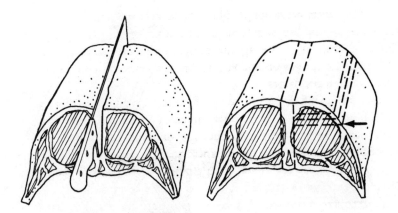

about 20 to 30 minutes, the rack 10 to 15 minutes) before being carved for serving.

If the lamb happens to have a stronger lamb odor than you like, this can be remedied before cooking. Boil 2 gallons of water; after it begins to boil, add 2 to 3 cups vinegar and continue to boil 2 to 3 minutes. Pour this hot vinegar-water over the lamb. Let stand about 4 minutes, drain, then start the roasting preparation.

ROAST PORK STUFFED WITH HUNGARIAN SAUSAGE
Serves 8

1 piece Hungarian or Polish sausage, approximately ⅔ inch in diameter and as long as the pork loin
3- to 4-pound pork loin, center cut, all bones except rib removed
1 medium-sized onion, skin on

1 small carrot
1 rib celery
1 quart water
2 cloves garlic, chopped
2 tablespoons Chef's Salt (see appendix)
1 teaspoon caraway seeds, bruised

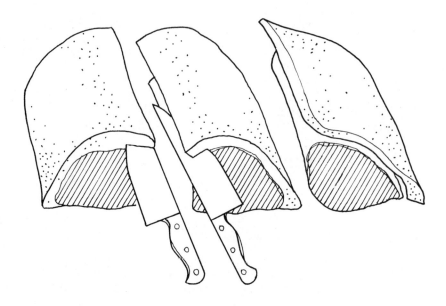

Straighten the sausage by rolling it tightly into aluminum foil, then placing it in the freezer for at least 2 hours.

Ask the butcher to remove all the bones from the pork loin except the rib bones. Cut off the fat part from the top of the loin (see illustration). Reserve the fat.

Preheat the oven to 350°. With a long, thin-bladed knife, carefully make a hole throughout the entire length of the pork loin, keeping to the middle as much as possible (or ask the butcher to do this for you).

Slice the onion (including the skin), carrot, and celery, and place in the bottom of a roasting pan. Pour the water over the vegetables and add the garlic.

Cut the fat trimmed from the pork loin into ¼-inch cubes and fry them until they turn dark brown.

Rub the Chef's Salt into the surface of the whole roast—top, bottom of ribs, and the two sides. Rub in the caraway seeds. Carefully insert the stiffly frozen sausage into the pork loin by starting at one end of the roast and gently pushing it in, turning side to side. It will help if you first insert the handle of a wooden spoon, or similar object, slightly smaller than the diameter of the sausage.

Place the pork, rib side down, on the vegetables and pour the smoking hot fat over the top. Cover the pan and roast 90 minutes to 1 hour and 45 minutes, or until a thermometer inserted into the thickest part registers 165 to 170 degrees. Baste every 15 to 20 minutes.

Remove the roast from the oven and place it on a serving platter. Let is stand in a warm place for at least 30 minutes.

Strain the liquid from the vegetables. Skim the fat from the juices, place the juices over medium heat, and reduce them to ⅓ the quantity. Serve as a clear sauce.

If you prefer a country pork gravy, reduce the liquid only to ½. Combine 1 cup milk and 2 tablespoons flour and add 4 or 5 drops of Kitchen Bouquet. Stir this mixture into the simmering pan juices. If you wish you may puree the vegetables and add all or part of the puree to the sauce; otherwise, discard the vegetables.

CHEF'S SECRET   Freezing the sausage makes it rigid enough to be inserted in the roast. The best way to cut the hole in the roast is to make a cross-cut using a very thin-bladed knife. First push the knife in, cutting vertically, then cut horizontally.

To increase the pleasant taste of the sausage throughout the pork, press holes in the sausage casing with a fine needle before freezing.

This dish is elegant and inexpensive for a buffet table. You never have to worry about the sausage falling out; as the pork cooks, the muscles contract and grip the sausage. Also, there is a natural gelatin present in the meat which acts as a glue to hold the meat and sausage together.

Among the dessert recipes you will find an excellent and unique hot dessert, Prunes Frederick, which I created and named in honor of one of the most brilliant people I ever worked with, Fred Robbins. Excellent just as it is, or over vanilla ice cream or on poundcake or spongecake, it is also outstanding as a side dish with roast pork. It lifts the roast pork from the ordinary into the extraordinary, and gives an inexpensive elegant accent that would be hard to achieve in any other way. The taste, texture, and color lend themselves to that perfect "little something" on a beautiful plate of roast pork, mashed potatoes, and a vivid green vegetable.

ROAST SUCKLING PIG
Serves 8 to 12

1 small suckling pig, about 16 to 22 pounds, inspected and government stamped
4 to 6 tablespoons Chef's Salt (see appendix)
2 pounds pure lard

1 quart beer
10½ ounce can chicken broth, undiluted
3 tablespoons flour
½ cup cold water

Prepare a cookie sheet, or other cooking utensil that is large enough to hold the suckling pig in a sitting position (lying on the belly with hind legs pulled up under the body and head resting stretched out on the forelegs). Brush the pan with shortening, line it with aluminum foil, then brush the foil with shortening.

Wash and dry the suckling pig inside and outside and rub the surface completely dry with towels. Rub the inside with Chef's Salt, being careful to avoid getting any salt on the outside of the skin. Tie the two hind legs together under the belly, leaving enough room between them so that the belly can lie flat. Tie the front legs together and insert a piece of wood in the mouth so the pig will roast with its mouth open. This will make it easier to insert an apple or lemon in the mouth before serving.

Preheat the oven to 375°. Thickly spread the lard over the entire surface of the skin, covering the back especially well. Place the suckling pig in the oven to roast. After about 1 hour, dip a towel in the beer and wipe the entire skin. Repeat this every 15 minutes; toward the end of the cooking time, which is about 3½ to 4 hours, wipe every ten minutes.

Remove the suckling pig from the oven when a thermometer inserted into the thickest part of the hind leg registers 175 to 180 degrees. Let it rest until cool enough to be handled.

Remove the wood from the mouth. Replace with an apple or lemon. Place the suckling pig on a serving platter and surround it with green parsley or other greens of your choice, or surround it with shoestring potatoes to resemble hay or straw.

Serve the suckling pig with a sauce made by scraping all of the beer and fat mixture from the foil-lined pan and diluting it with the chicken broth, then thickening it with the flour dissolved in cold water.

CHEF'S SECRET   Don't ever buy a non-inspected suckling pig; you never know. . . .

Where to buy? Simply look in the Yellow Pages for a Greek, Mexican, or German butcher and ask him. If he doesn't have a suckling pig, he will be able to tell you where one can be purchased.

If you plan to have the suckling pig for Christmas, New Year's Eve, or New Year's Day, it is advisable to place your order around Thanksgiving. Suckling pigs are always in high demand and short supply at this time of year.

When serving, present the whole suckling pig at the table; then take it back to the kitchen to carve. Don't try to carve it at the dining table.

To carve, first cut off the head by inserting a sharp knife about 1½ to 2 inches below the ears, in the middle, trying to hit the center of a joint between the neck bones. Split the suckling pig on either the right or left side of the backbone, cutting from the neck along the backbone to the tail. Lay down one half. Cut off the whole hind leg, then the front leg, using a shorter-bladed knife (see illustration). Now cut the rib part into serving-sized pieces. Slice or cut up the hind and front legs. Repeat with the other half.

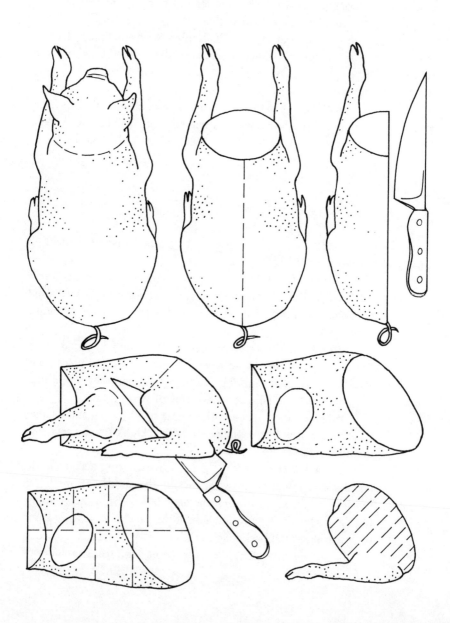

SZEKELY GOULASH
Serves 8

5 tablespoons shortening
(rendered from the
trimmings, if you like)
2 pounds pork butt,
trimmed and cut into
1-inch cubes
⅓ cup flour
1 tablespoon Chef's Salt
(see appendix)
1 clove garlic, mashed
to a pulp with ½
teaspoon Chef's Salt
1 cup finely minced onion
⅔ cup tomato juice
½ cup chopped green pepper

2 tablespoons Hungarian
paprika
2 to 2½ pounds sauerkraut,
drained, and rinsed
½ teaspoon caraway seed,
bruised
¼ teaspoon white peppercorns,
bruised
1 bay leaf
½ cup grated raw potato
1 pound Hungarian,
Polish, or similar smoked
sausage or ring bologna
1 cup sour cream
1 cup buttermilk

Heat 4 tablespoons shortening in a large skillet. Dredge the pork cubes in a mixture of flour, Chef's Salt, and garlic. Place in skillet with ⅔ cup minced onion and cook over low heat 20 minutes, stirring occasionally, until the meat browns.

Add tomato juice, green pepper, and paprika. Cover and simmer over low heat 1¼ to 1½ hours, or until the meat is tender. Add water as necessary to keep the meat barely covered, and stir occasionally to prevent the meat from sticking to the pan. Remove from heat and set aside.

In the remaining 1 tablespoon shortening, saute the remaining ⅓ cup onion until golden. Press the sauerkraut, reserving the juice, and rinse under cold running water. Press dry again by handfuls to remove all liquid, and discard this liquid. Loosen the sauerkraut with your fingers and add to the onions. Add caraway seed, white peppercorns, bay leaf, and water to cover. Bring to a boil over medium heat, then reduce heat and simmer 2½ hours. Grate the potato into the simmering sauerkraut and stir in gently. Taste and correct seasoning by adding some of the reserved sauerkraut juice if the taste is too bland.

To serve, gently mix pork goulash with cooked sauerkraut. Slice the sausage thin and stir it in until it warms through. Add some of the hot liquid to sour cream and buttermilk in a bowl. Stir, then add mixture to the goulash (in this way you avoid curdling the sour cream). Serve with plain boiled potatoes.

Instead of slicing the sausage into the goulash, you may saute the sausage pieces in a very little shortening over medium heat and use them to decorate the serving dish. You may also replace part of the sour cream, if you wish, with yogurt.

CHEF'S SECRET   The name of this goulash has a fascinating history. For more than a thousand years, a part of the Hungarian (Magyar) nation has called itself Szekely. The Szekelys live mainly in Transylvania, where they number about two million. Many persons assume that Szekely goulash is characteristic of their cuisine and is named for them.

Not so! The dish is named for a restaurant owner in Szeged, the second largest city in Hungary. This Mr. Szekely, who was a leading restaurant owner at the turn of the century, created the dish. People who imitated it called it Szekely goulash, honoring the inventor.

Like any other dish made with sauerkraut, this one improves if the sauerkraut is cooked the day before and heated gently the day it is used. The best way to heat it is in a baking dish covered with foil, or in an ovenproof casserole.

OLD-FASHIONED BLANKET OF VEAL
Serves 8

3 to 3½ pound breast of
  veal, cut into ½-inch
  pieces
6 cups veal or chicken stock
3 sprigs parsley
3 ribs celery, cut into
  2-inch pieces
2 teaspoons salt
1 bay leaf
20-ounce can tiny white
  onions

12 ounces fresh small whole
  mushrooms
4 tablespoons flour
6 tablespoons soft butter
3 to 4 egg yolks combined
  with enough cream to
  make 2 cups liquid
salt to taste
lemon juice to taste
white pepper to taste
chopped parsley for decoration

Blanch the veal in boiling water 5 minutes. Drain.

Combine the veal with the stock, parsley, celery, salt, and bay leaf in a large stock pot. Cover and simmer 1 hour.

Rinse the canned onions under cold running water. Do the same with the mushrooms. After rinsing, keep onions and mushrooms in ice water in the refrigerator for at least 30 minutes.

Remove the celery, parsley, and bay leaf from the stock pot. Add the onions and the mushrooms. Simmer 15 minutes longer.

Blend the flour and butter in a small cup. Add a few spoonfuls of the hot liquid to the butter-flour mixture. Then, using a wire whip, blend the butter-flour mixture into the veal liquid. Try not to break the pieces of veal. Cook on low heat until thickened. Remove from heat.

Blend the egg yolks with the cream. Stir into the sauce, and heat over low heat for one minute. Season with salt, lemon juice, and pepper. Ladle into a casserole and sprinkle with chopped parsley.

 CHEF'S SECRET   Be careful when mixing the softened butter-flour mixture and the hot liquid. It is best to wait for the cooking liquid to lose some of its heat, then add to the butter-flour mixture, teaspoonful by teaspoonful.

With a slotted spoon, move the meat away from the part of the pot where you will stir the butter-flour mixture in. This will help to prevent breaking the meat.

When you make this dish for the first time, it is probably advisable to first remove all the meat to a serving dish, then stir the egg yolk and cream into the thickened liquid to finish the dish. Do this very quickly over very low heat.

VEAL SCALOPPINE
(*Natural, a la Vermouth,* and *a la Milanese*)
Each serves 8

The word *scaloppine* actually means nothing more than "thin sliced," so veal scaloppine is just thin slices of veal. The great advantage of this dish is the quickness with which it may be prepared. Scaloppine Natural makes an elegant party dish, is relatively inexpensive, and is easy to learn how to fix.

Veal Scaloppine Natural:

8 thin slices veal, 4 to 6
    ounces each, cut across the
    grain; or 16 slices, 2 to 3
    ounces each
1 teaspoon Chef's Salt
    (see appendix)

2 tablespoons flour
2 tablespoons oil
4 tablespoons butter
⅓ cup water
2 lemons

With a mallet, gently pound each piece of meat, moving the mallet downward and at the same time outward, until the scaloppine tissues are broken down. Be careful not to tear the meat (see illustration).

Mix the Chef's Salt with the flour. Sprinkle each scaloppine sparingly with this mixture. In a large, heavy skillet, preheat half the oil and butter to the smoking point. Brown half the scaloppine quickly on both

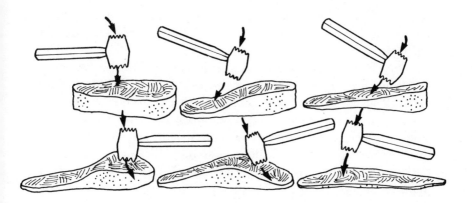

sides. Remove. Add the other half of the shortening, bring it to the smoking point, and brown the remaining scaloppine on both sides. Remove them and add to the frying pan ⅓ cup water. Scrape all the brown bits from the bottom of the pan. Squeeze the juice of ½ lemon into the pan. Keep stirring this mixture, scraping the bottom, for 1 more minute.

Return all the scaloppine to the pan and cook over medium heat for another 2 to 3 minutes. Serve the scaloppine at once with round slices of lemon cut from the remaining 1½ lemons.

Veal Scaloppine a la Vermouth:

1½ teaspoons Chef's Salt
    (see appendix)
2 tablespoons flour
½ teaspoon sugar
16 to 24 small slices of veal,
    2 to 3 ounces each
1 tablespoon finely minced
    shallots or scallions (white
    parts only)
2 tablespoons butter and
    2 tablespoons oil, or
    4 tablespoons oil

½ cup mixed red and white
    vermouth (preferably not the
    "cocktail" or "dry" white
    vermouth but the "golden"
    or sweet white)
pinch of oregano
1 teaspoon finely minced
    Italian parsley for decoration

Mix the Chef's Salt, flour, and sugar, and dredge the meat with the mixture. Lay the meat slices next to one another on absorbent paper, but don't overlap.

In a large heavy skillet, saute the shallots with the shortening until the shallots are limp and translucent. Increase the heat and add the scaloppine, all at once. Keep turning quickly with a spatula. As the color changes, pour the vermouth beside the meat (not over it). Using the spatula, lift the pieces slightly to let the vermouth flow under the scaloppine. Reduce the heat to medium. Carefully turn all the scaloppine. Sprinkle them with oregano and parsley. Turn the meat once more. Serve immediately.

Veal Scaloppine a la Milanese:

8 thin slices veal, 5 to 6 ounces each, cut across the grain; or 16 slices, 2 to 3 ounces each	2 tablespoons oil
	4 tablespoons butter
	⅓ cup water
	20-ounce can Italian-style tomato sauce
2 tablespoons flour	
1 teaspoon Chef's Salt (see appendix)	sprinkling of oregano to taste
½ teaspoon sugar	3 to 4 tablespoons grated Italian-style cheese

With a mallet, gently pound each piece of meat, moving the mallet downward and at the same time outward, until the scaloppine tissues are broken down. Be careful not to tear the meat (see illustration).

Mix together the flour, Chef's Salt, and sugar, and sprinkle each scaloppine sparingly with the mixture. Preheat half the oil and butter in a large heavy skillet until it reaches the smoking point. Brown half the scaloppine quickly on both sides. Remove. Add the other half of the shortening, bring it to the smoking point, then brown the remaining scaloppine on both sides.

Remove the scaloppine and add to the skillet ⅓ cup water. With a spoon or spatula, loosen all the brown bits from the pan. Return the scaloppine to the pan and pour in the tomato sauce. Let it heat through, turning the meat occasionally. Sprinkle on oregano to taste.

Place in a serving dish, scraping all sauce over the scaloppine. Sprinkle cheese on top. Serve with pasta or rice.

 CHEF'S SECRET   The great secret of making a good scaloppine is having a large heavy pot—an enamel frying pan, if possible—and slowly heating it through.

High heat and speed are very important. Don't give up if the scaloppine doesn't turn out perfectly the first time.

The small amount of sugar will not make the meat sweet, but it hastens and heightens the browning, and this improves the eye appeal.

If you cannot get scaloppine at your butcher's, buy a nice solid piece of veal hind leg. Look carefully to determine which way the grain is running in it. Wrap in aluminum foil and place in the freezer until it becomes very firm to the touch. Remove from the freezer and, with a very sharp knife, cut your own scaloppine against the grain. If the grain turns, which happens in certain parts of the leg, keep turning the meat.

VEAL TARRAGON
Serves 8

2 cups minced onion
4 tablespoons butter
1 clove garlic, mashed with
    2 teaspoons salt
2 pounds cubed veal
1 bay leaf
2 teaspoons tarragon
2 teaspoons sugar

1 cup white wine
⅓ cup vinegar
3 tablespoons chopped flat-
    leaf parsley
½ pound mushrooms
1½ cups milk
4 tablespoons flour
1 cup sour cream

Saute onions in butter until transparent. Mash the garlic and salt together with the flat surface of a knife until it turns to a pulp. Add to the onions, then add veal, bay leaf, tarragon, sugar, white wine, vinegar, and 2 tablespoons chopped parsley. Adjust heat to medium. Cover and cook until veal is tender, 30 to 40 minutes.

Add mushrooms and cook 2 to 3 minutes.

Mix milk and flour. Stir mixture into the veal. Correct seasoning if necessary.

Just before serving, mix the sour cream into the sauce and add remaining parsley. Serve with noodles or gnocchi.

CHEF'S SECRET   Adding some of the parsley while cooking and the rest at the last minute will serve two purposes. The part added during cooking will give out all its flavor and aroma, but it will turn brownish-gray and won't even be recognizable. The parsley added just before serving will give a beautiful green color accent and, as it warms through on the surface of the sauce, its oils will intensify and give a pleasant aroma to the dish.

Gnocchi is the Italian word for small dumplings, spaetzles, and several similar products.

4
POULTRY

The Bakery Restaurant proves an interesting point regarding assumptions about people's tastes. I often read that restaurants carry poultry (mainly chicken) on their menus because it is inexpensive, and people usually order it to save money.

We have always charged a fixed price for our meals. Beef, veal, lamb, poultry, and fish have always been sold for the very same price. Nonetheless, poultry has always been very popular. This proves to me that no one orders it, at least at *The Bakery Restaurant*, because they want to save money.

The most popular poultry on our menu has always been roast duckling. We serve it mostly the Hungarian way, with a very tart, sour cherry glaze instead of the obligatory orange sauce, and we always offer with it sweet and sour red cabbage. As odd as the combination of cabbage and cherries sounds, the moist, tender, crisp duckling seems to bring the two strange components together beautifully.

A few years ago we started to serve goose regularly. Now, if possible, we keep roast goose on the menu year round. At first it was an uphill struggle. If we roasted one goose a night, serving six to eight portions from it, we considered it good. Now we must figure about four times as much, which makes it very worthwhile.

Pheasant is also very popular, but it has a short season. We serve it for about three or four months, but during that time the amount of pheasant consumed is suprisingly high.

Chicken is still the most popular poultry with most home cooks, and the figures nationwide show a tremendous amount of chicken sold compared with all other kinds of poultry combined.

As party fare, pheasant and capon are the favorites of gourmet groups. Many important business dinners in our party room feature duck as one of the two or three items people want to choose from at small banquets where a choice is possible.

For the homemaker, one of the greatest advantages of poultry is the excellent soup that can be made from its byproducts with very little effort and no extra cost.

CHICKEN IN CHAMPAGNE SAUCE
Serves 8

3 tablespoons cornstarch
⅓ cup water
4 tablespoons butter
2 tablespoons other
   shortening
2 tablespoons Chef's Salt
   (see appendix)
2 fryers, 2¼ to 2½ pounds,
   cut into serving pieces
3 tablespoons concentrated
   orange juice

2 tablespoons finely minced
   shallots, or 1½ tablespoons
   finely minced scallions
   (white parts only)
1 teaspoon mace
½ teaspoon nutmeg
10½ ounce can chicken broth
1 teaspoon sugar
5 ounces fresh mushrooms
   (large, if possible)
2 cups champagne

Dissolve the cornstarch in the water. Preheat oven to 350°.

In a large skillet, melt the butter with the other shortening. Sprinkle Chef's Salt on the chicken pieces and, when the shortening is smoking hot, quickly brown the skin side of each piece of chicken. Remove chicken to a casserole and cover.

To the skillet add the orange concentrate, shallots, mace, nutmeg, and chicken broth. Stirring constantly, bring this mixture to a slow boil. Remove from heat, cool 4 to 5 minutes, then pour it over the browned chicken pieces. Cover the casserole and bake about 1 hour, then test for doneness.

Remove some of the sauce and stir into it the sugar and the cornstarch mixture. Bring to a boil, stirring constantly, and cook until thickened. Pour back into the casserole.

Quickly wash the mushrooms, cutting off the stems and reserving them for another use. Gently mix the mushroom caps among the chicken pieces. Add the champagne. Let the casserole stand in the shut-off oven or in a warm place for 1 hour. Then remove the pieces of chicken to a serving platter. Serve the sauce separately in a sauceboat.

CHEF'S SECRET The characteristic taste of the champagne sauce comes from the orange concentrate, mace, and the champagne. If you have no champagne available, substitute 1 cup dry white wine and 1 cup club soda. This mixture is a poor substitute for the champagne, of course, but it works.

If you were to pour the boiling sauce over the browned chicken pieces, the muscles would tighten up and get tough. That is why we recommend that you let the sauce cool a few minutes.

If you prefer, omit the mushrooms and add orange rind prepared as follows: Cut enough very thin strips of orange rind, the yellow part only, to have about 3 to 4 tablespoons. Boil the orange rind first in 2 cups water, discard water, then boil again in 2 more cups water. Rinse in cold water and soak in the champagne or wine-club soda mixture for about 10 minutes before mixing into the sauce.

CHICKEN PAPRIKASH
Serves 4

2½ to 3-pound frying chicken	1 cup finely chopped onion
salt and freshly ground black pepper to taste	3 tablespoons tomato puree
5 tablespoons sweet Hungarian or Spanish paprika	1 clove garlic
	2 teaspoons salt
5 tablespoons lard or shortening of your choice	2 cups chicken stock or water
	1 medium-sized green pepper
	1 cup sour cream

Cut out the backbone of the chicken and split into three pieces crosswise. Cut the neck in two pieces, cut off the drumsticks, and split the thighs lengthwise in half along the bone. Cut off two joints of each wing. Cut the breast crosswise in half, leaving the first wing joint on. Cut the gizzard into four pieces and the heart in half.

Sprinkle all the pieces of chicken with salt, black pepper, and 1 tablespoon paprika.

Melt 4 tablespoons of the fat in a large saute pan. When hot, put in the chicken pieces and very quickly saute over medium heat until the chicken meat turns white and is firm to the touch. Remove all chicken except the back, gizzard, heart, and neck. Keep warm.

Increase the heat and add the chopped onion, 2 tablespoons paprika, tomato puree, and the garlic which has been mashed with 1 teaspoon salt. Stir these ingredients until the fat sizzles. Add 1 cup stock, cover the pan, and cook until onions become pulpy.

Return the sauteed chicken and its juice to the pan. Add another teaspoon salt, the green pepper cut into finger-length slices, and the remaining stock. Cook, covered, an additional 25 to 30 minutes over medium heat, or until the chicken is tender.

In a small saucepan, heat the remaining tablespoon of fat and add 2 tablespoons paprika. Stir until heated through, being careful to prevent burning. Pour this over the cooked chicken.

Remove 3 large spoonfuls of cooking liquid from the pan. In a small bowl, stir this liquid into the sour cream. Pour the sour cream mixture over the chicken and remove from heat. Serve hot.

CHEF'S SECRET   If you follow the directions for the onions, you will have the perfect consistency and taste. Depending on the onion you use, the time it takes to turn into a pulp will vary. You must watch it carefully.

Only the best imported Hungarian or Spanish paprika will give the very special taste that Chicken Paprikash is famous for. If you can't get it in your regular grocery, look for it in a specialty store.

STUFFED WHOLE SPRING CHICKEN
Serves 8

2 spring chickens, 2½ to
   3 pounds each
½ pound ground beef
½ pound ground pork
2 ounces ham, chopped
4 ounces Hungarian sausage
½ cup chopped onion
1 tablespoon shortening
1 egg
3 to 4 tablespoons chopped
   parsley
¼ teaspoon marjoram
4 slices day-old white bread
¼ cup water or more if needed
salt and freshly ground
   black pepper to taste

½ teaspoon tarragon
⅛ teaspoon garlic salt
   (*not* garlic powder)
1 package fresh soup
   vegetables (carrots, celery,
   parsnips, etc.)
4 cups water; *or* 2 cups
   chicken broth and 2 cups
   water; *or* 2 cups chicken
   broth, 1 cup white wine,
   and 1 cup water
4 tablespoons shortening
1 tablespoon flour
1 tablespoon cornstarch

Remove from the chickens the bags with necks, giblets, hearts, and livers. Chop fine the livers, giblets, and hearts. Reserve the necks for later use.

In a mixing bowl, combine ground beef, ground pork, and ham with finely chopped livers, giblets, hearts, and half the Hungarian sausage chopped into pieces the size of green peas. Cut the other 2 ounces sausage into ¼ inch slices.

Saute onion in 1 tablespoon shortening until translucent. Work it into meat mixture. Add egg, parsley, marjoram, and bread broken into ¼ inch pieces. Work together with your hands, adding ¼ cup or so of water if necessary. Add salt and freshly ground black pepper to taste.

Divide the stuffing into two portions and stuff tightly into the cavities of the chickens. Rub tarragon and garlic salt into the skin over the breasts. Preheat the oven to 375°.

Wash, clean, and cut up the soup vegetables and distribute them in the bottom of a large roasting pan with a tight-fitting lid. Add the necks and sprinkle with a little salt and pepper. Pour 2 cups of the water (or other liquid) into the pan, then place the chickens over the vegetables.

Heat 4 tablespoons of shortening in a small pan until it starts to smoke. Spoon it carefully over the chickens (this will give the skin a beautiful crispness and color). Cover and roast 1 hour.

Remove chickens from pan. Strain pan juices and use vegetables and necks as you wish. Skim off fat. Put the chickens back in the roasting pan, heat fat to the smoking point, pour the fat over the chickens, and roast uncovered about 30 minutes.

Meanwhile, in a saucepan, mix flour and cornstarch with pan juices and remaining water (or other liquid). Whisk while bringing to a boil. Remove chickens from the oven and let stand in a warm place for 10 minutes. Split each chicken in four and place skin side up on a warm serving platter. Spoon on some of the sauce and serve the rest in a sauceboat.

CHEF'S SECRET   If you wish, tie the two legs together with white butcher string or soft, not-too-thin yarn, after the stuffing is done. It will hold the chickens in a nicer shape. You can also fold the wings under the back by gently lifting both wings at once away from the body, holding them with three fingers, and then pressing the second and third joints downward with your thumbs until they go under the back. Then push the first joints back to the body. The wings will stay folded and the breasts will look plumper.

You can stuff the chickens under the skin, instead of in the cavity, as follows: With your fingers, loosen the skin over the chicken breasts. Start at the neck and move your fingers toward the wings, then work from the breast bone to the inside of the thigh. Divide the stuffing into two portions and stuff it under the skin of the chickens.

ROAST DUCKLING
Serves 2 to 4

3 to 4 tablespoons lard,
    duck fat, or chicken fat
4½ to 5-pound duckling
1 tablespoon Chef's Salt
    (see appendix)
1 carrot, washed, scraped,
    and coarsely chopped
2 ribs celery, coarsely
    chopped

1 medium-sized onion,
    coarsely chopped
1 or 2 cloves garlic, thinly
    sliced
3 to 4 black peppercorns
1 small piece of bay leaf
sprinkling of marjoram

Preheat the oven to 325°.

Use a roasting pan with a tight-fitting cover. Put the lard into the roasting pan. Reach into the vent end of the duckling and remove the neck and giblets, which will be inside the body cavity. Rub the inside and outside of the duckling with Chef's Salt.

Place the duckling breast side down on top of the lump of fat in the roasting pan. Place the cut vegetables and garlic on and around the duckling. Add water to the pan to a depth of 1 to 2 inches. Add the peppercorns, bay leaf, and marjoram. Cover and roast 2 hours.

After 2 hours, take the roasting pan out of the oven and very carefully remove the duckling to a platter. Let it cool completely. If it is not completely cooled, the dish will not turn out properly.

To finish, split the duckling lengthwise by standing it on the neck end and, with a sharp knife, cutting from the tip of the tail directly down the center. To quarter, each half may again be cut (see illustration).

Place the cold, split duckling pieces, cut side down and skin side up, on a slightly greased cookie sheet. Return to a 450° oven for 18 to 22 minutes. Before serving, remove the first two joints of the wing, leaving only the third.

At *The Bakery Restaurant,* we always serve roast duckling with a tart cherry glaze (see page 208).

CHEF'S SECRET   The success of a roast duckling starts with the buying. For best results, buy the best. A 4½ to 5-pound duckling is the most satisfactory and economical size. It is

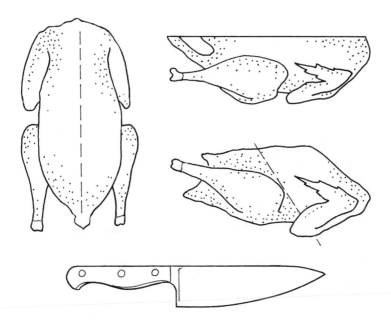

perfectly safe and even advisable to buy frozen duckling. Look
for the mark of government inspection on the package. Store in
a freezer until ready to use. Before using, let the duckling
defrost 48 hours in the bottom of the refrigerator, or submerge
it into a large container of lukewarm water 4 to 6 hours, changing the water hourly. After it has been defrosted completely and
the flesh feels soft, preparation may begin.

After the duckling has been removed from the roasting
pan to cool, it can be safely kept at room temperature all day. Or
if the weather is very hot and humid, store the duckling in the
refrigerator after it has cooled to room temperature. It is
important to bring it back to room temperature about an hour
before finishing. Do not reheat direct from the refrigerator.

Perhaps you wonder why fat is added to the duck, which is
a naturally fat bird. As the water starts to heat in the roasting
pan, the fat becomes liquid and forms an even surface over the
top of the water. The surface of fat has a boiling point of 360
degrees, while the water boils at 212°. Without the fat, the
water would create a vapor surrounding the duck in the covered

roasting pan. This would give the bird a steam-cooked, undesirable taste, and would prevent the fat under the duck skin from oozing out as it does in dry air.

ROAST TURKEY
Serves 8

For the turkey:

1 turkey, 10 to 12 pounds, ready to roast

4 tablespoons Chef's Salt (see appendix), mixed if desired with 1 teaspoon thyme or poultry seasoning

1 cup each coarsely chopped carrots, celery, onions, and turnips

1 clove garlic, sliced

1 teaspoon slightly bruised peppercorns

1 cup cold shortening (butter or oil)

1 large brown paper bag, without any printing on it, large enough to hold the turkey (don't use a "recycled paper" bag)

For the gravy:

giblets

pinch of Chef's Salt (see appendix)

pinch of thyme

pinch of oregano

1 tablespoon fat

2 cups water

2 cups cream or half-and-half

2 tablespoons flour (or more if you prefer a thicker gravy)

Preheat the oven to 325°.

Remove the giblets from the turkey, making sure that none is left in the neck cavity. Rub the turkey inside and outside with Chef's Salt, and place about one handful of the mixed chopped vegetables in the cavity. Place the remaining vegetables, garlic, and peppercorns in the bottom of a large roasting pan. Add enough water to have 1 to 1½ inches in the bottom of the pan.

Cover the turkey breast and legs evenly with the shortening, then place the turkey in the brown paper bag, close the bag, and set it on top of the vegetables in the pan. Roast 3 to 3½ hours, or until a meat thermometer inserted into the thickest part of the thigh registers 185 degrees. For the last ½ hour of roasting, open the paper bag and tear off as much of the paper as possible. Increase the heat to 425° and baste the breast every 8 to 10 minutes.

While the turkey is roasting, make the gravy. Wash and clean the giblets. Cut the heart, gizzard, liver, and as much of the meat from the neck as possible into pieces about the size of a cranberry. Sprinkle with a pinch of Chef's Salt, thyme, or oregano. Fry over high heat in the 1 tablespoon fat until brown, then pour 2 cups water in the pan, cover, and simmer slowly until needed for gravy.

When the turkey is done, remove from the oven, transfer to a serving platter, and keep warm for at least 1 hour before serving.

Strain the cooking liquid. Discard the turnip and spices, then press the remaining vegetables through a sieve. Add the pulp to the cooking liquid. Add the cooked giblets to the cooking liquid and bring the mixture to a boil. Stir in the cream or half-and-half mixed with the flour. Serve in a sauceboat.

POTTED GOOSE

1 goose, 8 to 10 pounds
2 10-½ ounce cans chicken
   broth
1 cup sliced carrot
2 cups sliced onion
2 cloves garlic, thinly
   sliced
1 or 2 sprigs green parsley

10 to 12 peppercorns,
   slightly bruised
1½ tablespoons Chef's Salt
   (see appendix)
4 tablespoons shortening,
   preferably lard, duck fat,
   or goose fat
2 to 3 cups warm water

Ask the butcher to cut the goose into four pieces. Don't attempt to cut the goose yourself as the bones are extra hard and dangerous. If you buy a frozen goose, the butcher can simply saw it into four sections. In this case, defrost the goose before you start the recipe by leaving it in the refrigerator overnight or placing it in the sink and running lukewarm water over it.

Preheat the oven to 325°. To a roasting pan add the chicken broth, carrot, onion, garlic, parsley, and peppercorns. Rub the goose parts with Chef's Salt and smear 1 tablespoon cold shortening over each piece. Place in the roasting pan. Cover and roast 4 to 5 hours, adding 2 to 3 cups of warm water during the cooking time.

The goose must be cooked until it falls off the bones when touched with a fork. Then remove it from the oven, lift it from the vegetables, and let it cool until it can be handled.

Pour the liquid from the roasting pan through a sieve. Press the vegetables through the sieve, leaving only the fibers. Discard the fibers.

Remove all flesh and skin from the goose. Discard the bones. Distribute the meat and skin into 6 to 8 plastic containers, pressing well down to the bottom. Carefully skim all fat from the cooking liquid and distribute the liquid over the goose flesh. Refrigerate, leaving the fat at room temperature.

In 3 to 4 hours, when the goose with the liquid starts to gel, distribute some of the fat evenly over the top of the plastic containers. Cool, then freeze. This confiture of goose may be kept refrigerated for 4 to 6 weeks or frozen up to 3 to 4 months. It is also an ideal gift. The rest of the goose fat can be stored frozen for up to a year or refrigerated for 1 to 2 months. Don't store too long; use it up for pates, sauces, and so forth.

ROAST GOOSE
Serves 8

1 goose, 8 to 10 pounds
4 tablespoons shortening
1 large clove garlic
3 tablespoons Chef's Salt
(see appendix)
1 teaspoon marjoram
(optional)

½ teaspoon caraway seed
(optional)
1 tart apple
1 onion
a few drops Kitchen Bouquet
1 to 2 tablespoons cornstarch
⅓ cup water

Preheat the oven to 350°.

Remove the giblets from the goose. Near the opening of the cavity you will find 2 large lumps of fat under the skin. Remove these, cut them into small pieces, add the 4 tablespoons shortening, and, in a small heavy pot over medium heat, render out the goose fat.

Mash the garlic with 1 tablespoon of the Chef's Salt and the marjoram and caraway seed. Rub the inside and outside of the goose with this mixture.

Cut the apple and onion into quarters and place them in the cavity of the goose. Add water to a roasting pan to a depth of 2 inches. Mix the remaining Chef's Salt into the water, then place the goose in the pan.

Strain the rendered goose fat and then heat it to the smoking point. Pour half of it over the breast of the goose, then turn the goose breast side down and pour the other half of the hot fat over it. Cover the roasting pan and roast 2 to 2½ hours, or until a thermometer inserted into the thickest part of the thigh and into the breast registers 180 degrees.

Remove the roasting pan from the oven and let it stand, covered, for about 30 minutes. Then remove the goose to a tray and let it stand at room temperature for at least 3 hours.

Pour the juices from the roasting pan into a fairly tall, narrow container to allow the fat to come to the top. Skim off as much as possible. Refrigerate the roasting liquid until you can remove all the fat.

Taste the juices; if salty, dilute with a little water. Add a few drops of Kitchen Bouquet and heat the juices to the boiling point. Mix the cornstarch with the ⅓ cup water and stir 1 to 2 tablespoons of the mixture into the juice, depending on how thick or thin you prefer the juice.

One hour before serving, preheat the oven to 475°. Heat 4 to 5 tablespoons of the goose fat to the smoking point. Place the goose on a low-edged pan, breast up, and pour the hot fat over the goose. Place in the oven and roast 30 minutes. Shut off the oven and leave the goose in for an additional 10 minutes. Then remove, place on a serving platter, and let stand in a warm place at least 20 minutes before serving.

 CHEF'S SECRET   The hot fat will make the goose skin very crisp. The salt added to the water in the roasting pan will prevent the juices from the goose flesh from oozing out, so that the goose remains juicy and tender.

ROAST QUAIL
Serves 8

8 quails
salt and pepper to taste
1 heaping teaspoon juniper
    berries, crushed (optional)
1 pound ground ham, or
    12-ounce can chopped ham

8 bay leaves
8 slices ranch-style bacon
    (thickly sliced)
10½ ounce can chicken
    broth, or ½ can chicken
    broth and 1 cup white wine

Preheat oven to 450°.

Split each quail down the back. Sprinkle with salt, pepper, and juniper berries.

If you are using canned chopped ham, chop it finely. Divide the ground ham or the canned chopped ham into eight equal portions. In the cavity of each quail, place 1 bay leaf and a portion of the meat. Wrap a slice of the bacon around each bird and tie with a string which is much longer than needed, so that it is not necessary to tie a knot.

Roast the birds breast side down 5 minutes. Turn the birds, baste each with 2 tablepoons of the chicken broth, and roast 10 minutes breast side up. Shut off the oven but leave the birds in the oven for another 8 to 12 minutes. Serve with Port Wine or Madeira Sauce (see Chef's Secret, page 218).

CHEF'S SECRET   Some homemakers have an aversion to canned meats that is absolutely unfounded. The canned chopped ham, or any canned meat that is packed under government inspection by a reputable company, will contain nothing but a very satisfactory quality of chopped ham. Its texture and taste will pleasantly counterbalance the taste of the quail without overpowering it.

For a festive way to serve the quail, prepare 1 package green noodles according to package directions. Brush 1 pound long macaroni with 2 to 3 tablespoons oil; toast it under the broiler on a cookie sheet, then cook according to package directions. When preparing the macaroni, keep turning them under the broiler, being careful not to let them burn. To serve, mix the green noodles and the prepared macaroni, butter the mixture, and make a nest for the birds on a serving platter.

ROAST PHEASANT
Serves 8

2 large pheasants
2 teaspoons salt
½ teaspoon freshly ground
    black pepper
¼ teaspoon crushed juniper
    berries
½ teaspoon paprika
3 or 4 carrots, coarsely chopped
1 large onion, coarsely chopped

2 or 3 ribs celery,
    coarsely chopped
2 bay leaves
4 to 6 tablespoons melted
    shortening, preferably lard
    or bacon drippings
2 to 3 cups water
bacon to cover pheasant quarters

Preheat the oven to 325°. If your pheasants are frozen, thaw them fully.

Rub the pheasants with a mixture of the salt, black pepper, crushed juniper berries, and paprika. Place the coarsely chopped carrots, onion, celery, and bay leaves in the bottom of a deep roasting pan large enough to hold the pheasants. Lay the pheasants breast side down on the vegetables and brush the skin with the melted shortening. Add the water to the roasting pan, cover, and roast about 2 hours.

Remove from the oven and let stand 10 to 15 minutes. Then remove the birds from the roasting pan, turn them breast down on a tray, and let stand at room temperature for at least 4 or 5 hours. Or, after cooling, cover them with plastic or foil and leave them in the refrigerator overnight.

Before serving, split each pheasant into quarters, cover the skin side with bacon, and roast skin side up at 450° for 20 to 25 minutes. Serve at once with Port Wine or Madeira Sauce (see Chef's Secret, page 218).

CHEF'S SECRET   If the birds are frozen, defrost by leaving in the refrigerator overnight. If you are in a hurry, defrost under running lukewarm water.

If you have a "great hunter" in the family, he will bring the birds home sometimes skinned—and probably tougher. In this case it is advisable to use an extra cup of water and to roast the birds a little more than 2 hours. You will also need more bacon to cover the pheasants.

If the bird brought home by the hunter turns out to be tough and inedible, don't give up. Cut it into small pieces, grind, then run through a blender and make a good pate from it.

Juniper berries are often unavailable in food markets, but try an ethnic pharmacy. You can buy as many as a pound at a time and keep them for years; they are not like other spices that rapidly lose their pungency. Be sure to crack them gently with a mallet in the corner of a kitchen towel before using. If you can't get any juniper berries, use an ounce of gin for each bird.

Regular sliced bacon will do for covering, but if you are lucky enough to have a friendly butcher nearby, buy a 1-pound slab of bacon and ask the butcher to slice it into rectangular pieces from the top toward the rind by laying it flat on the electric meat slicer. Place a double sheet of waxed paper, a little larger than the rectangles of bacon, between each and freeze what you don't use. This way the bacon will be available for other uses.

5

FISH & SHELLFISH

Perhaps the greatest change in taste trends in recent years has been the rapidly growing consumption of seafood.

Our type of continental restaurant used to carry a single fish dish, usually just as a polite gesture towards those few who, for one reason or another, wanted fish. It was never much of an attraction in our first decade, but then things began to change. Instead of one seasonal fish offering, on weekends we started to carry two or three, plus bouillabaisse on Fridays and Saturdays. Now on weekends we offer four or five fish dishes that are very popular.

The greatest danger in fish cooking is timing—mainly over-cooking—and a great deterrent is the incorrect belief that cooking fish is connected with strong odors. Our venerable but somewhat outdated cookbooks are a bit at fault on this point in that they indicate fish has a strong smell and they suggest ways to avoid or eliminate it.

They also suggest that you check freshness by looking in the eye of the fish, and testing the scales to see how firmly they are attached. This is somewhat anachronistic today when most fish arrives in the stores already cleaned, beheaded, deboned, or partially deboned. How can you look in the eye of a filet of sole, a halibut steak, or a headless shrimp?

I should also talk about freezing. Some restaurants, for unknown reasons, claim their fish is flown in fresh daily and never frozen. Such statements are dangerous and, let's face it, in many cases self-destructive. I don't maintain that nothing is wrong with frozen fish, or that it is equally as good as fresh. By no means. I would never want to serve frozen salmon in my restaurant, so we serve salmon only for the short months when it arrives fresh and is available in the stores. Salmon can stand icepacking, shipping, and proper storing for three to four days with very little damage.

I am not fond of frozen lobster tails either. I don't think we have served more than two or three portions in two decades. Whenever someone orders lobster in advance we always present the live lobster on a silver platter with fresh seaweed before the cooking starts (except for Lobster Parisienne, which needs several hours of preparation time).

I won't lie to my customers by saying our arctic perch, and the slipper lobster from which we prepare the sauce we serve with it, are *fresh*. The same can be said about pike, which is sometimes fresh from the northern parts of the lakes, sometimes frozen. And I must say that the frozen perch we receive from our supplier is sometimes superior to fresh.

If we serve Dover sole or turbot, I insist on receiving it frozen. I have been on vessels fishing for sole and turbot, and I have followed these two noble and delicate fish, fresh and frozen, from the hook of the fisherman to the frying pan both ways. They are both line fish, which means they are not netted but are caught on individually baited hooks on long fishing lines. After they are pulled into the small fishing vessels, you can see how the different methods work. The so-called fresh fish is carried to a larger boat where it is mixed with slushy ice. Then the boat goes to the harbor where the fish is separated from the ice, transferred to other containers with fresh ice, carried to the airport to wait for the next freight plane, flown across the ocean, inspected many times through customs, transferred through the broker to the wholesaler, packed in fresh ice, and trucked to the store. So "fresh" Dover sole gets to market a minimum of 70 (more likely 96) hours after it is pulled from the water.

On the other hand, frozen Dover sole goes from the small fishing vessel to a factory ship within a couple of hours. There it is gutted and pushed through a wind tunnel into the freezing compartment. In this tunnel a 40-mile-an-hour wind blows 20-degrees-below-zero air on the individually water-sprayed sole, which freezes so fast that in many cases rigor mortis sets in only in the frying pan. This frozen temperature keeps the fish as fresh as it was a couple of hours after it was lifted from the water.

Now I ask you respectfully, which fish is fresh, the fresh or the frozen?

BAKED GROUPER
Serves 8

4 tablespoons oil
3½ to 4 pounds grouper filets
1 tablespoon Chef's Salt
(see appendix)
2 tablespoons fresh chopped
parsley
1 teaspoon tarragon
1 teaspoon rosemary

½ teaspoon chervil
2 tablespoons butter
1 large bunch fresh green
parsley for decoration
2 large lemons cut into wedges
1 recipe Hot Herb Butter for
Fish (see page 213)

Preheat oven to 375°. Cover the rack of a broiler pan with aluminum foil. Brush 2 tablespoons oil on the foil.

Rub both sides of the fish with Chef's Salt. Mix chopped parsley, tarragon, rosemary, and chervil in a cup with butter and 2 tablespoons oil. Spread this mixture on the flesh side and place the fish, skin side down, on the foil. With a small, sharp knife, gently make 2 or 3 lengthwise cuts into the fish, being careful not to go deeper than half the thickness of the fish. Then cut it 6 to 8 times crosswise. Bake the fish 20 minutes.

Check doneness by inserting 2 forks in the thickest part of the fish and trying to pull it apart. If it flakes and is not translucent, the fish is ready. Remove it to a large serving platter. Surround with fresh parsley and lemon wedges. Serve with Hot Herb Butter, flambe it, and serve Sauce Louis (see page 206) on the side. Offer with it plain boiled potatoes and a fresh green vegetable.

CHEF'S SECRET   Grouper is not a well-known fish, but it is gaining in popularity because of modern freezing facilities around the Mexican Gulf, where most of it is caught. It is a delicately flavored, delightful fish. Don't overcook.

POACHED SOLE
Serves 8

2 quarts water
1 tablespoon salt
1 cup vinegar
10 to 12 black peppercorns
1 bay leaf
2 to 3 sprigs parsley

1 rib celery
1 carrot, sliced
1 piece lemon rind, 1 × 2 inches
8 filets of sole, 3½ to
    4 ounces each

Combine all the ingredients except the fish filets and bring to a boil. Boil 15 minutes over medium heat.

Place the filets in a shallow pan and ladle the hot liquid slowly over them. Over low heat, bring filets and liquid to a gentle boil. Remove from heat after 2 minutes and cover. Let stand 3 to 4 minutes, depending on the thickness of the filets. Serve immediately.

SAUTEED SOLE
Serves 8

4 tablespoons oil
4 tablespoons butter
salt and white pepper to taste

1 cup flour
8 filets of sole, 3½ to 4
    ounces each

In a heavy saute pan, slowly heat the oil and butter. Mix the salt and pepper with the flour and sprinkle both sides of the filets liberally with the mixture. Gently press the flour mixture into the filets, then lift by one end and shake off excess.

When the shortening is hot, place the filets in the pan, side by side. Turn over immediately. Gently shaking the pan, cook the filets over medium heat 3 to 4 minutes. Remove to a serving platter or to individual plates and serve immediately.

BAKED FILETS OF SOLE
Serves 8

2 to 3 tablespoons butter
salt and pepper to taste
8 filets of sole, 3½ to 4
    ounces each

1 cup white wine
1 cup water or 1 cup fish stock
    or Court Bouillon
    (see appendix)

Preheat the oven to 350°. Carefully brush an ovenproof dish with the butter.

Salt and pepper the filets and fold them in half across the width. Place them, slightly overlapping, in the dish.

Mix the white wine with the water or stock, bring the mixture to a rolling boil, and spoon the hot liquid over the fish. Cover and bake 15 to 25 minutes, depending on the thickness of the filets.

SOLE SAUTEED ENGLISH STYLE
Serves 8

4 tablespoons oil
8 to 10 tablespoons butter
salt and white pepper to taste

1 cup breadcrumbs
8 filets of real Dover sole,
    3½ to 4 ounces each

Heat the oil and 4 tablespoons of the butter together in a heavy saute pan or skillet. Melt the remaining butter separately.

Mix the salt and pepper with the breadcrumbs. Dip one side of each filet in the melted butter, then press it, buttered side down, into the breadcrumb mixture.

Place the filets, uncoated side down, into the hot shortening in the pan. Tilt the pan and spoon the shortening over the breadcrumb-covered side, using a long wooden-handled or plastic spoon. Remove the filets to a hot serving platter and serve.

CHEF'S SECRET   If you use frozen filets, defrost them by submerging them in lukewarm water after removing them from their cardboard box. If they are wrapped in cellophane or plastic, start defrosting them while they are still wrapped and remove the filets later.

More than 95 percent of all Dover sole is flown frozen into the United States. But all kinds of sole are not Dover. All soles and flounders belong to the same family, but the texture, flavor, and water content of Dover sole are entirely different from the others.

If you use real Dover sole, the fish handler will probably filet the fish for you.

In many fish stores and supermarkets, it is possible to buy individual frozen sole filets or, even better, fresh rex sole, lemon sole, or grey sole.

Uncooked sole filets are very easy to handle, but only true Dover sole remains firm after cooking. Therefore, be very careful in handling the cooked filets. With a fairly large spatula eased under the filet so that nothing hangs over the edge, you can carefully lift the fish from the pan or cooking dish.

The English style of sauteing requires some skill. Try it first with only one or two filets. In this case, of course, don't heat all the shortening at once. Learn to tilt the pan so that you can spoon the hot shortening easily, without touching the filets.

Sometimes sliced onions, scallions, or shallots are added to the court bouillon. I don't recommend this for sole. For other fish, salmon, for instance, yes, — but only sparingly!

NOVA SCOTIA SALMON SERVICE

Perhaps one of the finest gourmet delicacies ever devised is smoked salmon. In Europe the Scotch, and in the New World the Nova Scotia salmon are unsurpassed. But this delicacy can turn into a disaster if it is not served properly and with proper accompaniments. Just as chamber music is designed for a few selected instruments, smoked salmon is designed to be enjoyed with a few selected side dishes.

First of all, it should be sliced so thin that you can read through the slices. A Parisian restaurant once had a fabulous captain who could slice salmon tissue-thin. The owner, to prove the point, ordered some plates designed with newspaper reproductions on the surface—and the captain sliced the salmon so that one really could read the text through the slices. After a couple of years he left and opened his own small country restaurant. The owner never could find another man to master the slicing, so the plates have been in storage ever since. How do I know? I have one of the plates hanging in my office.

If you purchase smoked salmon that is machine cut and packed in oil, wipe off the oil with paper towels, place the slices between two sheets of strong plastic wrap, and very gently pound the slices until they are two or three times their original size and turn a very pale pink. Be careful not to destroy their texture. Remove the slices from the plastic with a wide metal spatula or with a slicer (a wide-bladed long knife with a rounded end, often used for slicing roast beef).

Always serve the salmon at room temperature, never cold. Accompany it with freshly chopped onion that has been soaked for 5 minutes or so in cold water with 1 or 2 teaspoons lemon, then gently pressed out in a towel. Serve also with rinsed capers, juicy ripe lemons cut in half and covered with a double cheesecloth to prevent the seeds from falling out during squeezing, and an excellent fresh rye or wheat bread with fresh sweet butter.

If you can't get sweet butter, take a stick of salted butter and break it in half. Put it in a bowl with 2 or 3 cups of room-temperature water and squeeze the butter with both hands, pressing and kneading until the salt and other chemicals go into a solution with the water. Then lift out the washed butter and put it in a strong, wet cloth. Gather the cloth until the butter forms a ball, then squeeze out all the water.

Be sure to have plenty of good chilled beer or a pleasant but dry, well-chilled white wine on hand.

Eating salmon like this is a heavenly experience, especially if you follow the rules for eating as well as those for service. To eat Nova Scotia salmon you must train your palate just as you must train your ears for chamber music. The first bite you take should be nothing but salmon, about the size of two postage stamps. Place it on the middle of your tongue if possible, without touching either your lips or tongue with the fork. Close your mouth and let your tongue and upper palate engulf the salmon and warm it to your body temperature. The volatile oils that preserve the frail scent of the smoked fish will start to evaporate, filling your mouth with a very pleasant, warm, sweet sensation. The mild saltiness will awaken all your taste buds.

Now start to chew the salmon very slowly, turning it with your tongue from molar to molar in the back of your mouth. Without opening your mouth, swallow. Now take a deep breath and have four or five short but powerful sips of the beer, or two sips of the wine, to rinse the fish taste from your mouth and to enjoy the fragrance and cooling effect of the beer or wine.

Next, take a small piece of bread with a touch of butter. Chew and swallow it. Take a second piece of bread, placing on it a piece of salmon. On top of the salmon put two or three small bits of the sweet onion, one or two capers, and a few drops of lemon juice. Don't use a fork. Lift the little canape by hand to your mouth. Bite into it right in the middle. Place both bites in your mouth. Close your mouth and chew slowly, playing sensuously with the food, turning it back and forth with your tongue. Enjoy the crunchy sensation of the onion, the mellow fragrance of the caper, the unique texture of the salmon, the bland coarseness of the bread, and the sweetness of the butter.

Close your eyes if you wish, as if you were listening to music. Keep repeating this procedure and you will decide, I'm sure, that the salmon was well worth the price you paid for it.

PAN-FRIED WALLEYED PIKE
Serves 8

8 fresh or frozen filets of
   walleyed pike, 6 to 8
   ounces each
2 cups flour
2 to 3 tablespoons Chef's Salt
   (see appendix), depending on
   taste

1 cup corn oil
1 cup other shortening,
   preferably butter
8 lemon halves for decoration
8 sprigs of parsley for decoration
1 portion Sauce Louis (see
   page 206)

If you use frozen filets, defrost either by submerging in lukewarm water or placing on a wire rack at room temperature for approximately one hour.

Mix flour and Chef's Salt thoroughly and dip the filets into the mixture, coating evenly and shaking off excess.

In a large skillet that will hold at least 2 but preferably 4 of the fish pieces at once, preheat the oil and butter over medium heat until a small breadcrumb dropped into it bounces to the surface and starts to fry immediately. Do not overheat.

Using a metal spatula with a wooden handle, ease 2 or 4 filets, flesh side down and skin side up, into the skillet. Cook 3 to 4 minutes, then turn them skin side down and finish cooking another 3 to 4 minutes. Remove to an absorbent paper towel, then to a warm serving platter. Decorate with lemon halves and parsley sprigs and serve Sauce Louis in a sauceboat on the side.

 CHEF'S SECRET   In the last few years pike has become extremely popular in our restaurant. Most of the time we can purchase fresh filets of walleyed pike from nearby waters, but sometimes we have to look for other sources of supply. I find that the imported walleyed pike from Holland is excellent. No wonder: it is a close relative to the finest fish in Europe, the fogas, which lives only in Lake Balaton in Hungary and costs an astronomical amount of money in restaurants in Paris, Vienna, Munich, and other places. The walleyed pike from Holland is the closest thing to it.

While we never serve frozen salmon or many other kinds of fish that I believe suffer from freezing, I never hesitate to serve those that do not, such as real turbot, mahimahi, and Dover sole, among others. Don't misunderstand: I don't like frozen fish, but something I like even less is lying to the customer. If the fish is frozen when it arrives at our restaurant, we always say so, and we plan to continue this policy.

In my test kitchen we found an excellent way to handle small amounts of frozen fish for defrosting, and we recommend it as follows: Place each piece of frozen fish in a plastic bag. Put 2, 3, or 4 individual portions, each in their bag, into a larger plastic bag and submerge the double-bagged fish in lukewarm water in a large container in the sink, and let some lukewarm water constantly run (not directly on the fish) so that the water in the container won't cool off. This way you can defrost the fish without water-soaking or overheating it. That the fish is still firm to the touch does not mean that it is still frozen. An average 8-ounce filet of any kind of fish is ready for the pan in 15 to 20 minutes if treated this way.

POACHED SALMON IN CHAMPAGNE SAUCE
Serves 8

8 salmon steaks, 5 ounces each
4 tablespoons butter
1 tablespoon flour
1 tablespoon cornstarch
1 teaspoon sugar
⅛ teaspoon mace
salt and white pepper to taste

1 cup half-and-half
1 cup dry champagne or dry
    white wine
1 egg yolk
8 slices black truffle or
    4 black olives (optional)

In a shallow pan, poach the salmon steaks in simmering, lightly salted water for 6 to 8 minutes, depending on their thickness. Remove them carefully with a wide spatula to a warm serving platter.

Melt the butter in a saucepan. In a bowl, mix the flour, cornstarch, sugar, mace, salt, and pepper. Slowly stir in the half-and-half, mixing until completely smooth and free of lumps. Pour this mixture into the warm butter and stir until it starts to bubble. Immediately remove from heat and stir in the champagne or wine, reserving 3 tablespoons of the champagne. When the champagne is completely mixed into the sauce, put the sauce back on low heat and stir until it boils again. Remove and let it stand in a warm place until serving time.

Just before serving, mix the reserved champagne with the egg yolk. Spoon a little of the hot sauce into the yolk-champagne mixture. Stir it and then pour slowly into the sauce. Spoon the sauce over the salmon. Decorate with truffles or halved olives and serve immediately.

CHEF'S SECRET   The mace enhances the champagne flavor, but too much of it will spoil the sauce, so be very careful when using it.

The egg yolk will give a desirable faint yellow hue to the sauce. If you wish to omit it, replace it by adding 1 teaspoon more cornstarch and 1 drop of yellow food coloring to the sauce. Of course, the cornstarch is added with the other dry ingredients.

If you use an ordinary white wine instead of champagne, add a few drops of lemon juice or orange juice and 2 to 3 tablespoons ginger ale or club soda to it before stirring the wine into the sauce.

POACHED TURBOT
Serves 2 to 4

Court Bouillon (see appendix)
2 tablespoons butter

2 filets of turbot, 1 pound
each, skin removed

Prepare the Court Bouillon.

Butter a deep ovenproof casserole and place the turbot filets in it, with the side from which the skin was removed up. Cover with the Court Bouillon, with at least 1 inch of the liquid above the surface of the filets. Cover the casserole and place it over low heat. Maintain the liquid at a simmer for 20 minutes. The flesh should flake when separated with a fork. Carefully lift the fish from the Court Bouillon and let it drain on a platter.

CHEF'S SECRET   Unfortunately, the law does not always protect the consumer as it should. Besides the fact that real turbot is a very expensive fish, other countries pack much lower-quality species and call them turbot. When you buy turbot, be sure that the fish you buy is extremely firm, snow white, and has no "watery" appearance. No bargains exist in turbot. The price per pound is comparable to that of lobster. Turbot, just like real Dover sole, firms up when cooked, so you won't have any difficulty in lifting the pieces from the Court Bouillon.

Leftover poached turbot makes the world's finest fish salad when mixed with chopped celery and mayonnaise. Keep this in mind while shopping.

ARCTIC PERCH WITH LOBSTER SAUCE
Serves 8

This dish is one of the newest additions to our menu. Arctic perch, a beautiful boneless, skinless, natural-shaped fish is readily available, relatively inexpensive, and, like most fish from arctic waters, has a clean, firm texture and taste.

We just saute it in melted butter, using about 2 tablespoons for each portion of 6 to 8 ounces, then serve it with a sauce that we make from slippery lobster — but you can make it from any raw lobster meat. The great advantage of it is that it is quick and easy to prepare. By adding the raw lobster meat at the last minute, the sauce develops a tremendous lobster flavor from very little lobster meat.

2 tablespoons corn oil
2 tablespoons finely chopped
    shallots or scallions, white
    parts only
1 cup water
2 tablespoons cornstarch
1 tablespoon Hungarian mild
    paprika
1 cup light cream
½ cup cooking sherry
pinch of sugar

1 teaspoon Chef's Salt
    (see appendix)
2 tablespoons butter at room
    temperature
4 ounces raw lobster meat,
    chopped, or 4 ounces raw
    peeled deveined shrimp,
    chopped
toasted, thin sliced almonds for
    decoration

In a saute pan, heat the corn oil. Add the shallots and saute 5 minutes or until they start to get limp and yellow. Add 2 to 3 tablespoons water and stir until it evaporates. Add more water and repeat until you notice that the shallots disappear and the mixture turns into an opaque pulp.

Mix the cornstarch and paprika into the light cream, and with a wire whip stir this mixture into the shallot mixture. Add sherry, sugar, and Chef's Salt, and keep stirring. Add about ½ cup more water, if needed, for an even, smooth, medium-thick sauce. Lower the heat and simmer, stirring occasionally, for 10 minutes.

Add the soft butter in small pieces, beating after each addition to the sauce. With a cooking spoon, fold in the chopped raw lobster. Simmer 2 to 3 minutes, then remove from heat, cover, and let the sauce steep for at least 10 minutes before serving. Correct seasoning by adding perhaps a little more salt or a little more sherry.

To keep this sauce warm in a water bath, cover the surface of it with a fitted piece of waxed paper to prevent a skin from forming on the top of the sauce. If you wish to have a contrasting texture, sprinkle some toasted thin-sliced almonds on top of the sauce just before serving.

SALMON SALAD
Serves 6 to 8, or many more as an hors d'oeuvre

For the salmon:

2 pounds salmon	1 or 2 bay leaves
7 cups water	1 small onion, sliced
1 cup vinegar	1 or 2 celery ribs
1 tablespoon salt	1 carrot, sliced
1 teaspoon crushed whole black peppercorns	

Wash the salmon and place it in a heavy pot with a tight-fitting lid. Add the remaining ingredients, cover, and bring to a boil over medium heat. Reduce heat and simmer gently about 5 minutes. Remove from heat and let stand under cover 10 minutes, then remove salmon carefully with a slotted spoon. Cool until easy to handle.

Remove the skin and the dark substance that runs between the upper and lower filets. Remove bone. Discard cooking liquid, bones, skin, and dark parts. Cover a metal tray or cookie sheet with aluminum foil and place salmon on it. Cover lightly with a plastic sheet or aluminum foil and freeze for several hours or overnight.

For the salad:

1½ pounds poached salmon	1 or 2 tablespoons champagne
salt and white pepper to taste	or white wine (optional)
2 cups mayonnaise	small pinch of mace
(see appendix)	1 cup diced celery

Remove the salmon from the freezer and let it stand at room temperature 10 to 15 minutes, or until you can cut it easily into ½-inch cubes. Sprinkle with salt and white pepper.

Sprinkle mayonnaise with champagne or white wine, add mace and celery, and fold together. Fold in salmon. Refrigerate at least 8 hours or overnight. To serve, shape the salmon salad with a wet spatula into any shape you like—a fish, a dome, a ring, or a loaf, or serve it in a bowl.

CHEF'S SECRET   I discovered some 15 years ago by accident that if I freeze the cleaned poached salmon for a very short time and cube it frozen before folding it into the mayonnaise, I will have a much better salmon salad with a beautiful contrast of the firm pink cubes and the lemon-yellow smooth mayonnaise. The short freezing after poaching does not destroy the fine texture and flavor of the fresh salmon.

As a rule I suggest only finely ground white pepper on fish, because I don't like the appearance of the black specks on it. This salmon salad is different. While the salad itself calls for white pepper, for the cooking of the fish I believe you need the pungent perfume of the crushed whole black peppercorns. The best way to crush the peppers is to put them in the corner of a clean kitchen towel, gather the towel up, and hit it gently 2 or 3 times with the flat side of a mallet.

SMOKED LAKE TROUT

This is not a recipe but rather a description.

For years we have been searching for an appropriate complimentary course we might offer to very special guests to show our appreciation. Because we serve a complete five-course meal and nothing is a la carte, we felt the extra offering should not be too filling but still should be something extraordinary.

After a long search and many tests, we obtained a very special smoked lake trout from our supplier. We have found that all over the United States it is possible to interest smoked fish houses in mildly curing and smoking 4 to 8 pounds average weight of lake trout.

We developed a technique to lift off the entire skin intact from the body of the smoked trout, remove the whole flesh, stuff an aluminum foil-covered paper replica of the body of the fish into the skin, brush it with melted gelatin, and reshape it to its original form. We mount this on parsley on a long, narrow silver fish platter and serve the deboned lake trout in about 1-ounce pieces on lemon slices, decorated with a piece of black olive. We offer with it our now legendary Sauce Louis (see page 206).

Sometimes it is impossible to get lake trout, so we have tried other smoked fish with more or less success. But whenever lake trout is available, we always turn back to it without fail. We find that, besides lake trout, whitefish, sable, sturgeon, and a few other commercially offered smoked fish are suitable for this type of service.

BOILED LOBSTER
Serves 4

4 live lobsters, 1½ to 2 pounds each
sea water, or water with 1 tablespoon sea salt per quart
handful of seaweed if available, or (European style) 1 teaspoon caraway
    seed per 2 quarts water

Method 1:

Place the lobsters in a large empty pot. Add water to cover plus one inch. Remove the lobsters, add salt, and cover. Bring to a rapid boil.

Plunge lobsters headfirst into boiling water. Add seaweed or caraway seed and cover the pot. When the water starts to boil again, set the timer for 10 minutes for 1½ pound lobsters, 15 minutes for 2-pound lobsters. When time is up, remove lobsters immediately and plunge into a mixture of ice cubes and cold water, or keep the pot under running cold water for 4 to 5 minutes to stop the cooking. Serve on a silver platter covered with a white napkin. Surround lobster with the green seaweed that was boiled with it.

Method 2:

Place the lobsters in an empty pot. Cover with warm tap water. Add salt and seaweed or caraway seed. Cover pot and bring to a rapid boil.

As soon as boiling starts, remove the pot from the stove. Proceed as in Method 1, using the same cooling times.

CHEF'S SECRET   I lived for seven years in New England and watched experienced chefs and outstanding homemakers use both methods with excellent results. If you are afraid of the lobster you will probably find the second method easier. Experienced cooks tend to like the first. The main point in both cases: Don't overcook.

Many experts suggest laying the boiled lobster on its back, armor down, and splitting it lengthwise down the belly. I see no advantage in this method. As a matter of fact, it can lead to disaster. The easiest, best method is to place the boiled lobster belly down on a carving board (never on a tabletop!) and insert a knife (with the cutting edge toward the tail) in the middle of the body armor about an inch behind the tip of the head. Plunge the knife with a firm downward thrust until the tip hits the carving board, then bring the handle of the knife with one swift movement down toward the tail, like a lever, so that the entire cutting edge is used.

If the lobsters are 2-pounders, precrack the two big claws in the kitchen with a good lobster cracker; but if they are smaller, let the guests have the joy of cracking and picking.

Live lobster is almost always shipped in seaweed. This kind of seaweed looks like canned spinach with little air bubbles inside the leaves, and it is dark black-green. But when you boil it, it goes through a miraculous chemical change and turns into an emerald green that makes a beautiful contrast with the red hue of the lobster.

Sea salt or Kosher salt is available in most supermarkets. It can be kept for years, so buy a package and use the rest for other occasions.

LOBSTER ARMORICAINE
Serves 8

4 live lobsters, 1½ to 2
   pounds each
½ cup oil
4 tablespoons butter
1 tablespoon finely chopped
   shallots
1 small clove of garlic,
   mashed to a pulp with
   1 teaspoon salt
2 ounces cognac or brandy
2 cups dry white wine

2 cups peeled, cored, and
   seeded fresh tomato, chopped
½ bouillon cube dissolved in
   2 tablespoons boiling water
1 tablespoon freshly chopped
   parsley, or 1 tablespoon
   parsley flakes
pinch of cayenne pepper
2 tablespoons cold butter
chopped parsley for decoration
   (optional)

Cut lobsters into pieces as follows: First cut the lobster lengthwise down the middle, then cut the tail halves crosswise so that each tail makes six pieces. Break off the claws, cut off the legs, and cut open the two large legs. Crack the claws. Split the armor in two. Remove and discard the sac. Collect all the soft parts, green liver, and coral in a plastic container. Save for later use.

In a heavy Dutch oven or skillet with a good tight lid, melt the oil and butter together until they are smoking hot. Add the lobster pieces all at once. Toss briskly over high heat until the shell is red. Pour off the fat and discard it.

Lower the heat. Sprinkle the shallots and crushed garlic over the lobster. Toss with a spatula.

In a small pan, warm the cognac. Light and pour it flaming over the lobster and kill the flames immediately with the white wine. Add the tomatoes, bouillon, parsley, and cayenne pepper. Cover and cook gently over medium heat about 20 minutes.

Remove all the lobster pieces. Cool so that you can handle them, then quickly remove the meat from the shell. Put it in a casserole and keep it warm. Save the half shells of the body to decorate the lobster meat.

Put the cooking liquid back on the stove over high heat. Add the chopped coral, green liver, and intestines to the sauce and add 1 tablespoon of the cold butter. Cook 2 to 3 minutes. Remove from heat and stir in the remaining cold butter bit by bit. Pour the sauce over the lobster. Sprinkle with additional fresh green parsley, if you wish, and serve immediately.

CHEF'S SECRET   This recipe may be more difficult to read than it is to prepare. I would advise you to read it two or three times and have all ingredients on hand before you begin. Before you even touch the lobster, prepare the tomato, garlic, shallots, wine, brandy, and butter. Taste the chopped tomatoes and if they are too acidic and leave a sour taste in your mouth, sprinkle them with a teaspoon of sugar.

It is hard to remove the lobster pieces from the shell if you don't have the right tools. A lobster pick, a shrimp fork, or a small sharp knife does the job best.

Don't throw out the pieces of shell. Cut them fine with lobster scissors and put them in a saute pan with 4 to 6 tablespoons of butter. Sprinkle with ½ teaspoon Spanish paprika. When the shells start to sizzle, pour on 1 can of chicken broth and 1 cup of light cream. Bring to a boil, strain, and cool. Then freeze and use as a base for lobster bisque. When you are ready to use it, remove the butter from the top and melt it in a soup pot. When it starts to sizzle, stir in 2 tablespoons flour and 2 tablespoons cornstarch diluted in 2 cups of cold milk. Then add the reheated stock-cream mixture. Bring to a very gentle boil, add a few tablespoons of sherry or a touch of brandy, and serve.

BOUILLABAISSE
Serves 8

For the liquid:

1 clove garlic, crushed
1 teaspoon salt
1 pound onions, chopped very
   fine
1 cup oil
2 green peppers, chopped very
   fine
2 ribs celery, thinly sliced
1 bay leaf, crushed
12 cups water
2 pounds fish bones and fish
   heads, or 1 pound inexpensive
   fish, such as smelt

1 cup tomato sauce, Italian
   style (preferably with
   peppers, onions, and celery
   bits)
2 fresh tomatoes, chopped
3 to 4 sprigs parsley
2 blades saffron (optional)
1 tablespoon Spanish or
   Hungarian paprika
½ teaspoon dried fennel

For the fish:

2 pounds red snapper filet,
   skin on
1 pound perch filet
1 pound pike filet
1 pound striped bass or
   black bass filet
1 pound whitefish or lake
   trout filet

1 pound shrimp in the shell
lobster or lobster tail, fresh,
   frozen, or canned (optional)
clams (littleneck or cherrystone)
   or oysters (optional)

For the hot sauce:

1 cup cold mashed potatoes
½ cup oil
½ cup strained cooking liquid
   from the fish stock
1 teaspoon or more Tabasco

1 to 2 cloves garlic
1 tablespoon prepared mustard
1 tablespoon Spanish or
   Hungarian paprika
salt to taste

Mash the garlic with the salt. In a large kettle, saute the onions in the oil about 10 minutes, stirring constantly. Add green pepper, celery, garlic, and crushed bay leaf. Pour in 2 cups of water, cover, and cook over very low heat, stirring occasionally so that the mixture does not stick to the bottom of the pan. Cook until the mixture turns into a pulp.

Add the fish bones and the remaining ingredients for the liquid. Bring to a slow rolling boil. Boil at least 2 hours. Strain, discarding everything from the strainer. Boil the strained liquid, covered, for another 30 minutes over very low heat.

Cut the filets of fish into bite-sized or serving pieces. Twenty minutes before serving, place the cut filets in a low casserole-type pot. Add the shrimp in the shell. If you use clams or oysters, before adding them wash off all the sand and then wash them again three times in a sieve under running cold water. If you use lobster, cut it up into chunks. Do the same with lobster tail.

Make the sauce by combining all the ingredients and then pressing them through a fine sieve.

Pour the boiling fish stock over the fish. Over high heat, bring to a rolling boil. Check the thickest piece of filet to see if the fish is done. Serve at once, offering sauce on the side. Also serve thin, freshly made, buttered garlic toast.

CHEF'S SECRET   Probably the most controversial of all soups in the world, this is simple to make and delightful to eat.

The onions cooked into a pulp add a thickness to the broth which cannot be achieved any other way. If you brown or fry the onions, they will not work as thickener. Be sure to add the water as soon as they begin to get limp.

Not all the fish mentioned can be purchased fresh at all times. It is possible to use some frozen fish, but, of course, if all are frozen, the taste will not be the same.

The hot sauce made with mashed potatoes enables everyone to add as much spice to his own dish as he desires or can tolerate, without forcing the others to eat the Bouillabaisse too hot or too mild.

In some restaurants in Marseilles, they omit the paprika and overload the broth with saffron. Having watched many American tourists' faces after they have eaten this version, I would not recommend it.

6
VEGETABLES

Years before we opened *The Bakery Restaurant*, I was sure of one thing: I would never serve green peas, except at banquets or private parties if people insisted on them as an alternate choice. I will tell you why.

As a young executive with Armour and Company, I was "on the road" for several years. I traveled about 40 weeks a year throughout several continents, many countries, and every state of the Union except North Dakota (I still don't know how I missed it). I ate in many fine restaurants in the United States. Silas Spitzer's Holiday Award Winners list was a permanent part of my travel kit, but somehow I always felt that even the greatest meal fell short when it came to the vegetables.

Fresh asparagus (which I love) or fresh broccoli (the only vegetable I cannot stand) with Hollandaise was perhaps the most appealing, if not the most imaginative, vegetable offered. Otherwise, year in and year out, from coast to coast, and from Duluth, Minnesota, to Galveston, Texas, it was nothing but green peas and green beans. I had more of these two vegetables than anyone could ever want.

It was a part of my job to talk to groups—restaurant owners, meat suppliers, grocers, nutritionists—and as a rule the meetings were either over lunch or dinner. The main course could be anything from a slice of gray shoe leather (roast sirloin) or a piece of pink rubber (broiled lobster tail). Once in a while a stuffed pork chop appeared, or a minute steak or ham steak (always with the obligatory canned slice of pineapple). But the vegetable was, without fail, either the limpest of French-cut green beans or the little mushy pellets misnamed as green peas. This was so even when an excellent sirloin steak, a great roast chicken, or tremendous barbecued baby ribs was the meat on the plate.

Eating these limp green beans and peas for years strengthened my resolve never to serve these vegetables. Somehow we have succeeded. When we put ratatouille on the menu as a hot vegetable to accompany our Beef Wellington, not one single restaurant in the Greater Chicago area served ratatouille in any form or shape. Kohlrabi, sugar-loaf cabbage with fresh dill, carrots in cream sauce with dill—these also could not be found on menus when *The Bakery Restaurant* started to serve them.

I have nothing against frozen vegetables, but we never serve them at *The Bakery Restaurant*. If we have to serve green peas as a second vegetable during the winter for an important group, I do prefer frozen peas, but this is really the only exception to my rule. We are fortunate to be able to buy good fresh seasonal vegetables throughout the year.

KOHLRABI
Serves 8

3 pounds kohlrabi
½ teaspoon sugar
4 tablespoons shortening
   (preferably half butter)
1 teaspoon salt
freshly ground black pepper
   to taste

½ cup freshly chopped
   flat-leafed parsley
2 cups chicken broth
3 tablespoons flour
1 cup heavy cream
1 cup sour cream
parsley sprigs for decoration

Peel the kohlrabi and cut it into pieces ¼ × ½ × ¾ inch. Rinse the pieces and let the water run off, but do not shake them dry.

Heat a large empty saucepan over high heat. Sprinkle the sugar into the middle of the hot pan. As soon as it turns brown, add the shortening. Adjust the heat to medium and add the washed kohlrabi, salt, pepper, and half the chopped parsley. Stir over medium heat for about 2 minutes. Pour in the chicken broth, cover, and simmer about 30 minutes or until the kohlrabi is tender.

Stir the flour into the cream. Stir this mixture into the kohlrabi. Add the remaining chopped parsley and remove from the heat. Let the kohlrabi stand in a warm place for at least 1 hour.

Just before serving, fold the sour cream into the kohlrabi and garnish with parsley sprigs.

CHEF'S SECRET   Buy small kohlrabi if possible. Avoid the large, light pieces that will probably be woody and empty. The ideal size to buy is 2 to 2½ inches in diameter.

Sometimes the root end of kohlrabi has a woody grain in the bulb itself. In this case, don't chop the bottom part. Save it for soup.

The little caramelized sugar in the empty pot will give an excellent taste to the kohlrabi without making it sweet.

If you wish, add 2 cups freshly shelled green peas or 1 package frozen peas, defrosted, to the kohlrabi about 30 minutes before serving.

SUGAR-LOAF CABBAGE
Serves 8

1 head firm white cabbage,
    2 to 2½ pounds
2 teaspoons salt
¼ teaspoon freshly ground
    black pepper
2 tablespoons cornstarch
6-ounce can tomato paste
2 cups tomato juice

¼ cup sugar (or more, depending
    on sweetness of
    tomato paste)
2 tablespoons wine vinegar
1 tablespoon chopped fresh dill
    or dried dill weed
    (or more, to taste)

Cut the cabbage into strips about ¼ × 1 inch. Place them in a large pot, add salt, pepper, and water to cover. Cover and cook over medium heat until tender, about 30 minutes. Drain in a colander, reserving 1 cup of cooking liquid and discarding the rest.

Cool the 1 cup cooking liquid, dissolve the cornstarch in it, and then add tomato paste, tomato juice, sugar, vinegar, and dill. Bring this mixture to a boil in the pot in which the cabbage was cooked, stirring constantly, then add the cabbage. Cover and remove from heat. Let stand in a warm place for 25 to 30 minutes before serving.

CHEF'S SECRET   Don't forget to mix the cornstarch thoroughly with the cool liquid *before* adding the tomato paste.

Sugar-loaf cabbage is firmer, tastier, and sweeter than regular white cabbage—but if you cannot get it, use the regular instead. The same dish is very good when made from large (8- to 10-inch) firm zucchini, peeled, seeded, and cut (or grated) into matchstick-size pieces.

If you have a small apartment with not much ventilation in the kitchen, first pour boiling water on the raw cabbage, cover, and let stand 10 minutes. Then drain, rinse, and cook in fresh water to cover with the salt and pepper.

SWEET-SOUR RED CABBAGE
Serves 8

3 heads firm red cabbage,
    about 3 pounds total
3 tablespoons lard, chicken fat,
    or duck fat
1 tablespoon finely minced onion
1 teaspoon salt
freshly ground black pepper
    to taste

½ cup sugar
¼ bay leaf
very light sprinkling of nutmeg
    (optional)
1 teaspoon caraway seeds
½ cup vinegar or more, to taste

Remove the outside leaves of the cabbage. Split each head in half and remove the core from each half. Split the halves into quarters. Place the quarters with a cut side flat on the cutting board and cut them into ¼-inch strips, or thinner, crosswise. Quickly wash the cut cabbage in cold water. Place in a colander and shake off all the water.

Melt the lard or fat in a large pot. Add the onions and cook until they turn glossy. Add the cabbage, salt, pepper, sugar, bay leaf, nutmeg, and caraway seeds. Pour in the vinegar. Gently toss the mixture together as you would toss a salad. Cook the cabbage over medium heat, uncovered, until it starts to steam.

Continue cooking over medium heat, stirring. When the liquid that develops starts to boil, reduce the heat to low and cook until tender, stirring occasionally. All the liquid must slowly evaporate; this is the only way to make the cabbage sweet-sour, tender, and a pretty purple. Pick out a few strips once in a while, let them cool a little, and taste them. You may wish to add more sugar or more vinegar.

CHEF'S SECRET   Buying red cabbage is similar to buying white cabbage. Look for the firmest, hardest heads. If three or four leaves are bursting through or have burst in the same place, watch out—the cabbage is oversoaked with water, which adds additional weight.

Never cover red cabbage while cooking. An unbearable odor would develop, the color would fade, and the cabbage would be inedible.

Although white cabbage dishes may be easily reheated, red cabbage is hard to reheat and the result is usually unsatisfactory.

FRENCH COUNTRY PEAS
Serves 8

4 tablespoons butter
1 tablespoon sugar
2 quarts shelled, fresh peas
½ teaspoon salt
6 thin slices or 3 ranch-style
    slices bacon, cut into
    ¼-inch pieces

2 cups shredded lettuce
1 teaspoon cornstarch
2 tablespoons water
1 tablespoon chopped parsley,
    for decoration

Place a heavy 12-inch skillet over high heat. Melt the butter. Sprinkle the sugar in the middle of the pan and let it brown. Once the sugar browns, add peas and salt. Stir, then push the peas around the inside rim of the frying pan, leaving the middle empty. Cover and adjust the heat to medium. Cook 5 to 7 minutes.

In another skillet, quickly fry the bacon pieces, stirring constantly and making sure that they do not burn. As soon as the bacon pieces start to brown, remove them from the heat. Strain and save the drippings for another use. Keep the bacon bits warm.

After cooking the peas 5 to 7 minutes, depending on their size, add the shredded lettuce, placing it in the middle of the pan. Cover and let the lettuce wilt for 2 minutes. Add the bacon bits. Stir the mixture together, then make another ring or wreath around the inside edge of the frying pan. Cover tightly and cook 2 more minutes over medium heat.

Pour the juices from the pan into a dish. Stir the cornstarch into the 2 tablespoons water, then dissolve the mixture into the pan juices. Pour this mixture back over the peas. Stir, then remove from the heat and keep covered 10 minutes. Sprinkle with chopped parsley and serve.

 CHEF'S SECRET   If you cannot get fresh shelled peas, use frozen peas. Remove them from the freezer and keep them refrigerated for several hours before cooking, or keep them at room temperature for 1 hour before using. If you do not have time to do this, place the frozen peas into a sieve or colander, start rinsing with cold water, and, as the peas start to separate, increase the water temperature until it is lukewarm. Shake dry and proceed as directed for fresh peas.

Peas come in many sizes, easily recognizable by comparison. The finest frozen peas are hardly bigger than the head of an old-fashioned kitchen match. The next grade compares in size to cranberries, and the common grade is even larger— about the size of a shelled hazelnut. Depending on which size you purchase or shell yourself, you can adjust the cooking time.

The caramelized sugar will not make the peas sweet but will enhance the good fresh pea taste.

The procedure of making a wreath with the peas is an oriental cooking method. The purpose is to let the heat waves and the steam circulate around the peas. The liquid collected in the middle of the pan quickly turns to steam, which condenses on the cover and drips down on the peas as they cook.

The tiny amount of cornstarch will not make the juice thick but will thicken it just enough to make the juice adhere to the peas, enhancing the flavor.

You may substitute a small amount of finely chopped ham for the bacon bits or, if you wish, omit the meat entirely. Instead of green parsley, you may sprinkle freshly chopped mint leaves on top.

This is the most popular banquet vegetable at *The Bakery Restaurant*. When we offer a choice of two vegetables, people always ask for green peas as one of the two. And this is the only vegetable we purchase frozen during the winter months.

LENTILS
Serves 8

4 cups dry lentils
12 cups water
¼ teaspoon finely minced garlic
1 tablespoon salt
4 tablespoons bacon drippings,
    lard, or other shortening
1 cup finely chopped onion
1 cup coarsely chopped carrot
1 bay leaf

1 tablespoon sugar
¼ teaspoon white pepper
1 piece smoked pork jaw, 8 to
    12 ounces, or the same
    amount of smoked picnic
    ham or bacon
4 tablespoons vinegar
sour cream and/or additional
    vinegar (optional)

Soak the lentils overnight in 12 cups water.

Mash the garlic with the salt. In a large pot, melt the shortening. Add the onion, carrot, bay leaf, garlic, sugar, and pepper. Cover and cook over medium heat 10 minutes.

Pour off the remaining soaking water, if any, from the lentils. Quickly wash the lentils.

After 10 minutes' cooking, add half the lentils, in small amounts, to the onion and carrot mixture, stirring constantly. Add the pork jaw, then add the rest of the lentils. Add enough water to barely cover the lentils. Bring the mixture to the simmering point, then adjust the heat to low and cook the lentils until tender.

Once the lentils are done, remove from the heat. Stir in the vinegar and let the lentils stand, covered, 15 to 20 minutes. To serve, offer sour cream in a sauceboat, or additional vinegar, or both.

CHEF'S SECRET   To test the lentils for doneness, use the same procedure that is used to test beans. Remove a spoonful of the lentils and gently blow on them. If the skin breaks and starts to peel back, the lentils are done.

Press the lentils through a food mill for a puree of lentils.

In classic French cuisine, lentils are the constant companion of roast pheasant, other gamebirds, roast suckling pig, and many other dishes. Venison and gamebirds are often served with three legumes—lentils, peas (yellow or dry green), and white beans—pureed separately and offered in small side dishes.

YELLOW WAX BEANS WITH DILL
Serves 8

2 tablespoons chopped onion
4 tablespoons shortening
6 tablespoons chopped fresh
    parsley
6 cups young wax beans broken
    into pieces
2 tablespoons flour
2 tablespoons cornstarch

1 teaspoon Chef's Salt
    (see appendix)
2 cups chicken stock
1 cup light cream or half-and-half
2 to 3 tablespoons wine vinegar
    or tarragon vinegar
¼ cup fresh dill weed
1 cup sour cream

In a saucepan over high heat, saute the onions in the shortening. Add 2 tablespoons parsley and washed, wet wax beans. Cover, adjust heat to medium, and cook, stirring occasionally, 15 minutes. If the water evaporates, add a few tablespoons but not more.

In a bowl, mix flour, cornstarch, Chef's Salt, chicken stock, and light cream. Blend smooth with a wire whip and slowly pour over the beans, stirring with a wooden spoon. Bring to a boil and adjust the heat immediately to simmer. Add the remaining parsley, vinegar, and fresh dill. Mix, cover, simmer 5 more minutes, and serve with sour cream.

CHEF'S SECRET   Wax beans have a distinctive flavor. The blandness of the other ingredients in this dish lets the true flavor of the wax beans come through beautifully.

If you wish, add a dab of sour cream to the dish before serving. Or if you want the dish to taste very festive, stir an egg yolk together with 3 or 4 tablespoons sour cream, place it in the serving dish, then slowly add the beans, mixing lightly.

CARROTS WITH DILL IN CREAM SAUCE
Serves 8

4 cups thinly sliced, fresh
    young carrots
1 cup water
2 tablespoons butter
1 teaspoon salt
½ teaspoon sugar

⅛ teaspoon white pepper
2 tablespoons flour
1 cup heavy cream
3 tablespoons freshly chopped
    dill weed

Place the carrots, water, butter, salt, sugar, and white pepper in a heavy saucepan. Bring the liquid to a rapid boil and cook until the carrots are tender.

Stir the flour into the heavy cream.

When the carrots are tender, pour the liquid off into another saucepan. Bring this liquid to a boil; then, stirring constantly, add the flour-cream mixture. Simmer the sauce slowly 10 to 15 minutes. After the sauce has cooked, add the freshly chopped dill and the carrot slices. Hold in a warm place for at least 15 minutes before serving.

CHEF'S SECRET   The amount of moisture in carrots varies, depending on where they are purchased and on their freshness. It is easy to adjust the liquid in the recipe after cooking. If there is too much, simply discard some; if not enough, add a small amount of water. To test the water content of carrots, bend one before cutting or slicing. If the carrot is easy to bend and slow to go back to its original shape, the moisture level is very low; if it snaps with a noise when bent or cut, and splits in a lengthwise direction, it is oversaturated with water.

For a lighter sauce, substitute 2 tablespoons cornstarch for the flour.

Fresh dill weed or tender young dill leaves are sold in season and may be frozen for a year-round supply. Holding the dill by the stem ends, dip a bunch in boiling water for 2 or 3 seconds. Immediately place in ice water to chill. Shake out some of the water but leave the bunch moist. Roll very tightly in aluminum foil and freeze. Once frozen, pack the aluminum-wrapped rolls in a plastic bag and store in the coldest part of your freezer. The dill will stay fresh for as long as a year. To use the frozen dill, remove it from the freezer just before it is needed. With a sharp knife, slicing crosswise, cut as much as needed. Repack and freeze the rest immediately.

DILLED BABY CARROTS WITH BROWN SUGAR
Serves 8

5 to 6 baby carrots per person
1 quart boiling water plus
   1 tablespoon salt
1 tablespoon butter

1 tablespoon oil
2 tablespoons chopped dill
4 tablespoons brown sugar

Wash and scrape the carrots. Ideally, they should be 2½ to 3 inches long and about ½ inch in diameter. Plunge the carrots into boiling salted water, boil 5 to 6 minutes, discard water, cover the pot, and keep the carrots warm.

Melt the butter and oil in a heavy skillet. Add the carrots and half the dill. After turning the carrots so they are coated with butter, sprinkle on brown sugar. When the sugar starts to melt, gently shake the pan back and forth, and turn the carrots with a spatula, until they are evenly coated.

Just before serving, sprinkle the rest of the dill over the carrots.

CHEF'S SECRET   The best way to scrape carrots is with a non-metallic scrubbing pad that takes off all the dirt but leaves on some of the skin.

Dill weed is very delicate and loses much of its fragrance if it is cut with a knife. Always snip it with a good pair of scissors.

Try adding some lemon zest and a few drops of lemon juice to the carrots. This will give them a new "life" and a new taste.

For small banquets, weddings, and other parties in our banquet room, we insert a toothpick into each carrot before boiling, leave them in the carrots during glazing, and replace the toothpicks with nice, bushy parsley sprigs just before serving.

PAN-ROASTED POTATOES
Serves 8

2 pounds potatoes
1 tablespoon caraway seeds
    (optional)
2 teaspoons salt
½ teaspoon freshly ground
    black pepper

1 tablespoon paprika
3 tablespoons butter
3 tablespoons lard
2 tablespoons finely chopped
    parsley for decoration

Wash and peel the potatoes, then wash them again. Cut them into uneven cubes, about 1 inch. Place them in a large pot with enough cold water to cover plus one inch. Add the caraway seeds and 1 teaspoon of the salt. Bring the potatoes and liquid to a boil over medium heat. As soon as the water starts to boil, remove the pot from the heat and let stand for 5 minutes. Pour off the water, place the potatoes in a bowl, and let them stand at room temperature until cooled.

Combine the remaining salt, black pepper, and paprika.

Place the butter and lard in a large, heavy skillet. Add the cold potatoes and sprinkle the top with the salt mixture. Heat slowly over medium heat, turning the potatoes gently with a spatula. Cook until the potatoes heat through and start to turn a light golden brown color. Remove to a serving dish. Sprinkle the potatoes with chopped parsley and serve.

CHEF'S SECRET   If you precook the potatoes according to the directions (removing the pot from the fire as soon as the water starts to boil, letting it stand for 5 minutes, then draining the water), the 1-inch cubes will be just barely cooked and will not have raw centers. If you immediately start to fry them without cooling to room temperature, they will become over-cooked and break. If you let them cool and slowly reheat them, they will be piping hot but not overcooked.

The paprika will give the potatoes a beautiful golden color with only a fraction of the amount of shortening which would otherwise be needed to achieve this color. Potatoes prepared in this way will not be greasy and will retain the real potato taste.

This is the only type of potatoes we have served since opening *The Bakery Restaurant*. People write love letters to us about them, asking for the recipe, and many guests ask for seconds, often assuring the waiters that they don't eat potatoes on other occasions.

RATATOUILLE
Serves 8

2 cups sliced onion
6 tablespoons oil
2 cloves garlic
1 teaspoon salt
2 cups sliced green pepper
1 pound zucchini cut into
    1½ × ¼ × ¼ inch pieces
2 cups eggplant, cut the same as
    the zucchini
1 package frozen green beans or,
    in season, 1 pound fresh
    green beans, cleaned
    and trimmed

4 to 5 tablespoons 4 percent
    white vinegar
15-ounce can tomato sauce
10½ ounce can tomato puree
2 tablespoons sugar
salt and freshly ground
    black pepper to taste
1 pound fresh tomatoes

In a large heavy pot, over medium heat, saute the onions in the oil until they turn glossy.

Mash the garlic with the salt and add to the pot with the onions. Add the green pepper slices, zucchini, and eggplant. Add the green beans if the fresh variety is used. Sprinkle the vinegar in the pot, cover, and cook 10 minutes, stirring occasionally. (If frozen green beans are used, add after the 10-minute cooking period.)

Add the tomato sauce, tomato puree, sugar, salt, and pepper to taste. Cover and simmer over very low heat 30 to 40 minutes, stirring occasionally to prevent the mixture from sticking to the pan.

Meanwhile, bring some water to a boil in a separate saucepan. One by one, drop the tomatoes into the boiling water. Remove after 2 to 3 seconds, and immediately rinse under cold running water to cool. Peel, core, and chop the tomatoes. Add the chopped fresh tomatoes to the mixture, gently stir, then remove the pot from the heat. Let stand in a warm place for at least 1 hour.

Correct seasonings, if necessary, by adding more salt, pepper, or sugar. Serve hot or chilled.

CHEF'S SECRET   This famous Mediterranean dish was developed as a way for the homemaker to use up vegetables on hand which, separately, would not be enough for the family. It is more often served cold as an appetizer or first course than hot as a vegetable.

The amount of sugar needed will vary depending on the acidity of the fresh tomatoes.

The vinegar sprinkled on the eggplant and zucchini will keep these two vegetables from turning soft during the cooking.

Frozen green beans are blanched or precooked during the manufacturing process and therefore do not need as much cooking time as the fresh beans.

To store ratatouille, be sure that the container is airtight and that no air bubbles exist. Always be sure to cover the top of the container with oil before placing it on the ratatouille. Then place it in the refrigerator.

When serving this dish as a cold appetizer, add some black olives if you wish, and be sure to have plenty of freshly ground pepper, good butter, and crusty French bread on hand.

At *The Bakery Restaurant* this is one of the most popular hot vegetables. Sometimes we add yellow wax beans, cauliflower, asparagus, fresh green summer cabbage, or tender young cucumbers to the basic vegetables—but never so much of anything to disturb the original character of the dish.

QUICK SAUTEED FRESH ASPARAGUS
Serves 4 to 6

1 pound fresh asparagus
¼ teaspoon brown sugar
   (or white sugar)
2 tablespoons butter

1 tablespoon corn oil
½ teaspoon salt
⅛ teaspoon finely ground
   white pepper (optional)

Wash and peel the asparagus. Cut off the bottom ends. Cut the asparagus on a diagonal to obtain thin, "French-cut" slices.

Place a heavy saute pan or skillet, with a tight-fitting lid, over high heat. Sprinkle brown sugar into the middle of the pan. When it is melted and the edges start to brown, add butter and oil.

When butter and oil are hot, add the cut asparagus, salt, and pepper. Stir quickly, then distribute the asparagus around edges of the pan so that the middle is empty. Cover and cook 2 minutes. Lower the heat to medium, lift cover, quickly stir asparagus, distributing it throughout the pan. Cover again, remove from heat, and let stand about 5 minutes before serving.

CHEF'S SECRET   The peelings and ends of the asparagus may be chopped, then run through a blender, adding just enough stock or water, as necessary. This mixture can be strained into a small container, frozen, and used in the future. Added to canned asparagus soup, it will make a quick, fresh-flavored soup.

Other fresh vegetables may be prepared in the same manner, such as fresh snow peas, fresh broccoli, fresh or frozen green peas, etc. The small amount of sugar does not sweeten the vegetables, it just enhances the flavor.

ZUCCHINI
Serves 8

4 pounds zucchini
2 tablespoons plus 1 teaspoon salt
1 small clove garlic
½ cup chopped fresh dill weed,
    or 1 tablespoon dried dill
    weed, or ½ teaspoon
    dill seed
½ teaspoon freshly ground
    black pepper
1 teaspoon sugar

½ cup vinegar
2 cups water
4 tablespoons shortening
    (preferably half butter)
3 tablespoons flour
1 cup milk
1 cup sour cream
paprika, finely chopped dill weed
    or parsley for garnish

Peel the zucchini and remove the soft, seedy inside parts with a spoon. Discard. By hand or with a grater, cut the squash into strips measuring ¼ × ¼ × 4 inches. Salt the strips with 2 tablespoons of salt and let them stand in a bowl for 2 hours.

Press the salty liquid that has accumulated from the squash. Quickly rinse the pieces of squash under cold water. Shake dry.

Crush the garlic with 1 teaspoon salt. Place the squash, dill, garlic, pepper, sugar, vinegar, and water into a heavy pot and cook over medium heat 20 minutes.

Melt the shortening in a heavy saucepan.

Drain the cooking liquid from the squash. Save 2 cups of the liquid. Mix the flour with the milk and add the mixture to the 2 cups cooking liquid.

When the shortening is melted, slowly pour in the flour-liquid mixture, stirring constantly with a wire whip. Cook until the mixture is smooth and thickened. Pour the thickened sauce over the squash, cover, and simmer over low heat 30 minutes.

Just before serving, fold in the sour cream. Sprinkle with paprika, fresh dill weed, or fresh, finely chopped parsley.

CHEF'S SECRET   Zucchini, in Italian, means "little gourd." But you may use the large, matured zucchini which is probably tastier than the smaller, younger squash.

The vinegar keeps the squash from cooking to a pulp.

Letting the squash stand with the salt removes much of the liquid from it, so that it will be firmer to the bite. It will not be salty if rinsed thoroughly.

7
CHEESE, PASTA, & RICE

This is what I call a "coalition" chapter. Each group of recipes in it is too weak to stand alone as a chapter, but the three together form a strong coalition. As in politics, coalitions make strange bedfellows.

Perhaps cheese is what holds the chapter together. Among the pasta dishes, Fettuccini, Galuska, and Spaghetti Bolognese contain cheese as one of their ingredients or garnishes. I also think that both Rice a la Grecque and Rice Pilaf are delightful with grated Parmesan or dried hard Swiss cheese.

CHEESE SERVICE

Cheese is the most abused of all food items, especially among the so-called "gourmet foods." On many occasions, even at the dinners of eating societies where they strive for propriety and perfection, a mortal sin is committed: the cheese is served direct from the refrigerator. This makes even the world's best cheese inedible.

In the wintertime, cheese should be kept at room temperature all day long on the day it will be served. In the summer, or during warm weather, keep it at room temperature for at least 2 hours before serving. Very "runny" cheeses, of which Camembert and Brie are the two most popular, can be left in their wrappings and should not be cut far in advance. But cheeses such as Edam, Port Salut, Swiss, and Cheddar can be precut, covered with a wet cheesecloth or absorbent paper towel, and then covered with plastic.

Not only by tradition, but for chemical reasons, cheese should never be served on any type of metal platter. Wood, marble, glass, plastic, fresh straw, or grape leaves are all proper foundations, and all emphasize the importance and elegance of the cheeses.

Travelers know that in elegant French, Swiss, or other restaurants, and in the homes of aristocrats and true gourmets where the service is the most beautiful silver, the cheese course is served on an old wooden plank or a piece of marble that has been in the restaurant or family for a decade or a century, even though the quality of the cheese is the very highest.

This custom has other than traditional reasons, as was demonstrated not too many years ago. A giant American corporation once purchased a small independent cheese company, built a magnificent new manufacturing facility, yet for more than a year could not produce a single piece of edible cheese. This manufacturer consulted a European cheese manufacturer from the old traditional school, who had recently changed his famous old factory to a new, automated manufacturing plant with great success. When the European arrived to look at the factory, he immediately asked what had happened to the old building. When he was told that the old building was still standing, though it was locked up and for sale, he felt relieved.

He told the manufacturers to remove as many of the old wooden surfaces from the former factory work tables, wall coverings, and storage shelves as possible, rush them to the new factory, and incorporate them all over. This suggestion worked a miracle, and the aroma and taste of the cheese, which was seemingly lost forever, is now the same as it was before the crisis. The fungi living on the wood through the years established a "working relationship" with the molds of the cheese, and the biochemical mixture gave the cheese its characteristic, inimitable flavor.

If you are interested in cheese, you can make a good test at home. Buy a piece of true Roquefort, Danish Bleu, Italian Gorgonzola, and if available, a piece of English Stilton. You will note that all four have a seemingly identical greenish-blue mold (which nowadays is mechanically injected to expedite ripening). But they are only similar, not identical, because they come from different natural caves where centuries of cheese manufacturing have established a very special strain of fungus or mold, which gives to each a matchless, unmistakable identity.

If you leave the four pieces of cheese together for a few days at room temperature, under a glass dome, you will notice that all four will lose their characteristics. The molds will all turn yellow or brown, and all the cheeses will acquire the same sharp, acid, unpleasant taste. This happens because the molds kill each other. On the other hand, if you keep the four pieces separately, each on a different plate under a small glass dish, each one will remain fresh, pleasant-tasting, and edible after the same length of time.

In France and elsewhere on the Continent, cheese is served with white, soft-centered, crusty bread, or with a juicy dark rye. In England it is served with special cheese biscuits. Both ways traditionally are correct, and both can be very pleasant. But one unforgivable thing is frequently found: stale, rancid, imported cheese biscuits are used just for tradition's sake.

If neither crusty French or Italian bread nor fresh, crisp cheese biscuits are available, freshly made, lightly buttered toast is the best substitute.

Fruits are the natural accompaniment for cheese. Apples and grapes are especially appropriate, but fresh figs, avocados, peaches, and other fruits are also delightful.

In England not only fruits but fresh celery hearts are offered with the king of all cheeses, the Stilton.

In France tiny radishes (the size of a peanut) and tender scallions, hardly thicker than wooden matchsticks, are offered with it.

Green, yellow, and red peppers accompany cheeses in Hungary, and in my native Transylvania black olives are a natural side dish with the excellent sheep and other cheeses, just as in Greece.

Wherever you travel, you will find something different. Here in the United States we are fortunate to be able to try them all.

FETA CHEESE MIX
2 to 2½ pounds

1 pound feta cheese
8 ounces cream cheese
1 cup butter
1 tablespoon prepared mustard
2 tablespoons Hungarian or
    Spanish paprika

2 teaspoons whole caraway seeds
⅓ cup finely minced onions
    or scallions
⅓ cup beer

In the bowl of an electric mixer, blend ⅓ of the feta cheese, grated or pressed into small crumbs with a fork, ⅓ of the cream cheese, and ⅓ of the butter. Use a paddle or dough hook if you have either.

When this mixture is smooth and blended, add the mustard, paprika, caraway seeds, and onions. Beat the mixture for 2 to 3 minutes, then stop, scrape the walls of the bowl, and add the second third of the feta cheese, cream cheese, and butter. Beat again for 5 minutes. Scrape the bowl and add the remaining cheese and butter. Set the speed to low and, while mixing, slowly pour in the beer. When all the beer is incorporated, set the speed to high and beat for another 2 or 3 minutes.

Remove and pour into a high mound in the middle of a serving platter. Chill. Sprinkle the top with some additional paprika if you wish, or with finely chopped parsley, or both. Surround with radish roses and serve with heavy rye bread or toast.

CHEF'S SECRET   This is a pleasant and surprisingly good cheese spread for cocktail parties or as a first course. In Europe it is made either with feta or with a similar cheese such as Brinza or Liptoi—all soft goat or sheep cheeses resembling baker's cheese or smooth cottage cheese. For variation, you may add a 2-inch piece of anchovy paste, or a tablespoon of rinsed, chopped capers, or 2 tablespoons of finely minced Hungarian salami.

In Austria and Hungary this cheese spread was called "Liptoi" cheese, or "Körözött Liptói" and was very popular. The finest sheep cheeses today are still from the Carpathian mountains, especially in the region of the city of Lipto, Czechoslovakia.

LIMBURGER CHEESE SPREAD
Serves 6 to 8

4 ounces ripe limburger cheese
4 ounces soft unsalted butter
1 tablespoon finely chopped
    green scallion

1 tablespoon finely chopped
    white scallion

In a blender, or with a fork, mix cheese and butter well. Fold in chopped scallions. Serve at room temperature with toast points, dark bread, or crackers as a cocktail spread or cheese course.

CHEF'S SECRET   This seemingly simple dish has a great American historical tradition. To my knowledge I own the world's only large manuscript collection that contains culinary manuscripts exclusively. These are handwritten or typewritten and signed letters, notes, and documents by and about famous people connected with food, eating, dining, and drinking. I have something food-connected from almost every President of the United States.

One of the most amusing pieces in the collection is a letter written by President Harding. He writes about a dinner at which he loved the pheasant and the venison but resented the absence of Limburger cheese with onions.

Following the presidential directive, I created this recipe and served it with great success to many guests as *The Bakery Restaurant*, among them the Chicago chapter of the Commanderie de Bordeaux. They had their 17th annual dinner at *The Bakery Restaurant* in 1977.

Fine gourmet groups and food and wine lovers have requested many times since then this simple but delightful and very "macho" cheese course.

WARNING   The Limburger cheese must be ripe. The best way to ripen it if you buy it "green" is to pack it into several layers of paper, then into a brown bag, then put the brown bag in a plastic bag and keep it at room temperature overnight.

The best member of the onion family for this cheese spread is the scallion, but if you cannot get any you may substitute onions. In this case, rinse the chopped onions in lukewarm water, then wring them dry in a clean towel before mixing them into the cheese.

POTTED CHEESE

1 pound soft or semi-soft cheese,   1 tablespoon brandy or
    such as Port Salut   good bourbon

Grate the cheese through the large holes of a four-sided kitchen grater into the mixing bowl of an electric mixer that has a paddle or dough hook. Do not use a wire whip.

On slow speed, mix the cheese with the liquor until it forms a ball. Slowly increase the speed until the ball falls apart and sticks to the sides of the bowl. Remove the cheese from the bowl with a rubber spatula and press it tightly into an old-fashioned cheese crock.

Cut a piece of white paper exactly to the size of the opening of the cheese crock. Dip the paper into the liquor used in the cheese, then place it on the cheese and press it down firmly. Be sure no air pocket remains. Close the lid tightly on the pot and refrigerate. The cheese will keep in the refrigerator for 6 months to 1 year.

CHEF'S SECRET   This is an old American recipe from a cookbook *The Improved Housewife or Book of Recipes by a Married Lady,* printed in Hartford, Connecticut. In my library I have the sixth edition of this book from 1845, and we now know that the married lady's name was Mrs. A. L. Webster. You can imagine how popular the book was if the sixth edition was printed 135 years ago.

In Mrs. Webster's time, this was a way of preserving the cheese. Today it simply enhances its flavor. It is so good that I have to warn you, you may become addicted to it!

STILTON SPREAD
Serves 12 to 15

8 ounces ripe imported English Stilton	8 ounces soft unsalted butter

Cut the Stilton into small pieces or, even better, press it in a soup bowl with a fork. Cut the butter into very thin slivers and mix the two, using a paddle or dough hook if you have one, until the butter and cheese are thoroughly blended. Transfer to a tasteful container and serve at room temperature, if possible with freshly toasted imported English cheese biscuits and hearts of celery.

 CHEF'S SECRET   With all honors and compliments to the French for their cheeses, I personally think that not one of them is even a close second to a good Stilton. An elegant sight is to see how Stilton is prepared and served in one of the old London clubs.

The whole cheese is tied into two large, snow-white napkins which are folded in a special way to surround the cheese from which the top crust has been cut off. Next to it on the silver tray is a special cheese spoon. The inside of the cheese has been graciously dug out by the butlers for service, or the guest digs into it himself to his heart's content!

Stilton is eaten in small quantities with celery hearts, which as a rule are offered in large water glasses next to the cheese while the biscuits are hurried to the table at the last minute, either in a special covered silver container or on a silver tray protected by folded napkins.

Recently I have seen in several clubs that the Stilton is filled with a large amount of a faintly green, creamy spread. I am told this is a mixture of Stilton cheese with Devonshire butter, and is preferred by many people because it is milder, so even gentlemen with high blood pressure can enjoy it! When I tried it, I immediately fell in love with it, and at *The Bakery Restaurant* we have served it on many occasions, harvesting great praise.

The traditional classic accompaniment to Stilton is an old port, but you commit no heresy if you enjoy it with a glass of good imported beer, especially if you mix it with a little Guinness Stout for body and color. It also goes with claret, as the English call the light red wines they prefer.

ALSATIAN NOODLES
Serves 8

4 quarts water with 4 tablespoons
    salt
8 tablespoons corn oil
1½ pounds noodles

6 tablespoons butter or lard
½ teaspoon salt
¼ teaspoon white pepper

Set water with salt to boil. When it starts to boil, add 2 tablespoons oil. Let oil coat the top and adjust heat so that water boils gently. Add 1¼ pounds noodles slowly, by handfuls, waiting 10 seconds between each addition. When all noodles are in, stir with a wooden spoon that reaches to the bottom of the pot. Cover, but leave about a ½-inch opening between pot and lid. Stay and watch; within a minute or so the water will start to foam and run over. Remove lid and stir noodles again with wooden spoon. Adjust heat somewhat lower and keep boiling as long as the package instructions indicate. Rinse if it is suggested.

In a skillet large enough to accommodate the noodles, heat the butter or lard with the remaining oil. Crush the remaining ¼ pound noodles (wrapped in a clean kitchen towel) with a rolling pin until they resemble crushed cornflakes. Saute in the hot shortening, stirring constantly until they turn golden brown. Slowly add boiled noodles and mix gently with 2 forks so as not to break them. Sprinkle salt and white pepper on top. Heat through and serve.

CHEF'S SECRET   At *The Bakery Restaurant* we always serve Alsatian noodles with Beef Stroganoff. Guests often ask me what is sprinkled on top of the noodles. When I tell them "noodles," they are surprised—until I explain how the dish is made. The interesting thing is that the taste of the toasted raw noodles will be so surprisingly and pleasantly different from the boiled noodles that your guests will think they are some kind of nuts or specially treated almonds.

The best noodle for this dish is the ½-inch wide "broad" egg noodle. Of course, you can make it from other types just as well. The important thing is that you use the very same noodles crushed as boiled.

The oil swimming on top of the boiling water will coat the noodles with a very thin layer of fat molecules as you drop them in. The outside surface will start to cook and firm up while the fat molecules are still adhering to it. As the noodles that have sunk to the bottom of the pot start to heat up, the oil will coat them so that they will not stick to each other, but they won't become greasy either.

You can use the same method when cooking other pasta. Lasagne, for instance, is much easier to prepare if the pasta stays separate while cooking.

FETTUCCINI A LA ROMANO
Serves 8

1 pound imported fettuccini,
    or 1 pound fettuccini-type
    noodles (preferably the long
    variety)
2 tablespoons oil
1 small clove garlic,
    slightly crushed

1 cup butter
6 ounces grated Swiss cheese
    (preferably Gruyere)
6 ounces grated Romano
    or Parmesan cheese
1 cup heavy cream
freshly ground black pepper

Cook the fettuccini until just barely tender—al dente—according to package directions. Try not to break the long noodles.

In a large, heavy skillet, over medium heat, warm the oil with the garlic. As soon as the garlic edges turn yellow, remove and discard it. Add half the butter to the oil and let it melt. Add half of each type of cheese, stir, then add the noodles. Gently, but firmly, keep turning the noodles, cooking over medium heat.

Make a well in the middle of the pan and pour the cream into it. Fold the noodles and cheese into the cream.

Quickly place the mixture on a hot serving platter. Place the unmelted butter and the rest of the two cheeses on top. Rush to the table, give a good grinding of fresh black pepper, fold it once more, and serve.

CHEF'S SECRET   Do not be afraid to use the garlic. It will not give a garlic taste to the noodles.

Not all the cheeses of Rome are available here. After many tests I have found that the most satisfactory and most "Roman" result comes from the mixture of Gruyere and a good Parmesan. If possible, make the dish close to the dining table so the guests can watch. If a person is clever at using two forks and at lifting long noodles in the air and dropping them down, he can easily win the reputation of a master chef without knowing anything about cooking.

GALUSKA (SPAETZLE)
Serves 8

water with salt	3 cups flour
4 eggs	1 teaspoon salt
1 cup milk	4 to 6 tablespoons butter

Fill a large pot about two-thirds full with water. Add approximately 1 teaspoon salt for each quart of water used. Cover and bring the water to a boil, then set the heat so the water remains at a gentle boil.

With a fork, beat the eggs with the milk. In a large mixing bowl, combine the flour and salt with the beaten egg mixture. Stir with a wooden spoon until the batter is smooth and all the flour is incorporated.

With a tablespoon, spoon the dough into the boiling water, taking an amount about the size of an almond each time. Continue until all the dough is used.

Cover the pot three-quarters of the way, leaving an opening so that the steam and foam can escape as the Galuska cook. Stir occasionally. Cook until all the Galuska are on top of the water. Test one of the larger Galuska by cutting through it to be sure that no raw center remains. Pour into a colander and immediately rinse quickly and briefly with cold water. Shake as dry as possible.

Place the Galuska in a skillet and distribute the butter over the top. Let it melt, then gently turn the Galuska with a spatula and keep them warm until ready to serve.

CHEF'S SECRET   Do not overwork the dough, as this will result in hard, chewy Galuska.

To cut down on your work, pour ⅓ of the dough onto a dinner plate. Hold the plate close to the edge of the pot with the simmering water and quickly spoon the almond-sized portions into the water by first dipping the spoon into the water and then taking the dough from the edge of the plate. If you use this method, no dough will stick to the spoon and all the Galuska will be approximately the same size.

PINCHED DUMPLINGS (CSIPETKE)
Serves 8

2 cups flour
1 teaspoon salt
½ teaspoon baking powder
1 egg

2 tablespoons ice water
2 quarts water with 1 tablespoon
  salt
2 tablespoons butter or shortening

Sift together twice the flour, salt, and baking powder.

Beat the egg with ice water until frothy. Pour into flour mixture and mix with your hands, using all ten fingers and pressing the flour and liquid firmly together. It will not be easy, because this dough, when it is ready, must be extremely hard (harder than modeling clay). If you just can't manage it, add another tablespoon water, but definitely not more than one. When the mixture turns into a very firm ball, remove from the bowl and keep kneading with the heels of your palms until it turns into a firm, elastic dough.

Bring the salted water to a boil in a pot that has at least a 3-quart capacity. With your thumb and index finger, pinch off pieces of dough the size of raisins, and drop them one by one into the water. Continue until about ⅓ of the dough is in the pot. Stir with a wooden spoon. Repeat with remaining dough. Wait until the water boils again before each addition. Lower heat and simmer 10 to 15 minutes, or until the chewy little dumplings no longer have a raw center.

Drain, rinse quickly, fold in butter or shortening, and serve with Cream of Potato (see page 64), Wax Bean (see page 69), or another soup of your choice.

 CHEF'S SECRET   After the dough is ready, you can do the pinching and spread out the little pieces of dough on a kitchen towel or paper towel, then cook when you are ready. You can keep the dough covered with a cloth for 2 to 3 days at room temperature.

"Pinching" in Hungarian is *csipni,* so the name *Csipetke* coming from this verb means simply "the little pinched pieces."

SPAGHETTI BOLOGNESE
Serves 8

8 to 12 ounces ham,
    coarsely chopped
2 cups coarsely chopped onion
½ cup thinly sliced carrots
1 cup thinly sliced green stalk
    of celeriac, or 2 cups thinly
    sliced pascal celery
1 cup butter
1 cup olive or corn oil
1 pound ground pork shoulder
1 pound ground beef
1 cup or more Italian white wine
    or tart domestic white wine
10½ ounce can beef consomme

10½ ounce can chicken broth
2½ cups water
pinch of nutmeg
pinch of coriander
¼ teaspoon or more freshly
    ground black pepper
salt to taste
1 pound chicken livers
4 tablespoons cornstarch
2 cups heavy cream
spaghetti, cooked according to
    package directions
grated Parmesan or Romano
    cheese

After measuring the ham, onion, carrots, and celeriac, chop each finely, then mix them together in a bowl and set aside.

Melt 1 tablespoon of the butter and 1 tablespoon of the oil in a heavy skillet or saucepan over medium heat. Add the finely chopped ham-vegetable mixture and cook, stirring occasionally, until the mixture starts to brown. Remove from heat and transfer to a large saucepan. Keep warm.

In the same skillet, heat 1 tablespoon of the butter and 1 tablespoon of the oil. Alternately add small amounts (about the size of a walnut) of the pork and beef, starting with the pork. After each addition, break the meat up with the edge of a large spoon so that no lumps remain. Continue until all the meat has been added and no pieces are larger than the size of a green pea.

Increase the heat to high. Add the wine and bring the mixture to a boil, stirring with a spatula or cooking spoon. Boil until almost all the wine and the liquid which oozes from the meat have evaporated and the meat starts to brown in its own fat.

Transfer the browned pork and beef mixture to the large saucepan. Add the consomme, chicken broth, and 2 cups of water and bring to a vigorous boil. Reduce the heat to very low, cover, and simmer 30 to 35 minutes, stirring occasionally. Add the nutmeg, coriander, pepper, and salt.

In the same skillet you used before, melt the remaining butter and oil over high heat and saute the chicken livers 3 to 4 minutes. Remove them from the heat and, as soon as they are cool enough to handle, chop them into small cubes.

Dissolve the cornstarch in the remaining ½ cup water and add to the sauce along with the chopped chicken livers. Cover and cook over very low heat about 10 minutes. Stir the cream into the sauce and continue heating until the cream has warmed. Taste and add salt if needed. Serve over spaghetti and top with grated cheese.

CHEF'S SECRET   For a perfect dish, it is better to under-cook than overcook the spaghetti. Do not use spaghettini, but you can serve this sauce over macaroni or mostaccioli.

If possible, try to buy prosciutto or a prosciutto-type, salty, dry ham, such as Southern country ham or Westphalian ham. If you must use regular ham, try to get a lean piece.

There is a great difference in the taste and aroma of the green stalks of the celeriac or celery root, which are dark green, thin, very fragrant and pungent, and the crisp, whitish or yellowish-green, much less pungent pascal celery. If you use the pascal celery, use the greener outside stalks.

Using the same skillet is a great advantage, but make sure nothing sticks to the pan because it will burn during the next step. If you have to clean the pan between steps, do not wash it; just wipe it with paper towels.

This sauce freezes well, especially if the cream is not added. When you want to use the frozen sauce, heat it in a water bath—this will take longer but will keep it from burning. Once it is heated, stir in the cream and continue heating just until it is warm enough to serve.

BARLEY WITH WILD RICE AND MUSHROOMS
Serves 6

⅔ cup regular pearl barley
3 cups water with ½ teaspoon salt
½ cup wild rice
4 cups water with ½ teaspoon salt
2 tablespoons shortening
2 tablespoons butter or margarine
⅛ teaspoon freshly ground
    black pepper
½ bay leaf

2 chicken bouillon cubes
¼ cup hot water
½ cup finely chopped celery
½ cup finely chopped mushrooms
⅓ cup finely chopped onion
⅛ teaspoon garlic salt
3 tablespoons finely chopped
    parsley

Wash and drain the barley. Cook barley and rice separately in salted water for approximately 1 hour, or until liquid is absorbed.

In a heavy skillet, heat the shortening to smoking. Add 1 tablespoon butter. When melted, add rice, barley, pepper, and bay leaf. Mix well.

Soften bouillon cubes in hot water. Add to rice mixture. Pat down in skillet. Keep turning and patting until mixture is browned.

In another skillet, melt remaining 1 tablespoon butter. Saute celery, mushrooms, onion, and garlic salt in butter. Stir into rice-barley mixture. Add 1 tablespoon parsley and mix thoroughly. Pat down in skillet and turn after 1 minute. When mixture is browned, stir in 1 tablespoon parsley. Remove from heat. Before serving, garnish with remaining parsley.

As a variation, 1 cup regular pearl barley cooked in 4½ cups salted water may be substituted for barley and wild rice.

CHEF'S SECRET   Be sure to let the wild rice soak in not-too-cold water at least a couple of hours before you start to cook it. If possible, soak it for longer, perhaps overnight.

Dark, dehydrated, not-too-fresh mushrooms are better for a dish like this than the snow-white firm fresh mushrooms.

They will not look as good, but the aroma and pungency will be much stronger. If you are fortunate enough to live in an area where so-called "oyster" mushrooms are sold, use them.

This recipe works well doubled, and freezes very well. If you want to freeze half, defrost it slowly in the refrigerator overnight and heat in a lightly buttered casserole under cover at 350° for about 45 minutes.

RICE A LA GRECQUE
Serves 8

1 medium-sized onion,
   finely minced
1 clove garlic, slightly crushed
3 tablespoons butter
2 cups rice
½ teaspoon salt
water
8 ounces Italian sausage

10-ounce package frozen peas
2 tablespoons chopped pimiento
   or fresh red bell pepper,
   if available
butter for brushing the bowl
Greek or black olives for garnish
parsley sprigs for garnish

Saute the minced onion and garlic in the butter until the onions turn glossy. Discard the garlic. Add the rice to the pan with the onions and stir until the rice turns slightly yellow. Add the salt and slightly less water than required according to package directions and bring to a boil. Simmer until the water is absorbed and the rice is tender.

Form the sausage meat into balls the size of a cherry, then fry in a separate skillet until browned.

Cook the peas according to package directions. Add the sausage and peas to the cooked rice mixture. Gently toss together and heat through. Add the chopped pimiento or bell pepper.

Lightly butter a bowl and press the rice mixture into it. Turn out onto a serving platter. Garnish with olives and parsley sprigs and serve immediately.

CHEF'S SECRET   This recipe, to the best of my knowledge, is one of the original recipes of Escoffier. Of course, it is adapted from a restaurant form to a household recipe, and there are other minor changes. It is the finest accompaniment for roast capon, roast chicken, or roast turkey. It is also excellent with squab or veal.

To keep this dish as colorful as possible, undercook the peas. Leave the pan uncovered during the cooking so they will remain vivid green.

If you cannot get Italian sausage, buy regular sausage and, for each 8 ounces of meat, dilute ½ teaspoon oregano and ¼ teaspoon ground coriander in 2 tablespoons water. Mix the water-spice mixture into the sausage meat and form the balls. If only link sausage is available, sprinkle it before frying with the amount of spices indicated above.

Escoffier added white "pearl" onions or "tiny" onions to the dish. You may add them when you add the peas.

RICE PILAF
Serves 8

2 cups long-grain rice
2 tablespoons oil
3 tablespoons butter
1 tablespoon finely minced onion
½ teaspoon salt

⅛ teaspoon freshly ground black pepper
3 tablespoons freshly chopped parsley
4 cups boiling water

Preheat the oven to 375°.

Wash the rice in a colander. Cover the colander with a lid or a plate and shake to dry the rice as much as possible. Let it stand for a few minutes and shake again.

Heat the oil and 1 tablespoon butter with onion, salt, pepper, and 1 tablespoon parsley in a heavy metal casserole over medium heat. When the onions start to turn yellow, add about ⅓ of the rice and stir with a wooden spoon to coat it with the shortening. Repeat twice more until all the rice is in the pan. Stir until the rice heats through, turns opaque, and starts to crack and pop.

When the rice starts to turn yellow, add the boiling water in small amounts, being careful not to burn your hand with the steam. Keep stirring with the wooden spoon as you add the boiling water. Cover and bake 45 minutes to 1 hour. Stir once after 30 minutes and again after 45 minutes.

Before serving, fluff the pilaf with two forks. Add the remaining 2 tablespoons butter and let it melt into the rice, then add the remaining parsley.

 CHEF'S SECRET   As a child, I watched an old Turkish woman make this rice in the home of a classmate. She used more butter and more oil than this recipe calls for, and the end result was greasier than this version. Nevertheless, I have always found that this type of rice goes very well with Western-style dishes. It is very different from the Oriental method of cooking rice, though its taste resembles fried rice. The basic recipe given here can be prepared with many variations. For example:

Add to the above ingredients 4 tablespoons red zane corinth (a Mediterranean raisin, tiny and dark, resembling the English red currant).

Add 4 tablespoons chopped, sliced, or slivered almonds, plain or roasted.

Add 4 tablespoons pine nuts or pistachios.

If you don't have a metal casserole or serving dish, fry the rice in a skillet, add water, and then transfer to a glass or china ovenproof dish.

8

SALADS

California is the home state of cults, religious and otherwise. I admire that state more than anything else for its salad cult.

We know that salads did not originate in California. In my library I have an Italian book, *Archidipno; overo, dell'insalata, e dell'vso essa, trattato nuovo, curioso, e non mai piu dato in luce* by Salvatore Massonio, vintage 1600, which offers exclusive salad recipes. But the strong position that salads hold on the American dinner table, both in homes and restaurants, is definitely due to California's influence. The big and elaborate salads, the simple and intricate combinations, the dressings as we know them—all have something to do with California. This is true from the most American and most popular of elegant salads, Caesar Salad, which was invented on the California-Mexico border, to the Waldorf Salad, which combined in New York's Waldorf-Astoria three great products from sunny California—apple, walnuts, and celery.

At *The Bakery Restaurant* we serve only one kind of salad at a time, and each year we try to serve our unique and much loved celery root or celery knob remoulade for as much of the year as possible. When it is not available we serve an assorted mixed green salad with our Herb Salad Dressing. As I mentioned in the Chef's Secret following that recipe, it comes from an old American cookbook in my collection, and was simply called "Another Dressing." I adapted it for modern-day use, and I feel that the boiled cornstarch gives enough texture so that the dressing is rich and smooth with much less oil than another dressing would require for the same consistency. This is what I think makes it so popular.

The carrot-blueberry salad, to the best of my knowledge, is my own invention, and I am quite proud of it. I always feel that blueberries deserve many other places on the menu besides their role as a dessert.

THE BAKERY'S HERB SALAD DRESSING
2 quarts

2 cups water
1 cup white vinegar
2 tablespoons prepared mustard
⅛ teaspoon freshly ground
   black pepper
⅛ teaspoon white pepper
2 teaspoons salt
½ cup sugar
6 tablespoons cornstarch mixed
   with 1 cup cold water

1 cup oil
4 cups ice cubes
any 4 or 5 or all of the
   following herbs, 2 to 3
   tablespoons of each,
   according to your taste:
   tarragon, dill, scallions,
   rosemary, parsley (curly or
   flat), watercress, marjoram,
   sage, chervil, celery tops

Bring to a boil the water with the vinegar, mustard, black and white pepper, salt, and sugar. When it comes to a boil, gently stir in cornstarch-water mixture. Bring to a boil, adjust heat to medium, and cook, stirring, until the mixture thickens and becomes opaque.

Remove from heat and pour into a large bowl. Add half the oil, stirring constantly. Then add half the ice cubes, half the oil again, and the second half of ice cubes. Keep stirring until the ice cubes are melted. Refrigerate.

Add the herbs of your choice and mix when ready to serve.

CHEF'S SECRET   This dressing will keep for two to three weeks in the refrigerator. If you were to add the herbs before storing, the dressing would keep for three to four days at the most.

It is difficult to get fresh herbs all the time. Therefore, at *The Bakery Restaurant* we add some fresh and some dry herbs, depending on season and availability. If we add dry herbs, we always moisten them first with a few drops of vinegar and water, waiting a couple of minutes until they absorb the liquid.

This recipe is from a very old American cookbook which calls it "Another Dressing." At *The Bakery Restaurant* we sprinkle over this dressing some finely chopped hard-boiled eggs and grated feta cheese. Warning: once the cheese and eggs are mixed into the dressing it should not be kept more than a day.

BIBB LETTUCE
Serves 8

pinch of salt
1 clove garlic
pinch of sugar
freshly ground black pepper
4 to 6 tablespoons fresh oil

juice of 2 lemons, diluted with a
    small amount of water
4 heads Boston or 8 heads
    Kentucky bibb lettuce

Sprinkle the bottom of a wooden salad bowl with salt. Cut the garlic in half and gently rub it on the salt, then discard the garlic.

Add the sugar and a little black pepper to the bowl. Pour in the oil. Then, with a fork or wire whip, dissolve the spices in the oil.

Pour in the lemon juice-water mixture, stirring constantly. Pour the mixture from the bowl into another container. Keep at room temperature.

Very quickly wash and dry the lettuce. Remove the outside leaves if necessary, then place the lettuce in the wooden bowl and chill.

Just before serving, vigorously stir the dressing and pour it over the salad. Toss gently and serve immediately.

CHEF'S SECRET   There are generally two kinds of bibb lettuce available throughout the United States: Boston bibb and Kentucky bibb. Boston is tender and almost lemon yellow on the inside. Kentucky is hearty, leafy, and darker green but also very tender and tasty. It is a sin to use an overpowering dressing on either one.

If you have a wooden mortar and pestle, of course you do not have to make the dressing in the salad bowl. But the bowl itself improves and will last longer if you keep rubbing the inside with garlic, because of the oil in the garlic.

The best way of drying the bibb lettuce or any other vegetable is to use a French wire basket which is designed for this purpose. If you do not have such a basket, just put the lettuce in a large absorbent kitchen towel which is about 20 inches by 20 inches. Fold the four corners together and, making a full circle with your arm, shake out the water.

If you chill the dressing or chill the lettuce with the dressing on it, the oil will become firm and separate and will not coat as nicely as when kept at room temperature. Of course, if you wish, you may substitute a good-quality vinegar for the lemon juice.

CARROT BLUEBERRY SALAD
Serves 8

2 cups carrots, cubed to the
    size of blueberries
2 tablespoons vinegar
1 pint fresh blueberries
1 egg yolk
1 teaspoon prepared mustard
juice of ½ lemon
1 teaspoon sugar
½ teaspoon salt

1 cup sour cream
lettuce leaves
1 tablespoon snipped
    dill weed or chopped
    fresh parsley
2 slices whole wheat bread,
    toasted
2 tablespoons butter

Place carrots in a small saucepan, cover with water, and bring to a boil over high heat. Remove and let stand 5 minutes. Discard water. Add vinegar. Shake carrot cubes under cover and let cool in the vinegar.

Wash, pick over, and chill blueberries. In the bowl of an electric mixer, blend egg yolk, mustard, lemon juice, sugar, and salt. Fold in sour cream by hand.

Gently fold drained carrot cubes into the sour cream mixture. Then fold in blueberries, being careful not to break them. Arrange lettuce leaves in a salad bowl and place carrot-blueberry mixture on top. Sprinkle with snipped dill. Chill.

Trim crusts from the toast. Cut into small cubes. Heat butter in a small skillet over medium heat. Add toast cubes, increase heat, and turn with a spatula or slotted spoon until cubes turn deep brown. Stay with it—don't let them burn. Sprinkle cubes on top of the salad and serve, if possible, while the bread cubes are still warm.

 CHEF'S SECRET   As the carrot cubes cool in the vinegar, they will acquire a pleasant flavor that will make an excellent contrast with the mild fragrance of the fresh blueberries. If you like your salads more on the tart side, add more vinegar to the carrots or sprinkle some on the blueberries before chilling.

To make the salad more colorful, save 10 to 20 blueberries and the same number of carrot cubes and sprinkle them on top of the toast cubes.

CELERY KNOB REMOULADE
Serves 8

3 to 4 large celery knobs
    (celeriac), about 2 to
    2½ pounds total
1 teaspoon salt
⅔ cup vinegar
3 tablespoons Dijon-style mustard

salt to taste
¼ teaspoon white pepper
⅔ cup oil
juice of ½ lemon
2 to 3 tablespoons freshly chopped
    parsley

Peel the celery knobs and cut them into thin julienne strips (⅛ × ⅛ × 2 inches). Sprinkle the strips with the salt and vinegar and let stand for 15 minutes. Drain.

Blend together the mustard, a little salt, and white pepper. Using a wire whip, gradually beat in the oil. Add the lemon juice.

Toss the celery with the remoulade sauce and place it in a serving dish. Sprinkle the top with the chopped parsley.

 CHEF'S SECRET   Celery knob, or celeriac, is available from November through April throughout most of the United States. If you do not see it in the grocery, ask for it. If the produce manager does not have any on hand, he can pick up a half-bushel for you. Seeds for celeriac are also readily available and easy to grow.

If you want your celery remoulade to be snow white, while you are cutting the julienne strips have a plastic bowl with enough cold water mixed with vinegar to cover the celery. Keep both the peeled uncut celery and the thin julienne strips in the vinegar-water until you start to make the salad itself.

In different cookbooks—even in my own—you will find many recipes for remoulade. I am afraid no such thing as a "real" or "true" remoulade sauce exists. Whatever concoction you make with mustard, vinegar, water, and spices can be called remoulade.

CRAB-APPLE
Serves 8

8 large Rome Beauty apples
juice of 2 lemons
16 fresh pitted dates, cut into
    ¼-inch slices
2 4- to 5-inch celery ribs,
    peeled and cut into
    ⅛-inch slices
2 cups mayonnaise (see appendix)

3 to 4 tablespoons bourbon
1½ teaspoons prepared mustard
1 teaspoon Worcestershire sauce
1 pound Dungeness crabmeat
    (use claws for decoration)
lettuce leaves
leafy celery tops

Cut a slice ½ to ¾ inch thick from the top of each apple. Rub the surfaces with lemon juice. Refrigerate the tops (see illustration).

    With a melon-ball cutter, scoop out 4 or 5 balls from each apple. Sprinkle with lemon juice. Remove the core of each apple to enlarge the cavity. Sprinkle the insides of the apples with lemon juice. Refrigerate.

Combine the apple balls, dates, and celery in a small bowl.

Gently fold together the mayonnaise, bourbon, mustard, and Worcestershire sauce. Add half of this to the combined fruit. Chill for 1 hour.

Before serving, gently fold the crabmeat into the mayonnaise-fruit mixture, and place ¼ of the mixture into each apple. Spoon the remaining mayonnaise mixture on top of each apple. Replace tops.

Serve each apple on a bed of lettuce leaves and garnish each with a few crab claws and celery tops.

CHEF'S SECRET   To have nice, completely round balls from the apple, follow the illustration. It is important that you first press the whole circumference of the cutter into the apple and, turning the wrist left to right, keep pressing until you feel (or check by removing the cutter) that you have the upper half of the ball perfectly shaped. Then, with a clockwise movement, still pressing, turn the cutter 180 degrees, then remove. You can use this method for other fruit balls.

On enlarging the cavity after you have enough apple balls, see the procedure described on page 263.

IVORY EBONY SALAD
Serves 8

any lettuce of your choice,
    such as Kentucky bibb,
    Boston bibb, romaine, leaf
    lettuce, or a mixture, enough
    for 8 portions depending on
    the size of the salad you want
1 can hearts of palm

white vinegar
½ pound black Greek olives
    (not canned black olives)
salad dressing of your choice,
    or vinaigrette
8 parsley sprigs

Wash and spin or swing dry the greens and arrange either in a salad bowl or individual serving dishes.

Open the can of hearts of palm. Rinse thoroughly by running cold water gently into the can for 4 to 5 minutes, then remove piece by piece, rinse under running cold water and place in a shallow dish. Add enough cold water to cover, and for each cup of cold water add 1 tablespoon plain white vinegar. Chill.

With a small sharp paring knife, cut each olive in half lengthwise, removing the pit with the tip of the knife without cutting into the flesh. To serve, tastefully arrange crosscut slices of the ivory-colored hearts of palm and the ebony-colored olives either before or after adding the dressing, depending on the type of dressing you use. Garnish with parsley and serve.

CHEF'S SECRET   This is one of the simplest and most attractive salads. Sometimes we cut the hearts of palm once across the middle lengthwise, then split them into 4 or 8 long pieces depending on the thickness of each piece. Other times we arrange alternating slices of hearts of palm and olive halves on the edge of the salad plate. You can try many variations.

This salad is beautiful at wedding dinners where we always emphasize the occasion by cutting half-inch-thick slices of the heart of watermelon with a 2-inch heart-shaped cookie cutter, placing on each salad a watermelon heart, but always giving two hearts to both the bride and the groom. Watermelon is very easy to carve. We often carve the initials of the couple's first names in their pairs of watermelon hearts. At one magnificent wedding, which was perhaps the most lavish we ever gave, we carved the initial of every guest into the watermelon heart (don't ask how much the bill was for that party!).

LIMESTONE LETTUCE WITH TOMATO VINAIGRETTE
Serves 8

2 large ripe tomatoes
1½ tablespoons sugar
2 teaspoons salt
⅛ teaspoon white pepper
⅛ teaspoon garlic salt
2 to 3 tablespoons chopped
    green parsley or dill,
    or a mixture of the two

⅔ cup oil
⅓ cup white vinegar
8 small or 4 large heads
    limestone lettuce,
    washed and trimmed

Spear one tomato at a time on a fork and dip into boiling water for about 30 seconds. Remove and hold under cold running water or plunge into ice water. Peel, quarter, and discard seeds and liquid.

Cut tomatoes into small cubes. Place in a bowl and sprinkle with sugar, salt, pepper, garlic salt, and chopped parsley or dill. Gently toss and chill.

In an electric mixer add oil and vinegar alternately, drop by drop, beating constantly at highest speed until blended. Pour over marinated tomato cubes. Spoon over lettuce and serve.

 CHEF'S SECRET   Adding the vinegar and oil drop by drop while beating at highest speed will bring the two ingredients into suspension. The dressing will be creamy and won't separate. This thick, opaque mixture with the tomato cubes folded in gives a beautiful appearance to the lettuce. It coats every leaf. The soft texture of the tomatoes, the creaminess of the dressing, and the fresh crunchiness of the lettuce will provide three very desirable textures.

SHREDDED CARROTS WITH LEMON
Serves 8

2 cups water
1 cup seedless raisins
4 cups shredded carrots
½ cup fresh lemon juice
¾ cup salad oil

2 teaspoons salt
pinch of white pepper
½ teaspoon dry mustard
1 teaspoon paprika
dash of cayenne pepper

In a small saucepan, bring the water to a boil. Add the raisins, cover, and turn off the heat. Let the raisins stand in the warm water for at least 20 minutes. Drain.

Place the raisins and shredded carrots in a serving bowl.

With a wire whip, combine the lemon juice, oil, salt, pepper, dry mustard, paprika, and cayenne. Pour this dressing over the salad and refrigerate at least 2 hours before serving.

CHEF'S SECRET   This salad has been the rage of French gourmets for the last decade, appearing on menus in the most elegant places.

This is the type of recipe you can modify and develop into something uniquely your own. For instance, you can replace the raisins with chopped pitted prunes, or you can substitute chopped pitted dates, figs, or any other dried fruit for part of the raisins. If raisins or other dried fruits are too rich for your diet, you can use ¼-inch cubes of a celery stalk that has been peeled before chopping.

9
SAUCES

In one respect, cookbook authors are not very different from other authors. They hardly finish one book and they are already thinking about the next one.

Somewhere in my future is a book called *The Funeral of the Roux*. I imagine a beautiful color photograph for the dust jacket — six or seven smiling chefs standing around an open grave, slowly lowering with ropes a large pot of roux. The book will describe what I believe is the greatest revolution in the kitchen in recent times — the revolution in sauces.

Several years ago I had a talented young man working with us, who has since become a successful restaurant owner. His credentials were impeccable. He was a graduate of the Culinary Institute, studied for a year in Europe, then spent more than a year as an apprentice with my dear friend and colleague, the late Albert Stockli, at his unsurpassed country inn, Stonehenge, in Connecticut.

The young man's references and recommendations were so excellent that even though we did not need an extra person in the kitchen, we hired him. Everything went well until I told him one day to melt some butter in a heavy saute pan, make a mixture of light cream, cornstarch, and flour in the electric blender, and, when the butter got hot and bubbled, stir the cream mixture into it. He asked me to repeat my instructions, then he told me that he was very sorry, he wouldn't do it, and he was resigning immediately because this was not the way to make a white sauce.

Most chefs are hotheaded and so am I. My first reaction was to wish the young man good riddance, but then I changed my mind. I persuaded him to let me call Albert Stockli at Stonehenge, present him with the problem, and ask his opinion. Stockli listened carefully, and then he said "Louis, I really don't know why I didn't think about this myself. I'm sure you are not the only one who does it this way, instead of starting with a roux blanc, and I see no reason why the method could not produce an excellent light sauce."

The young man stayed with us for a long time before he went on to further his education, which led him finally to his goal, owning and operating his own renowned restaurant, Robert's Place, in Charleston, South Carolina.

Sauces are extremely important. So are culinary methods. But you should never lose sight of the fact that people don't eat methods, they eat results. If a new and different method can offer excellent results, invention is in order for the saucier.

AIOLI (GARLIC SAUCE)
Serves 8

1 large boiled potato
1 slice day-old (or older)
    white bread
4 to 6 cloves garlic, chopped
4 tablespoons finely chopped
    flat-leaf parsley
¼ cup blanched crushed almonds

3 to 4 tablespoons red wine
    vinegar
1½ to 2 cups oil
1 teaspoon salt
¼ teaspoon freshly ground
    black pepper

Peel and mash boiled potato. Place ⅔ cup mashed potato in a bowl. Tear the bread into pieces and add to the potato.

Place the garlic, parsley, almonds, and part of the potato mixture in a blender. Add vinegar and ½ cup of oil and blend to a paste. Slowly add the rest of the potato mixture and blend again, alternating with the remaining oil until the mixture is the consistency of a thick mayonnaise.

Add salt and pepper to taste, and, if you like, a few more drops of wine vinegar.

 CHEF'S SECRET   This recipe sounds questionable but tastes heavenly. A "large" potato is a U.S. Grade A, No. 1 baking potato, and this is the best kind for this sauce. (Incidentally, you can use a baked potato just as well as a boiled one.) The sauce will keep in the refrigerator in a tightly covered jar for as long as 2 weeks.

This sauce is excellent with roast, braised, boiled, or grilled meats, especially lamb, beef, and pork. It is also good with plain boiled or broiled fish, and with cold meats.

COLD CUCUMBER SAUCE
Serves 4

1 large cucumber, peeled and
    cut in ¼-inch cubes
light sprinkling of salt, garlic salt,
    and freshly ground black
    pepper to taste

1 cup sour cream or yogurt
chopped dill weed

Sprinkle spices on cucumber cubes and chill thoroughly at least 30 minutes. Just before serving, fold into sour cream or yogurt and sprinkle generously with chopped dill weed or other herb. (If you use tarragon, be thrifty—it's pungent.) Serve with fish.

CHEF'S SECRET   If the cucumber is too seedy and the center is too soft, scrape it out with a tablespoon or melon-ball cutter before cubing. But if the seeds are immature and the center firm, you can cube the whole cucumber.

    Never chop the fresh dill on a board with a knife as you would other herbs. Always snip it with a pair of scissors right over the dish you are preparing. The volatile oils of dill are very delicate, and chopping destroys a large part of the fragrance and also the texture of fresh dill.

HUNGARIAN MUSTARD SAUCE
About 5 cups

4 cups water
1 cup prepared mustard
⅓ cup vinegar
½ cup sugar
⅛ teaspoon white pepper

¼ teaspoon salt
⅓ cup cornstarch
1 cup water
¼ cup port, Madeira,
    or cream sherry

Combine 4 cups water, ½ cup mustard, vinegar, sugar, pepper, and salt in a saucepan and bring to a vigorous boil over high heat. Stir with a wire whip when it starts to boil, and keep stirring for a minute or so.

Mix cornstarch into 1 cup water and slowly pour mixture into boiling liquid, stirring constantly. Adjust heat to medium and continue to cook until mixture is thick, smooth, and opaque.

Remove from heat and cool 10 to 15 minutes, stirring occasionally. Stir in remaining ½ cup mustard and wine. Cool to room temperature, then chill. The sauce will keep refrigerated 2 to 3 weeks.

CHEF'S SECRET   This sauce is popular with the different kinds of Hungarian fresh sausages that are simmered in water or heated in a skillet and eaten hot. It also makes an excellent sandwich spread instead of mayonnaise or butter.

If you wish, use a Bavarian-type mustard that has a pale gray color with small dark specks in it for at least half the mustard required by the recipe. It will give an excellent flavor.

If you don't wish to use an alcoholic beverage, add ¼ cup orange juice or other fruit juice instead of the wine.

HUNGARIAN PAPRIKA "KETCHUP"
2 cups

½ cup dry white wine
¼ cup plus 1 teaspoon sugar
2 tablespoons salt

¼ cup Hungarian paprika
2 tablespoons cognac
½ cup tomato puree

Stir all ingredients together. When well blended, add enough boiling water to yield 2 cups. Cool and chill. It will keep refrigerated for several weeks. Serve with eggs, sausages, and hot or cold meats.

CHEF'S SECRET   The amount of salt and sugar will depend on the wine you use. Leave out some of both and taste 2 to 3 hours after preparing.

OXFORD SAUCE
2 cups

2 teaspoons finely chopped
    shallots
⅔ cup port wine
⅔ cup red currant jelly
1 teaspoon sugar
zest of 1 orange and 1 lemon
    (see appendix)

juice of 1 orange
juice of ½ lemon
1½ tablespoons cornstarch
dash of cayenne pepper
dash of ginger

In a small saucepan, scald the shallots in boiling port wine for 1 minute. Remove from heat, add the jelly and sugar, and let them dissolve.

Remove the zest (outer peel) from the orange and lemon with a potato peeler. Cut the strips of zest into very fine julienne strips. Boil these 2 minutes in water to cover. Drain. Discard the water.

Squeeze the juice from the whole orange and half the lemon. Mix it with the cornstarch in a small cup. Add this juice with the julienne strips to the wine and jelly. Bring the mixture to a boil over medium heat, stirring constantly. Season with cayenne pepper and ginger. Cool at room temperature. Keep in refrigerator. If necessary, add more port wine to dilute the sauce to proper consistency. Serve with cold meats.

 CHEF'S SECRET   Shallots are not available at all times or in all places. If you cannot get them, substitute 2 tablespoons finely chopped onion which has been boiled in 1 cup water for 2 minutes, drained, and rinsed with cold water. Or omit onion and add a light sprinkling of onion powder or onion salt.

Red currant jellies may differ in acidity or sweetness. You may have to add more or less than 1 teaspoon sugar.

REMOULADE SAUCE

1 tablespoon capers
2 to 3 tablespoons prepared
    mustard
1 tablespoon finely chopped
    sweet pickle
1 tablespoon finely chopped
    dill pickle

1 teaspoon mixed chervil and
    tarragon, according to taste
1 tablespoon chopped fresh parsley
1 teaspoon anchovy paste
2 cups mayonnaise (see appendix)

Rinse the capers under cold running water. Fold all the ingredients into the mayonnaise and serve with cold meats or lobster.

GREEN SAUCE (SAUCE VERTE)

1 cup coarsely chopped fresh
    spinach
2 tablespoons finely chopped
    fresh parsley
1 tablespoon chopped scallions
    (green parts only)
    or chopped chives

½ teaspoon tarragon
½ teaspoon chervil
juice of ½ lemon
1 tablespoon vinegar
2 cups mayonnaise (see appendix)

Place all the ingredients except the mayonnaise in an electric blender and puree them together. Fold the green liquid slowly into the mayonnaise. Refrigerate. (The mixture will be somewhat runny but will become firm when refrigerated.) Serve with fish.

SAUCE LOUIS
2½ cups

2 eggs
3 tablespoons prepared mustard
3 tablespoons sugar
½ teaspoon salt

⅛ teaspoon white pepper
juice of 1 lemon
1 teaspoon vinegar
2 cups sour cream

In a medium-sized bowl, using a wire whip, blend together the eggs, mustard, sugar, salt, pepper, lemon juice, and vinegar. Slowly fold in the sour cream. Keep refrigerated. Serve with fish and cold meats.

CHEF'S SECRET   This is probably the simplest and quickest, but most elegant, sauce. It can be made in 20 seconds without even coming near the stove.

It is important that all ingredients except the sour cream be mixed together vigorously by hand with a wire whip or mixed in an electric mixer at the highest speed. On the other hand, the sour cream must be gently folded into the sauce with a rubber spatula or scraper; fold the mixture over the sour cream, then fold some sour cream under the mixture. If the commercial sour cream is beaten, it will become runny and will separate, and you will not get the same silky texture and consistency.

You can make this sauce using sour half-and-half or yogurt, but not every brand of yogurt will give exactly the same results.

WHIPPED CREAM-ORANGE MARMALADE SAUCE
Serves 8

1 cup heavy cream
pinch of salt
3 ounces prepared horseradish

3 ounces orange marmalade
juice of ½ lemon

Whip the heavy cream with the pinch of salt to very stiff peaks. Combine the horseradish, orange marmalade, and lemon juice, and very gently fold the mixture into the stiffly whipped cream. Chill until serving time.
Serve with cold venison, ham, or other meat.

CHEF'S SECRET   This surprising mixture sounds strange but tastes delicious.

Try to measure the horseradish with some of the liquid from the jar. If the horseradish has no liquid, increase the amount of lemon juice to 1 whole lemon. You will need a certain amount of moisture to help incorporate the orange marmalade into the horseradish. If you make the sauce ahead of time, in 4 or 5 hours all the orange marmalade-horseradish mixture will sink to the bottom, so gently fold the mixture together again before serving.

This sauce freezes very well. But be sure to defrost it by leaving it in the refrigerator overnight instead of trying to defrost it at room temperature.

BILL BEECHER'S WILD ONION SAUCE
2 cups

2 tablespoons bacon drippings
2 tablespoons oil
½ cup finely minced wild onion, including green parts
1 teaspoon salt
1 teaspoon sugar

1½ cups red wine
1 cup beef consomme or beef stock (see appendix)
2 tablespoons flour mixed with 1 tablespoon Kitchen Bouquet

In a heavy saucepan over high heat, heat bacon drippings and oil until smoking hot. Add wild onion and stir 2 to 3 minutes. Lower heat to medium, add salt, sugar, and 1 cup red wine. Stir, cover, and cook 30 minutes, lowering the heat if the liquid evaporates too fast.

After 30 minutes add consomme and flour mixed with Kitchen Bouquet. Bring to a boil over medium heat, then simmer the sauce over very low heat, uncovered, for at least 45 minutes. Press through a fine sieve, stir in the last ½ cup of red wine, and serve with steaks or barbecued, broiled, or grilled meats.

CHEF'S SECRET   Wild onion is much more common in the United States than one would think. If you cannot find it, substitute half shallots and half chives, adding ⅛ teaspoon garlic salt—*not* garlic powder. If you cannot get shallots, substitute the white parts of scallions.

When I first made this sauce I was privileged to receive the first bunch of wild onions I had ever handled from Dr. William Beecher, director of the Chicago Academy of Sciences. I am grateful not only for the wild onions but for his friendship, which has lasted now for over two decades. I am proud to be a trustee of the Chicago Academy of Sciences and to work with Bill Beecher on many special projects.

CHERRY GLAZE FOR ROAST DUCK
About 6 cups

2 large cans (6 cups) pitted
   sour cherries with juice
½ cup sugar (or more, depending
   on the sweetness of
   the wine)
1 stick cinnamon

1 slice lemon peel, ½ by 1½
   inches
2 cups red wine
7 tablespoons cornstarch
6 tablespoons cold water
sugar and salt to taste

Place half the cherries and all the juice from one can in a large saucepan with sugar, cinnamon, and lemon peel. Bring to a boil and boil 3 minutes. Add the red wine and again bring to a boil, then remove from heat. Immediately cover and let steep 5 minutes.

After 5 minutes, remove the lemon peel and cinnamon. Add the remaining cherries from the first can.

Blend all the cherries from the second can with half of the juice from that can in an electric blender until smooth.

Bring the rest of the cherry juice from the second can to a boil and thicken it with the cornstarch diluted in the cold water. Stir until the mixture is thickened and clear. Cook over low heat for 2 to 3 minutes.

Combine the three mixtures and serve warm or cold. Correct seasoning by adding sugar and salt, if necessary.

CHEF'S SECRET   The body of the sauce will be full, with small flakes of cherry flesh. These flakes are characteristic of the sauce, but if you wish to avoid them, after liquefying the second can of cherries in the blender, strain the liquid through a fine cloth to collect the fibers of the skin and flesh.

If you have some imitation cherry flavoring on hand, add a small drop. It also helps to add a few drops of red food coloring, very carefully, just before serving. After all, ladies wear lipstick, why shouldn't food?

If you are lucky enough to live in an area where frozen, pitted sour cherries are available, by all means use them instead of the canned variety.

CHICKEN STOCK BECHAMEL
Serves 6 to 8

¼ cup butter
2 tablespoons flour
1 tablespoon cornstarch
1 cup light cream

1¼ cups chicken stock, or
    a 10½ ounce can chicken
    broth
salt and white pepper to taste

In a medium-sized heavy saucepan, heat the butter over medium heat until it starts to foam. Dissolve flour and cornstarch in the light cream, mixing until well blended. Pour this into the foaming butter, stirring constantly, until the sauce has thickened. Adjust heat so that it doesn't scorch.

Stir in the chicken stock and continue to cook over low heat for at least 5 minutes. Season with salt and pepper. Strain through a sieve. Keep warm until ready to serve.

 CHEF'S SECRET   If the chicken stock is not strong enough, add half a chicken bouillon cube and a very small amount of celery seed.

If you want an exceptional Bechamel, finish it just before serving as follows: Stiffly whip ½ to 1 cup whipping cream (depending on how rich you want it) with a pinch of salt. Tablespoonful by tablespoonful, fold some of the hot Bechamel into the whipped cream to warm it gradually, then fold the whipped cream mixture into the sauce. Serve immediately. Don't use a wire whip for this folding; a rubber or plastic spatula works best.

VARIATIONS   This sauce is very versatile and can be easily varied with the addition of small amounts of concentrated flavoring. For instance, it makes an exceptional sauce for fish, fowl, or veal with the addition of 1 tablespoon anchovy paste and 1 tablespoon rinsed capers. (Always rinse capers under running cold water before using, to get rid of the chemical taste of the liquid from the jar.) Or you can add 1 to 2 tablespoons French mustard with 1 heaping teaspoon curry powder; or 1 ripe banana mashed with a fork together with 1 teaspoon curry powder; or 2 tablespoons grated Parmesan and 2 tablespoons grated Swiss cheese; or 3 to 4 tablespoons processed cheese grated with 1 or 2 tablespoons Parmesan.

DILL SAUCE
Serves 8

4 tablespoons shortening,
    preferably half butter
1 cup firmly pressed, chopped,
    fresh young dill weed
1 teaspoon sugar
½ to 1 teaspoon salt
2 cups chicken stock or
    chicken broth

4 tablespoons flour
1 cup milk
1 cup light cream
4 tablespoons vinegar
juice of ½ lemon
¼ teaspoon white pepper
1 cup sour cream

Melt the shortening in a heavy saucepan over medium heat. Add dill, sugar, and salt. Stir until the dill heats through. Add the chicken stock and bring to a boil.

Mix the flour with the milk and half the light cream. Pour this mixture into the boiling liquid, stirring constantly. Reduce heat, add vinegar, lemon juice, and white pepper, and simmer at least 20 minutes, stirring occasionally.

Before serving, mix the other half of the light cream with the sour cream. Slowly spoon some of the hot sauce into the mixture to warm it, then add the sour cream mixture to the sauce. Cover and keep in a warm place about 5 minutes before serving. Serve with boiled meat or poultry.

 CHEF'S SECRET   If you like a thicker or thinner sauce, simply increase or decrease the flour.

The dill weed you need is the baby dill sold in bunches and resembling carrot leaves. Don't confuse this with the dill weed sold in the fall for pickling, which consists of large stems and dill flower umbrellas, with a little fuzzy leaf here and there on the stem.

If you have to prepare the sauce from the pickling type of dill weed, prepare as follows: With a sharp knife, chop enough dill for 1 cup, firmly packed. Bring 2 cups water with 3 to 4 tablespoons vinegar to a boil. Add the chopped dill stems, cover, remove from the heat, and let stand about 1 hour. Strain, discard the liquid, and add 4 to 5 tablespoons finely chopped parsley to the prepared dill; then proceed with the recipe.

HORSERADISH SAUCE
Serves 8

6-ounce jar prepared horseradish
4 tablespoons butter
2 tablespoons sugar
4 to 5 tablespoons vinegar
½ teaspoon salt
¼ teaspoon white pepper
2 cups chicken or veal stock,
    or chicken broth

1 teaspoon prepared mustard
3 tablespoons flour
1 cup milk
1 cup light cream
1 cup sour cream

Place the horseradish in a clean, wet kitchen towel. Gather the towel with one hand, forming a ball, and twist with the other hand to get rid of all the liquid in the horseradish. Then hold the ball under cold running water, gently pressing with one hand, and rinse. Squeeze dry.

Place the butter in a saucepan and heat it. When warm, add the horseradish with the sugar, vinegar, salt, and pepper. Stir. Slowly add the stock. Bring to a boil, then add the mustard.

Blend the flour into the milk and half of the light cream. Stirring constantly, add to the sauce.

Blend the remaining light cream into the sour cream. Once the sauce boils again, slowly add some of the hot mixture to the sour cream mixture to warm it. Then add the warmed mixture to the sauce. Remove from heat and let stand covered in a warm place at least 25 to 30 minutes before serving. Serve with boiled meat.

CHEF'S SECRET   The horseradish, when treated as suggested, will be close in flavor to fresh horseradish. If you can get fresh horseradish, and if you have a special horseradish grater (available in gourmet or oriental shops), by all means use fresh horseradish.

To avoid crying while you grate fresh horseradish, breathe through your mouth and try not to look at the grater. Turn your head away as much as you can. If you do sniff some and suffer a painful sensation, which can last for minutes and make one break into tears, simply press a slice of bread to your nose and breathe through the bread, exhaling first. Surprisingly, the pain from the volatile oil of the horseradish will leave immediately.

HOT HERB BUTTER FOR FISH
1 cup

1 cup butter
1 lemon
2 tablespoons cold water
1 teaspoon tarragon
1 teaspoon rosemary

1 teaspoon basil
4 or 5 sprigs fresh parsley, dried
2 to 4 tablespoons cognac
    or brandy

Heat butter in a small saucepan. With a lemon zester or a small grater, scrape off about ½ teaspoon lemon zest. Add to butter and stir.

Cut the lemon, squeeze juice through a sieve into a cup. Put 1 tablespoon water in each lemon half; stir it with a spoon to scrape off all the flesh of the lemon. Press through a sieve.

Add tarragon, rosemary, and basil to lemon juice. Stir. Spoon mixture into the butter. Stir and keep herb butter hot.

Dip the dried parsley sprigs into the cognac or brandy and place the sprigs on the fish. Heat the remaining cognac and ignite it in the pan. Ladle flaming cognac over the fish so that the cognac-dipped dry herbs ignite and burn to ashes. Wait until the flames die, then spoon the hot herb butter over the fish, stirring constantly to distribute the herbs evenly.

 CHEF'S SECRET   Buy some fresh green parsley with long stems, if possible. Tie the stems about 3 inches from each other on a piece of yarn. Hang the yarn in a dry place in the kitchen. In 2 to 3 days the parsley will wilt. The sprigs should then be wrapped in aluminum foil and kept 3 or 4 hours in a 200 degree oven. (The best time to do this is after you have used the oven for baking and the heat is off.) Or, if you used the oven on the day the parsley is ready, place the foil with the parsley in the oven, leave the door open for 4 or 5 minutes, then close it and leave overnight.

You can keep the parsley in the kitchen, in a place where it won't break, for as long as two months. When needed, the sprigs will be bone dry. They will soak up the cognac very quickly and will burn into ashes with a pleasant aromatic smoke in a few seconds. This ash is very tasty on the fish. You can also do this with branches of tarragon, basil, rosemary, or any other herb.

If you are not sure whether your herbs are dry enough before dipping into the brandy, keep as many as you will need in a small dry pot or pan somewhere on or above the stove when you start to prepare the fish. If the cognac or brandy won't ignite, warm it up and try again. If it still won't light, someone may be watering your brandy.

MUSHROOM SAUCE
2 cups

2 cups (8 ounces) mushrooms
3 tablespoons butter
2 slices finely chopped bacon
½ cup finely chopped onions
½ teaspoon Chef's Salt
   (see appendix)
2 tablespoons flour

10½ ounce can chicken broth
½ cup white wine
1 teaspoon Worcestershire sauce
1 teaspoon ketchup or
   tomato puree
2 tablespoons freshly chopped
   parsley

Quickly wash, towel dry, and slice mushrooms thin.

In a heavy saucepan, melt butter, add bacon and onions, and cook over high heat until onions and bacon bits brown. Through a sieve, stir in Chef's Salt mixed with flour. Keep turning onions, then add all mushrooms at once and keep turning the whole mixture until the mushrooms brown.

Combine chicken broth, white wine, Worcestershire sauce, and ketchup. Stir into the saucepan at once. Adjust heat to low and simmer 15 minutes. Cool until lukewarm. Blend smooth in electric blender. Reheat and add parsley. Serve as is, or add cream or sour cream.

CHEF'S SECRET   This is a different kind of mushroom sauce, excellent on quickly sauteed thin slices of veal, or on pork, boiled beef, roast poultry, or fish. At *The Bakery Restaurant* we use it often, mainly at parties and banquets, when we offer two to three kinds of sauces with roast sirloin or roast tenderloin.

ORANGE SAUCE FOR POULTRY
Serves 8

1 cup chicken stock or
   chicken broth
1 envelope unflavored gelatin
3 or 4 tablespoons orange peel,
   cut in long, thin strips
2 cups boiling water

3 tablespoons sugar
juice of 2 oranges
juice of 1 lemon
4 tablespoons butter mixed with
   3 tablespoons flour

Set the stock to boil. Add gelatin when stock starts to warm. When it boils, adjust heat and simmer.

Cut enough orange peel (the skin only, without the white pulp) into very thin strips 1 to 1½ inches long. Drop into boiling water and boil 5 minutes. Drain and discard boiling water. Rinse boiled orange rind in cold water and let drip dry in a sieve.

Place sugar in a large saucepan and brown it over medium heat until it melts and turns the color of yellow straw. Add orange juice, lemon juice, and simmered stock.

In a saucer or small bowl, mix with your fingertips the butter and flour. Drop hazelnut-sized pellets into the sauce, stirring it constantly until all the butter and flour mixture is used. Adjust heat to low and simmer the sauce another 10 to 15 minutes over low heat. Add orange peel and let stand in a warm place until serving.

CHEF'S SECRET   This is a basic, versatile sauce that may be used for duckling, squab, guinea hen, or other fowl. Of course, if you wish, you may use it just as well on chicken, capon, or turkey.

If you like a darker brown color, add a teaspoon or so of Kitchen Bouquet. Or if you want the color to be more orange, grate into the simmering stock about ½ teaspoon or so of carrots.

If you don't want the sauce to be too rich, or if you use a natural stock from the poultry you roast yourself, omit the butter-flour mixture and stir into the boiling stock 2 tablespoons cornstarch diluted in ½ cup cold water.

The gelatin won't jell, but it will give a "heavy" texture to the consistency of the sauce without enriching it.

If you wish to glaze the poultry, reduce ½ cup of this sauce over high heat to one-half its volume and spoon the thickened sauce over the bird.

PAN DEGLAZING
Serves 4

1 cup water, beef or chicken stock, consomme, or wine, or any combination of these	1 to 2 teaspoons flour, if needed appropriate spices to correct seasoning

Pour off the fat from the frying pan, leaving only a few drops in the pan. Pour in the liquid and, over medium heat, scrape the bottom of the pan, loosening all particles adhering to the bottom and dissolving them in the liquid.

CHEF'S SECRET   Pan deglazing is mentioned in many of the 15,000 cookbooks I have, but I have never found any explanation of how or why deglazing is done.

When frying or sauteing meat, poultry, or fish, the recipe often calls for deglazing the pan after removing whatever was cooked in it. When you fry in shortening or saute in a combination of shortening and liquid, the metal pan expands from the heat. When the foods you fry are placed into the pan, they are cool. The surface of the pan shrinks from the quick cooking, then expands again as the food reaches the temperature of the surrounding fat.

While the meat is frying, liquids oozing from its cut surface, as well as solids if it is dusted with flour, fine bread crumbs, or corn meal, will stick to the pan. These particles are very tasty and in most cases contain ingredients which will caramelize from the heat and will have an intense, pleasant taste and also a desirable dark color.

If you pour all but a few drops of the fat from the pan, nothing remains but these tasty particles. When you pour stock, wine, or water into the pan and start to scrape with the flat edge of a metal spatula while heating the pan, all particles will loosen and start to dissolve, transferring their flavor and fragrance to the liquid.

If you sprinkle some flour into the fat and stir until the flour starts to brown, and then add the liquid, you will have a much thicker sauce-like substance instead of the pan juice. Either of these substances, spooned over the meat, poultry, or fish prepared in the pan, will enhance the taste and appearance.

There are many possible variations. Sherry, port wine, or Madeira wine may be added to the deglazed pan. Sauce prepared from the deglazed pan is the most appropriate and natural accompaniment for food prepared in the same pan.

QUICK BURGUNDY SAUCE
2 cups

1 tablespoon sugar
4 tablespoons shortening
2 tablespoons grated onion
2 tablespoons flour
1 tablespoon cornstarch
1½ teaspoons Chef's Salt
    (see appendix)

1½ cups beef consomme
1 tablespoon Kitchen Bouquet
1 cup red wine
red food coloring (optional)
1 tablespoon butter

In a saucepan, melt sugar over medium heat until it starts to brown and bubble. Add shortening and onion, stir, and cook 5 minutes.

Stir flour, cornstarch, and Chef's Salt into 1 cup beef consomme. Slowly pour into onions and shortening, stirring constantly with a wire whip. Cook until it thickens.

Combine Kitchen Bouquet, red wine, and remaining ½ cup consomme. Stir into sauce. Adjust heat to low and simmer, covered, 30 minutes, stirring occasionally. Add a few drops of red food coloring, if you wish, then strain through a fine sieve into a water-rinsed pan. Add butter, bit by bit, stirring. Correct seasoning with Chef's Salt or a pinch of sugar. If needed, thin with 1 to 2 tablespoons red wine. Serve with poultry or meat.

CHEF'S SECRET   The caramelized sugar will help to caramelize the onion quickly and will also counteract the acidity of the wine.

Some flour thickens much more than others, varying in the same brand from store to store as well as in different brands. So be careful, and measure the flour exactly.

You can, if you wish, add to the sauce: 1 to 2 tablespoons tomato puree, or ½ teaspoon mustard, or 1 to 2 teaspoons Worcestershire sauce, or less consomme and more red wine, or 1 to 2 teaspoons red currant jelly, or 1 to 2 tablespoons commercial barbecue sauce.

For Italian-style dishes, add ¼ cup minced green peppers and ¼ cup minced mushrooms cooked with the onions.

RED WINE SAUCE
Serves 8

1 cup Sauce Espagnol (see page 307)	chopped or sliced mushrooms, quickly sauteed in very little butter (optional)
6 to 8 tablespoons red wine	light sprinkling of sugar

Bring the Sauce Espagnol almost to the boiling point (when first or second bubble appears) over medium to high heat. Add the red wine and mushrooms, correct seasoning with sugar, and serve. Serve with all kinds of meats.

 CHEF'S SECRET   For variety, you can add to a basic red wine sauce 4 tablespoons melted currant jelly and 2 to 3 tablespoons red corinths (currant-like berries from the port of Corinth); or 2 ounces of ham sliced into thin strips, about the size of half a matchstick, and the same amount of black truffles cut the same way; or 4 ounces beef marrow cut into small discs and poached in slightly salted water.

When you are stirring with a wire whip, the rounded end of the whip never reaches the bottom rim of the pan where the sides and bottom come together. Some imported and domestic enamel-coated pans have a rounded bottom for easy stirring, but if you use a conventional pan, buy a special wooden kitchen spoon that has one straight and one rounded side, forming a point. If you don't have this kind of spoon you can use a spatula designed for the same purpose. It is important to scrape around the corners of the pan.

In the old days, wine used in cooking was boiled until it was reduced to ⅓ or ¼ the original volume, and then incorporated into the sauce in the beginning. This was because a cheap cooking wine was used. We believe that the new technique of using a good wine (the same wine to be served with the dish) and adding it at the end of the cooking period is much more suitable for today's palate.

RED WINE SAUCE "CUMBERLAND" FOR BEEF WELLINGTON

3 cups

For the stock:

1 medium onion, finely minced
1 clove garlic, finely minced
2 pounds beef scraps, fat and lean
1 carrot cut into half-inch dice
2 ribs celery, diced into
    ½-inch pieces
1 tablespoon salt

1 pound marrow bones
1 tablespoon flour
1 bay leaf
1 teaspoon black peppercorns,
    bruised
4 quarts water

For the roux:

⅓ cup flour

⅓ cup shortening

For the sauce:

½ cup red wine
¼ cup currant jelly
2 cups sauce base (stock and
    roux mixed)

¼ cup dry red currants
additional salt, if needed
Kitchen Bouquet (optional)
red food coloring (optional)

In a heavy saucepan, saute the onion and garlic with the fat parts from the scraps. When the onions become translucent, add the carrots, celery, salt, and enough water to cover the mixture. Cover the pan and cook rapidly until all the liquid evaporates.

Add remaining meat scraps and marrow bones. Sprinkle with flour and stir over medium heat until all particles brown. Transfer to a soup kettle. Add bay leaf, peppercorns, and 4 quarts water. Bring to a rapid boil, then lower heat and simmer 3 to 4 hours, skimming frequently. Strain liquid and skim again. Discard all solids. Cool.

Make a roux by mixing the flour and shortening and stirring over medium heat. When it starts to brown, remove the roux from heat and slowly add the cooled stock. Strain and return to a medium-sized saucepan. Bring to a boil, then lower heat and cook until the mixture is clear and glossy, skimming frequently. The amount will reduce to about 6 cups. This mixture can be refrigerated for up to a week, or frozen for 2 to 3 months.

To finish the wine sauce, combine the red wine and currant jelly. Stir this into 2 cups of the sauce base. Add the currants, bring to a boil, and simmer 10 to 15 minutes. Correct the seasoning and, if you wish, add Kitchen Bouquet and a few drops of red food coloring to achieve a reddish brown color.

 CHEF'S SECRET   This is how the sauce for Beef Wellington should be made if you use the whole tenderloin, either having the butcher trim it and give you all the scraps, or doing the trimming at home.

Making the red wine sauce is time consuming, and it needs care and attention. A large part of its success depends on how quickly you can adapt this method to your own cooking utensils. The pot itself is important. A heavy aluminum, cast iron, or enamel-coated pot will bring much better results than a thin, light utensil.

Also, it is important for the bottom to be straight and flat, and it must be very clean. If the outside bottom, in direct contact with the heat, is dirty, the flour-sprinkled bones and scraps will burn down because any dirt and grease on the bottom will act as a much faster and higher heat conductor than the clean area.

TARRAGON SAUCE
Serves 8

4 to 5 tablespoons butter
¼ cup firmly packed, fresh,
    chopped tarragon leaves
1 cup white wine
1 cup chicken stock or broth

juice of 1 lemon
salt, pepper, and sugar to taste
2 cups water
6 tablespoons cornstarch

In a saucepan, melt the butter. Add the tarragon and all other ingredients except 1 cup water and the cornstarch.

Bring to a boil. Combine the cornstarch and the remaining water and add to the boiling mixture. Bring to a boil again, reduce heat, and simmer at least 30 minutes, covered, before serving.

CHEF'S SECRET   This sauce may be served with lamb, veal, or poultry. Of course, the cooking liquid from the meat may be used instead of water. The only exception is the juice from lamb, which is never used in this country.

This sauce may be frozen, but once defrosted it must be diluted with a little water and beaten with a wire whip.

GRAVIES

A gravy differs from a sauce in that a gravy is made from ingredients derived from the dish it accompanies. For instance, turkey gravy is made from the giblets and pan roasting liquid of the roast turkey. Chicken gravy, beef gravy for pot roast or other slowly roasted dishes, or the gravy of a stew, goulash, or fricassee are all part of the dish.

A sauce, on the other hand, is made from a stock turned into an Espagnol and used as a base with other ingredients, or from a white stock, fish stock, or stock from whatever dish the sauce accompanies. Therefore, with the exception of Giblet gravy we will not offer gravy recipes in this chapter on sauces. You will find them as part of other recipes.

GIBLET GRAVY
6 cups

1 onion
giblets from a turkey or chicken
    (neck, heart, gizzard,
    and liver)
1 bay leaf
2 teaspoons salt
1 rib celery, coarsely chopped

pan drippings from the
    roasted fowl
3 tablespoons cornstarch
½ cup flour
Kitchen Bouquet
salt and freshly ground black
    pepper to taste

Cut the onion into four pieces. Place all the giblets, except the liver, in a medium-sized saucepan. Add bay leaf, onion, salt, and celery. Cover with cold water and cook at a low boil about 2 hours. Add liver for the last 20 minutes of cooking time.

Strain the stock from the giblets. Reserve the stock.

Remove all the meat from the neck. Finely chop the giblets and the neck meat. Discard the vegetables.

Place the pan drippings in a tall cylindrical container so that the fat will float to the surface. Skim off ½ cup and put it into a heavy-bottomed saucepan to heat. Discard the remaining fat. Measure the fat-free drippings and add enough of the giblet stock to make 6 cups liquid. Dissolve the cornstarch in the liquid.

Stir the flour into the fat and cook over medium heat until bubbly and golden brown. With a wire whip, stir in the liquid and cook until thickened, stirring constantly. Add giblets and continue to cook over low heat about 20 minutes. Stir occasionally.

Add enough Kitchen Bouquet to give the sauce a deep brown color. Season with salt and black pepper.

CHEF'S SECRET   If you like a more robust taste for giblet gravy, saute the cut-up gizzard and heart with 1 tablespoon finely chopped onion in 2 to 3 tablespoons fat, with a sprinkling of salt, over high heat until brown. Then reduce heat to low and simmer about 10 minutes, stirring occasionally. You can add the neck meat once the heat is lowered. Then cook the giblets according to the recipe.

CHOCOLATE SAUCE
About 2 cups

¼ cup unsalted butter
1 cup sugar
½ cup good-quality cocoa
1 cup milk
1 tablespoon cornstarch

¼ cup cold water
½ cup chocolate syrup
    (preferably Hershey's)
¼ cup brandy

In a very heavy saucepan, melt the butter with the sugar and cocoa until the mixture starts to caramelize. Immediately add the milk, stirring constantly. The hard lumps will dissolve as the liquid comes to a boil.

Dilute the cornstarch with the water. Pour this in a slow stream into the boiling syrup, stirring constantly. Remove from the heat and cool to room temperature. Add the chocolate syrup and brandy. Refrigerate.

CHEF'S SECRET   The saucepan must be very heavy in order to melt the butter and chocolate with the sugar until the sugar starts to caramelize. This mixture not only browns but begins to harden. The caramelized sugar will "toast" the cocoa somewhat, and the butter will get a "burned butter" taste. These are the secret flavor components of the sauce.

You can double or quadruple this recipe without changing the proportion of the ingredients, but it will take a little longer. However, if the family likes chocolate sauce, it is worthwhile. The sauce may be kept, refrigerated, up to 2 weeks.

VANILLA SAUCE
About 4 cups

3 cups milk
⅓ cup sugar
1 tablespoon unsalted butter
3 tablespoons cornstarch

5 tablespoons water
3 egg yolks, lightly beaten
1 teaspoon vanilla
pinch of salt

In a heavy saucepan, bring the milk, sugar, and butter to a boil.

Dissolve the cornstarch in the water. Pour this mixture into the boiling liquid, stirring with a wire whip. Simmer 2 to 3 minutes. Remove from heat.

Add lightly beaten egg yolks to the hot mixture, stirring with a wire whip until they are completely blended. Add the vanilla and salt. Serve warm or cold.

CHEF'S SECRET   Note that the recipe calls for 1 tablespoon unsalted butter and a pinch of salt. It would NOT be the same to use salted butter and omit the salt. Salted butter presents no problem when used with salty and pungent dishes, but it definitely gives an undesirable flavor to sweet sauces.

Before placing the milk, sugar, and butter in the saucepan, rinse the pan with water and leave it wet. Once the mixture starts to form a "skin" that covers the top, start stirring and continue to stir until it boils.

Separate the yolks from the whites as carefully as possible. Be sure not to get any egg white in the sauce because it will immediately solidify and leave unpleasant lumps. The best way to avoid these lumps is first to gently beat the yolks in a small bowl with 3 to 4 tablespoons of the hot mixture, then add the warmed egg yolks to the hot sauce.

10
BREADS

Long before we opened we decided to look for the very best bread for *The Bakery Restaurant*. The success of our restaurant could never have been achieved without the bread we served—a French box bread from the Toscana Bakery on Sheffield Avenue, just a few minutes walk from our restaurant.

Many readers are too young to understand how greatly the Second World War and the Korean conflict influenced the eating habits of Americans, especially with regard to bread. Tens of thousands of soldiers learned to enjoy the great crusty breads of Europe, especially those in France and Italy; the moist, fragrant, heavy, dark breads of Scandinavia, Germany, Austria, and the Middle European countries; and the light, different breads of the Near East, not to mention the rice of the Far East, the tacos and tortillas of our southern neighbors, or the tondoori bread of India. It became fashionable to serve limpa and pumpernickel, roggenbrot and hardtack. Sesame-seed-covered Euphrates wafers revolutionized the cracker industry. We knew we needed an excellent bread to accompany our meals.

We tried every rye from Rosen's through Cicero and 3 O'Clock. We visited small Italian, Greek, Mexican, and Polish bakers. Finally we found the perfect solution, the Toscana Bakery. We could never have achieved our success without their high-standards of professionalism and good friendship.

When the Chiappa family closed it in 1980 because they retired, we cried. We found another excellent bread since, but we miss our daily contact with Tina, Mama, and the rest of the family!

BREADS AS SERVING CONTAINERS

One of the simplest solutions to the homemaker's question, "What shall I serve it in?" is to buy a round or football-shaped rye, Italian, or Viennese bread, cut off the top, remove all of the soft inside or as much as necessary, and use the bread itself as a container.

For instance, to remove the inside from a 2-pound rye, carefully cut around with a grapefruit knife. Separate it from the bottom by putting all ten fingers in the part farthest away from you. Move your fingers, pressing toward your stomach, and remove the inside in one piece if possible. Fill the bread with a cheese mixture or a thick cheese spread or dip. Cut small finger-sized pieces or triangles from the bread that was removed from the center, and arrange them around the filled bread.

You can also fill a bread with barbecued hot-dog tidbits, meatballs, or liver pate. Or it can be used instead of the usual patty shell as a container for chicken a la king or creamed chicken.

The bread container will be unique and elegant, and there will be no dish washing. But don't try to fill the bread with dishes that contain too much liquid, as seepage may result.

Round rolls, Kaiser rolls, or oblong, ready-to-bake or bake-yourself rolls are ideal for individual edible containers. For breakfast, bake an egg or two surrounded with partially cooked bacon inside a well-buttered, hollowed-out roll. Or remove the inside of a roll, brush it with butter, and toast it under the broiler, then heap scrambled eggs in it. For dessert, remove the insides of Kaiser rolls, brush the hollows generously with butter, sprinkle with cinnamon sugar, and bake until crisp. Just before serving, place a baked apple in each, fill each with a scoop of vanilla ice cream sprinkled with cinnamon, or spoon some applesauce into each and top with a scoop of lemon sherbet.

Better yet, devise your own combinations.

BREAD DUMPLINGS
Serves 8

3 tablespoons butter
2 tablespoons bacon drippings
    or lard
4 cups ½-inch bread cubes made
    from day-old French,
    Italian, or Vienna bread

3 cups flour
1 teaspoon salt
1 cup scalded milk
3 eggs
freshly ground black pepper
    to taste (optional)

Place 2 tablespoons of the butter and the bacon drippings or lard in a large skillet. Toast the bread cubes in this shortening.

Mix the flour with the salt in a deep bowl.

To the hot milk, add the remaining butter. Pour this mixture slowly into the bowl with the dry ingredients, stirring constantly. As the mixture starts to cool, break in the eggs. Keep stirring until all ingredients are incorporated. Beat with a wooden spoon, adding a little warm water if necessary, until the mixture turns into a smooth dough somewhat stiffer than ordinary pancake dough.

Fold in the bread cubes. Sprinkle with a little pepper if desired.

With wet palms, form 16 dumplings and drop them into a pot filled ⅔ full with lightly salted boiling water. Cook about 10 minutes after you drop the last dumpling into the water. Remove the pot from the heat and let the dumplings steam for another 3 to 5 minutes. Remove the dumplings with a slotted spoon and sprinkle them with melted butter or lard, or spoon some sour cream over them, depending on what they will be served with.

CHEF'S SECRET   This recipe is a basic one. You can vary it by adding 2 tablespoons finely chopped onion sauteed in the shortening before adding the bread cubes, or 2 tablespoons finely chopped onion and 1 tablespoon chopped fresh parsley sauteed the same way. Instead of using 3 tablespoons butter and 2 tablespoons bacon drippings or lard, cut 4 to 6 slices of bacon into ¼-inch bits and fry the bacon bits with 2 tablespoons butter, then toast the bread cubes with the bacon bits.

Be sure the pot you use is large enough to allow the dumplings to move about freely; if it is not, cook only half the dumplings at a time.

CORNBREAD
Serves 8

½ cup sifted flour
1½ cups yellow cornmeal
1 teaspoon salt
1 teaspoon sugar
3 teaspoons baking powder

3 eggs, lightly beaten
1 cup milk
¼ cup heavy cream
⅓ cup melted butter
bacon fat to grease skillet

Preheat the oven to 400°. Combine the flour, cornmeal, salt, sugar, and baking power.

Mix the eggs into the milk. Add the dry ingredients, beating with a wooden spoon until thoroughly blended. Stir in the cream and butter.

Grease a small iron skillet with bacon fat and place it over high heat until it starts to smoke. Remove the skillet from the heat and spread the batter evenly in it. Bake 30 minutes, or until the cornbread is well browned.

 CHEF'S SECRET   This cornbread is an old original Southern recipe. The bacon fat gives it an especially good flavor.

For success, it is important that the heavy iron skillet is heated. If you do not have an iron skillet and you use a glass baking dish, the dish cannot be preheated in the same way. In this case, pour about 2 to 3 tablespoons bacon fat into the dish and place it on a cookie sheet in the oven as you start to heat the oven. Let it stay in the oven until the temperature reaches about 400°. Then pour the batter slowly into the heated dish, adding only about 1 to 2 tablespoons at a time so the temperature of the dish will not drop.

MINIATURE ROLLS
About 48 rolls

2 cups milk	8 cups flour, sifted
2 tablespoons sugar	6 egg yolks
1 package active dry yeast	grated zest of ½ lemon
½ cup warm water	½ cup butter

Scald ¾ cup of milk. Add sugar to the scalded milk, then cool to lukewarm.

Dissolve the yeast in warm water. Add the milk mixture and ⅓ of the flour. Mix into a soft dough. Sprinkle the top with flour and let rise in a warm place.

When double in bulk, punch down, and incorporate the egg yolks, lemon zest, and remaining flour. Knead with your hands until the dough starts to come off your hands by itself. Now, break the butter into small pieces and work it into the dough. When all the butter is incorporated and the dough no longer sticks to your fingers or the bowl, sprinkle the top with a little flour, cover with a towel, and let rise in a warm place until double in bulk.

Gently and lightly roll the dough out on a floured pastry board to ½-inch thickness. With a pastry wheel, cut tiny rectangles, 1 × 1½ inches or 1 × 2½ inches. After the rectangles are cut, form each into a little ball by pinching the four corners together; or make little ovals by pinching two corners together; or, if you wish, brush the tops with additional melted butter and fold them in half like Parker House rolls.

Place the little rolls on a lightly greased cookie sheet and let them rest in a warm place for 10 minutes. Preheat the oven to 375°.

Bake the rolls 10 to 12 minutes, depending on their size.

CHEF'S SECRET   This dough produces excellent dinner rolls that are very suitable for freezing. But if you plan to freeze them, underbake them somewhat so they will not become hard when you reheat them.

You can make these rolls for a party two days ahead of time, and store them in a well-sealed plastic bag at room temperature. Just reheat them in the oven for 3 to 4 minutes before serving.

If you want the rolls to be shiny, mix 1 egg yolk with a little powdered sugar and lightly brush the top of each before baking. If you like, melt some butter and brush the rolls with the melted butter as soon as you remove them from the oven.

If you prefer a variety, brush the tops of each with the egg yolk mixture and sprinkle poppy seeds on the ovals, sprinkle caraway seeds and coarse salt on the rounds, and press a half almond into the Parker House-style, or sprinkle with chopped almonds.

If you plan to make them ahead of time, do not brush the top with the egg. Instead, butter the rolls as soon as you remove them from the oven after reheating them, immediately before serving.

MUFFINS
12 muffins

2 cups flour
2 teaspoons baking powder
½ teaspoon salt
2 tablespoons sugar

1 cup milk
1 egg, well beaten
¼ cup melted butter

Preheat the oven to 400°. Combine the flour, baking powder, salt and sugar. Add the milk, egg, and melted butter to the dry ingredients. Stir, but do not beat.

Pour the batter into well-buttered muffin pans, filling each about ⅔ full. Bake 20 to 25 minutes.

 CHEF'S SECRET   The secret of muffins is in the method of combining the ingredients. The batter should not be overmixed and should never be beaten, just stirred. As soon as all the dry ingredients have been moistened, the batter should immediately be poured into the well-buttered pans.

Even if you use paper muffin cups, brush the pans with butter and brush the insides of the paper cups after inserting them in the pans.

This basic recipe may be altered by adding soaked, dried, and blanched raisins or black currants, or chopped pecans or other nuts. In case you are adding as much as ½ cup of any of these ingredients, add an additional 2 to 3 tablespoons milk and ¼ teaspoon baking powder.

QUICK BREAD
2 loaves

1 cup milk	1½ cups warm water
2 tablespoons sugar	7 cups sifted flour
1 tablespoon salt	3 tablespoons melted butter
1 package dry yeast	

Scald the milk, then add the sugar and salt. Cool to room temperature.

Dissolve the yeast in warm water, then add it to the milk mixture. Add 3 cups flour and beat until smooth. Add the melted butter and all but

½ cup of the remaining flour. Turn the mixture onto a lightly floured board and knead until the dough is smooth and satiny.

Brush the inside of a large bowl with shortening. Place the dough in the bowl, cover it with a towel, and set it in a warm, draft-free place for an hour or until it has doubled in size. Punch the dough down and turn it out again onto a lightly floured board. Divide it in half and let it rest for a few minutes uncovered.

Generously brush two loaf pans with shortening. Shape the dough to fit the pans and place it in the pans. Cover the pans with a towel and let the dough rise again until double in size. Preheat the oven to 400°.

Bake the loaves 15 minutes to set the crust, then reduce the heat to 375° and bake an additional 30 minutes. Let the bread stand at room temperature until cool to the touch, then remove from the pans.

 CHEF'S SECRET   Be sure to check the date stamp on the yeast. If it is near the end of the suggested period of usefulness, it is better to lose the price of the yeast than the product to be made from it.

The best tool for beating the milk-yeast mixture with the flour is an ordinary wooden kitchen spoon. Buy a new one and use it only for mixing doughs. You will see how easy it is to work with once you become accustomed to it.

Before kneading the dough, wash your hands, rinse them in cold water, and dry them quickly. Do not rub your hands enough to warm them up. This sounds like a paradox, but you must knead the dough strongly yet light-handedly. This means that the downward movement when pressing with the heel of your palm should be strong, but when you lift the dough your hands should hardly touch it, so that the dough will not stick to them. Keep turning the dough in a circular motion while kneading it. First knead on one side, then turn upside down and knead it again. Form it into a ball, press it into a tubular shape, then fold the two ends back toward the middle and keep kneading until you have one large elastic mass without any folds or creases showing. The surface should be completely smooth.

Punching the dough down means hitting it with the full palm of your hand to break the air bubbles that developed during the yeast's first fermentation. The air will escape, and the dough will lose its volume. When the dough rises a second time, the air bubbles will be smaller and more evenly distributed.

SWEET ROLLS
12 rolls

1 package active dry yeast
¼ cup warm water
½ cup milk
¼ cup soft butter
1 tablespoon sugar

¾ teaspoon salt
2 large eggs
2 cups sifted flour
extra melted butter for brushing

Dissolve the yeast in warm water.

Scald the milk. Stir in the butter, sugar, and salt. Cool to lukewarm.

Combine the eggs with the yeast and the milk. Add the flour. Beat the dough vigorously until smooth. Cover and let rise in a warm, draft-free place for about 1 hour or until it doubles in size.

Preheat the oven to 375°. Stir the dough well. Spoon it into greased muffin pans, filling each about half full. Let rise again in a warm place until double in size.

Bake the rolls about 20 minutes. Remove from the oven and brush each roll with melted butter.

CHEF'S SECRET   Be sure that you do not mix the yeast and egg into the milk before it cools to lukewarm. If the milk is too hot, it will impair the yeast's ability to rise and may partially cook the eggs.

Brushing the rolls with the melted butter while they are very hot enables the butter to seep into the rolls, making it unnecessary to serve butter with them. If you want them to be especially good, carefully remove each one from the pans and quickly brush the bottom with melted butter before buttering the top, then place them back in the pans and brush the tops.

11
DESSERTS

We don't bake our own bread, but we have never purchased a piece of pastry. All the pastry we serve at *The Bakery* is made on the premises.

Our all-nut tortes, made from finely ground nutmeats, without any flour, quickly became famous and extremely popular. The only contender in popularity was a later addition to our dessert offerings, *The Bakery Restaurant's* own Fresh Banana Eclairs and our Brownie Bottom Bourbon Pie. The latter is an adaptation of the old American classic brownie combined with an Americanized version of an old European classic, a Bavarian cream made with fine Jim Beam bourbon instead of the obligatory brandy. When I served this pie to visiting European pastry experts from Austria, Germany, and Switzerland, they loved it, and I felt I had contributed something very American to the international repertoire of fine desserts.

Blueberries are another very American delicacy that is enjoyed and praised by foreign visitors. Our most popular fruit dessert has always been our Pears Helene, a classic recipe made from fresh pears poached in their own light syrup.

Entertaining at home with family, friends, or special guests, you must remember how important the dessert is. The human brain works in an interesting way: It always remembers first what happened last. A cup of incomparable Stewart's coffee, with an excellent dessert selected by the guest from a reasonably large selection (at least three or four items), will always be favorably remembered.

If you entertain important guests at home, offer a choice of at least two desserts. Some people love chocolate, others can leave it.

Some people appreciate rich, gooey desserts while others would rather have something fruity and less caloric. Offering a choice will please everyone—and I'll tell you another Chef's Secret: Most likely everyone will eat from both.

BAKED ALASKA
Serves 8

1 pound spongecake or poundcake (homemade or commercial)	1 pint raspberry sherbet
	10 egg whites
1 pint vanilla ice cream (preferably brick style)	1 cup granulated sugar
	1 cup powdered sugar

Select the plate or platter you will use to serve the Baked Alaska. Cover it with a piece of paper and draw a line around the inner edges of it. Cut this out and copy it onto a piece of strong cardboard. Test to be sure the piece of cardboard will fit on the serving plate, then cover it with aluminum foil and place it in the freezer.

Cut enough ½-inch slices of the cake to cover a surface approximately 6 by 8 inches. Arrange on the foil-covered cardboard and freeze.

Cut the vanilla ice cream into slices and cover the cake, leaving a ½-inch border around the edges. Refreeze.

Mound the sherbet over the vanilla ice cream, rounding and smoothing the top. Freeze again.

Put about 7 of the egg whites into a mixing bowl with a little of the granulated sugar and start to beat them. As they get frothy, slowly add the rest of the granulated sugar and about ⅔ of the powdered sugar. As soon as the egg whites are stiff and start to get dry, stop beating. Add the remaining egg whites and the rest of the powdered sugar and start to beat again. Continue until they are stiff and shiny.

With a wide rubber spatula, cover the ice cream and the cake completely with this meringue, using about ¾ of it. Place the remaining meringue in a pastry bag fitted with a star tube and decorate the top with swirls, curls, and stars. Freeze until ready to use.

To serve, preheat the oven to 500°. Sprinkle the top of the meringue with powdered sugar, through a sieve, and place in the oven for about 1 minute. Check the Baked Alaska and turn it around to bake another minute if the front is not as brown as the back. Serve immediately, slicing with a knife dipped in hot water.

CHEF'S SECRET   It is very important to refreeze the Baked Alaska after each step of preparation, especially when you make it for the first time. Later, when you feel you have mastered the task, you will probably not have to refreeze it after each step.

If you follow the steps for making the meringue, you will have the stiffest and easiest-to-use meringue ever. Dusting the top of the meringue with powdered sugar before baking it will hasten the top's browning and improve the looks of the dish.

If you wish, you can use the egg yolks to make a special sauce to be served with the Baked Alaska. In an electric blender or mixer, mix the 10 egg yolks with 10 tablespoons sugar until the mixture turns lemon colored and fluffy. Add one cup cognac, brandy, or other liqueur, starting drop by drop and then increasing the amount to a thin stream, beating constantly. Spoon the sauce over the Baked Alaska after the portions are served, or spoon some on each serving plate before leaving a slice of the Baked Alaska on the plate.

I don't think we have ever had a week at *The Bakery Restaurant* since it opened in 1963 without at least one order of Baked Alaska, but sometimes we have 4 to 5 orders on a single night.

We use our almond sponge as a base and, if the guests request it, we flambe the Baked Alaska with preheated cognac at tableside.

CHOCOLATE MOUSSE
Serves 8

1½ cups Hershey's chocolate syrup
2 tablespoons brandy
2 envelopes gelatin dissolved in
    ⅓ cup water

1 cup boiling water
3 egg whites
2 cups whipping cream
2 tablespoons cocoa

Pour chocolate syrup into a mixing bowl. Stir in brandy.

In a saucepan, mix the dissolved gelatin into boiling water. Cool saucepan by dipping it into a larger pan of cold water. Keep stirring until syrupy.

Stir the gelatin into the chocolate syrup. Whip the egg whites to soft peaks and gently fold into the chocolate mixture.

Whip the cream stiff. Sprinkle the cocoa through a fine sieve into the whipped cream and then fold it in. Whip again a few seconds. (Do not overbeat or it will collapse.) Fold the whipped cream into the chocolate mixture. Transfer to individual serving dishes, chill, and serve.

CHEF'S SECRET   In my lifetime I have been served the strangest and most diverse desserts called chocolate mousse. But I think this recipe is closest to the genuine texture and flavor of the "real" chocolate mousse. Of course, I could give you a recipe where everything starts "from scratch," but I feel that the exact consistency and flavor of Hershey's chocolate syrup is very hard to duplicate at home. And if you are able to duplicate it, what do you achieve by duplication?

The cocoa whipped into the heavy cream fortifies the chocolatey "mouth feel." The cocoa will dissolve in your mouth during eating, making your taste buds convey a much more chocolatey feeling.

FRESH BANANA ECLAIRS
Serves 8 to 12

1 portion Pate a Choux
   (see page 283)
2 envelopes unflavored gelatin
½ cup plus 3 tablespoons water
2 cups heavy cream
6 to 8 tablespoons sugar
2 to 3 tablespoons rum,
   or few drops rum extract

4 ripe bananas
3 ounces semisweet chocolate
2 tablespoons sliced,
   toasted almonds
chocolate sauce (see page 225)

Preheat the oven to 425°.

Spoon the dough into 2 long giant eclairs, the length of a cookie sheet (approximately 12 inches long). Bake the eclairs, without opening the door, 20 to 25 minutes. Reduce the heat to 350° and bake 20 minutes longer. Reduce the heat again to 325° and bake an additional 10 minutes.

Dissolve the gelatin in 3 tablespoons water. Bring the ½ cup water to a boil and stir in the gelatin mixture. Cool in an ice-water bath until it starts to gel.

Meanwhile, whip the heavy cream with half the sugar to stiff peaks. Gently fold the rum or rum extract into the cooled gelatin. Pour the gelatin over the surface of the whipped cream and gently fold it in.

Press the bananas to a pulp with a fork. Stir in the remaining sugar. Fold this banana mixture into the whipped cream, using a spatula. Chill.

When the eclairs have cooled, split them in half lengthwise, parallel with the bottom. Remove and discard the soft inside parts. With a pastry bag fitted with a star tube, fill the bottom of the eclairs with the banana cream. Chill in the freezer at least 1 hour.

Melt the chocolate in a small saucepan and brush the top parts of the eclairs with the melted chocolate. Sprinkle the almonds over the chocolate while it is still warm. Let dry.

With a sharp knife, cut the top half of each eclair into serving-sized pieces. Place the top pieces on the cream-filled bottom halves and finish cutting through. Serve with chocolate sauce.

CHEF'S SECRET   This pastry is good only when it is made from fresh bananas that are so ripe that the skin is almost brown (at least more than half brown), thin, and soft. Do not try to make it from light, firm-skinned bananas. It will not have any taste at all. If you cannot get ripe bananas, store unripened ones in a brown paper bag for 2 to 3 days to allow them to ripen before trying to use them.

Do not try to run the bananas through a food mill, as they will turn into a liquid and will not serve the purpose. If gently pressed with a fork, they will retain their consistency.

GATEAU ALLARD
Serves 8

For the gateau:

1 pound heavy-crusted white bread (Italian, Vienna, French, or a round white bread), at least 1 day old	1 cup sour cream
	2 quarts fresh raspberries
	2 cups sugar

For covering the gateau:

1 cup sour cream	2 tablespoons brown sugar

For the sauce:

2 cups sour cream	3 to 4 tablespoons brown sugar
½ cup half-and-half or light cream	

Remove the crust from the loaf of bread, leaving only the white inside part. Slice into ⅓- to ½-inch slices.

With plastic wrap, line the inside of a straight-sided casserole or 2-quart souffle dish. Using the smaller slices of bread, line the bottom of the dish, spreading some sour cream on top of the slices.

Quickly wash the raspberries and shake very dry in a towel. Reserve a few of the nicest for garnish. Divide the raspberries into as many parts as layers of bread you will have. Add a layer of bread to the dish and sprinkle in some of the sugar on top of the bread. Add a layer of raspberries, then another layer of bread spread with sour cream — the sour cream side toward the raspberries. Sprinkle the top side of the bread with sugar, and repeat this for as many more layers of bread that you have, leaving the largest slices for the top.

Press the gateau gently with a plate somewhat smaller than the souffle dish. Refrigerate at least 6 hours.

To unmold, dip the casserole or souffle dish in enough very hot water to come almost to the rim for 2 to 3 seconds, then lift out the cake together with the plastic sheet (opened beforehand) onto a large platter. Chill again, then spread sides and top with a mixture of sour cream and brown sugar.

Decorate the top with a few nice fresh raspberries and, if available, a few green leaves. Serve very cold with a sauce made by gently stirring together sour cream, half-and-half, and brown sugar.

CHEF'S SECRET   For the last two decades Allard has been one of the most famous luncheon places in Paris. It is among the very few Parisian restaurants where until recently the chef and all the cooks were females. The Gateau Allard is simple but extremely delicious. It is so famous that during the raspberry season people come all the way from Brussels just to eat it.

Utmost care should be taken that the raspberries are not watery. You must wash them, but wash them quickly by just sprinkling some cold water over them; then immediately place the berries into an absorbent kitchen towel and swing them dry. Do not shake them, because the berries will break in the towel. Of course, the bread, when pressed down, will break the berries, but the juice will be absorbed in the bread.

If you think the raspberries are not sweet enough, add more sugar.

The bread must be at least a day old; two-day-old bread is even better.

The cake definitely improves if it is made one day ahead.

I received instructions how to make this gateau from Monsieur Allard more than twenty years ago. Since then many of my former workers and pupils and many restaurant owner readers of my first cookbook are using this, my adaptation of Gateau Allard, as their own. To widen the circle, I call attention to the fact that this cake can be made very successfully not only with frozen raspberries but also with fresh and frozen strawberries, fresh or frozen peaches, fresh ripe apricots, etc.

In many places a pre-sliced, round Italian bread is available, which in my experience serves the purpose of this recipe very well. Cut the crust off with a kitchen scissors, and lay the slices with the straight (bottom) part together into pairs, with alternating layers at right angles. The cake will never fall apart and will be very easy to handle.

WATERMELON ICE
Serves 10 to 12

1 piece cardboard, 12 × 12 inches
masking tape
aluminum foil
2 cups heavy cream
pinch of salt
2 to 3 tablespoons sugar

2 10-ounce packages frozen cranberry-orange relish
½ gallon vanilla ice cream, brick style
1 pint lime sherbet

Prepare the mold: Fold the cardboard in half to form a V-shaped opening with 6-inch sides. Reinforce the fold on the outside with masking tape. Secure the opening of this V by placing tape on each side from top to bottom. Line the V with aluminum foil (see illustration).

Whip the cream to stiff peaks, adding the salt and sugar. Chop the frozen relish and fold it into the whipped cream. Chill. Pile this mixture into the foil-lined mold, forming a half-moon shape to resemble the inside of a watermelon.

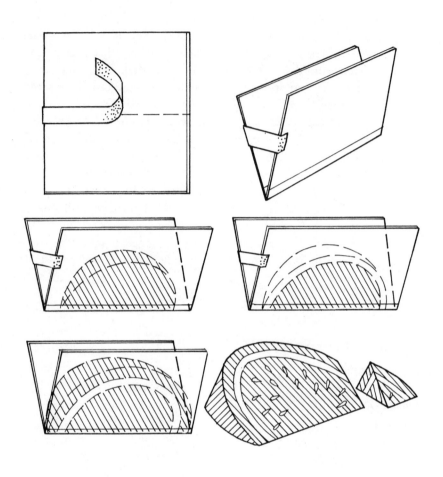

Cut a ¾-inch-thick slice from the long side of the ice cream. Cut it diagonally to make two triangles. Place these triangles, with their large ends together, around the cranberry mixture. Pat them into place. Place the mold into the freezer and let it freeze until it is firm.

Smooth the lime sherbet over the ice cream to resemble a watermelon rind. Freeze again.

To serve, remove the cardboard-foil frame. Place the mold on a serving platter and slice it crosswise into 10 to 12 pieces.

CHEF'S SECRET   This is one way to make a very festive-looking, elegant, but easy dessert without a fancy mold or special equipment. If you do not intend to use it right away, pack it in plastic wrap and then in aluminum foil and keep frozen until later.

If you want to be very fancy, press some chocolate chips into the red cranberry portion of the mold to resemble seeds of a watermelon.

Instead of the lime sherbet, you may use creme de menthe or pistachio ice cream for the green layer.

BREAD PUDDING
Serves 8

1 pound loaf French bread
5 cups milk
pinch of salt
⅓ cup sugar
2-inch piece of vanilla bean,
    split lengthwise, or a few
    drops of vanilla extract

8 eggs
½ cup white raisins,
    soaked 1 hour in hot water
1 tablespoon butter
½ cup dry white breadcrumbs
    (see appendix)

Preheat oven to 375°. Cut 8 very thin slices from the ends of the loaf of bread. Cut each slice in half and set aside. Cut the remainder of the loaf into ½-inch cubes.

Combine milk, salt, sugar, and vanilla bean. Bring to a boil, remove from heat, and pour over bread cubes. Let stand about 10 minutes. Remove vanilla bean.

Beat 4 eggs lightly with an electric mixer at medium speed. Add a cup or so of soaked bread and beat until well mixed. Fold egg mixture into the soaked bread.

Drain raisins and pat dry. Separate remaining 4 eggs. Add the egg yolks and raisins to the bread mixture. If you use vanilla extract, add it now. With a strong spatula or wooden spoon, mix well. The mixture should be free of large lumps.

Beat the egg whites until stiff and fold into the bread mixture.

Coat an ovenproof dish with butter and sprinkle evenly with breadcrumbs. Add the bread mixture. Arrange half-slices of bread on top, pressing them ⅔ down into the pudding so that just a part of the crust peeks out for decoration. Bake about 30 minutes, or until nicely golden brown.

Serve the pudding hot, warm, cold, or chilled with a vanilla sauce, whipped cream, a fresh fruit sauce, or some raspberry or currant jelly heated with an equal part of water in a small pan over medium heat.

If you prefer a sweeter bread pudding, add a little more sugar. If you like the taste of lemon, omit the vanilla and grate some lemon rind into the bread mixture instead.

CHEF'S SECRET   Be sure to use day-old, but preferably two-day-old, bread for this pudding. The type of French bread that you buy ready-to-bake and then bake yourself is perhaps the only one I would suggest *not* to use. French breads from commercial bakers are somewhat lighter and the crust is a bit different than the ones you bake at home from the frozen or refrigerated stage. The pudding is excellent when made with sourdough French bread.

It is always more effective to have a shorter piece of vanilla bean split lengthwise than to have double the same length without splitting it. The best way to keep vanilla bean is in a jar of powdered sugar. Another good way to keep vanilla beans is in alcohol, rum, pure grain alcohol, or bourbon whisky, if you don't like the rum taste. In Viennese and Hungarian pastry shops, the inimitable flavor of most of the pastries comes from the vanilla-flavored rum used for the butter creams, whipping cream, and the jams and jellies.

CREPES SUZETTE
8 crepes

8 crepes (see page 35)
4 tablespoons butter
4 tablespoons sugar
juice of 1 orange
juice of ½ lemon
grated zest of 1 orange and 1 lemon
    (see appendix)

1 teaspoon cornstarch diluted
    in ⅓ cup cold water
½ to 1 cup orange liqueur
2 ounces brandy, cognac, or a
    good-quality bourbon

Fold the crepes in half, then in half again so they resemble a slice of pie. Keep them warm.

In a heavy pan, melt the butter and the sugar together with the orange and lemon juice. Add the grated zest of the orange and lemon and continue to heat. Add the cornstarch mixture and bring to a boil. Add the orange liqueur. As soon as the mixture starts to bubble, add the folded crepes. Allow the crepes to heat through, turning once.

In a separate small saucepan, heat the brandy, cognac, or bourbon.

Ignite the crepes as follows: Remove 1 teaspoon of the hot brandy and light it with a match. Gently pour the flaming brandy back into the pan to ignite the whole amount. Then pour all the flaming brandy over the crepes and serve as soon as the flames burn out.

CHEF'S SECRET   If you wish to flame the crepes in front of a group of guests, first try to ignite a small amount of the spirit you plan to use in the kitchen. You will avoid embarrassment. Sometimes even the best brandy will not light.

BASIC SOUFFLE

Serves 4

1 cup milk	1 teaspoon vanilla or other
½ cup granulated sugar	flavoring
2 tablespoons butter	8 egg whites
3 tablespoons flour	2 tablespoons powdered sugar
3 egg yolks	additional powdered sugar

In a small saucepan, bring half the milk to a boil with 2 tablespoons of the granulated sugar and 1 tablespoon of the butter.

Dissolve the flour in the remaining ½ cup milk. Add to the boiling milk, stirring constantly, and cook over medium heat until the mixture turns into a medium-thick cream sauce. Remove from heat and cool at room temperature. It will become somewhat stiff.

About 1 hour before serving, preheat the oven to 425°.

Add egg yolks and vanilla or other flavoring to the cream sauce.

Start to beat all but 2 of the egg whites in an electric mixer. Slowly add the remaining granulated sugar and beat until the whites form soft peaks. Add the remaining 2 egg whites and beat until they become firm and shiny.

Prepare a 2-quart souffle dish by brushing the inside of it with the remaining 1 tablespoon butter and generously dusting it with the 2 tablespoons powdered sugar.

Fold ⅓ of the beaten whites into the cream sauce, then pour this mixture evenly over the remaining beaten whites. Gently fold the mixtures together with a spatula, folding in one direction, 10 to 12 times. Don't worry if some pieces of egg white are still showing; it is important not to overmix.

Pour the batter into the prepared souffle dish. Bake without opening the door for at least 15 minutes, then slowly open the door and rotate the souffle a half turn. Close the door and bake another 15 to 20 minutes.

Reduce the heat to 250° and leave the souffle in the oven for 3 to 4 more minutes. Remove and dust the top with powdered sugar. Serve immediately.

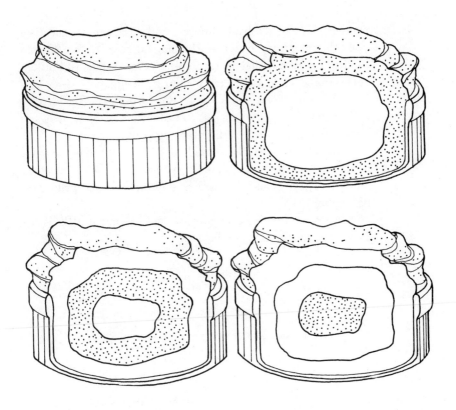

CHEF'S SECRET   It is no mystery to make a souffle. I do not believe it requires all the rigmarole some people think.

In old times, the thick white sauce with sugar used to be called "panda," but this expression is no longer used. You can make the cream sauce in the morning and let it stand at room temperature all day (except, of course, in extremely hot weather).

If you wish, you can incorporate many other ingredients into a basic souffle. You can soak leftover spongecake in brandy or sherry and then add small chunks or crumbs to the batter. Pour about one-third of the batter in the bottom of the souffle dish, add some of the spongecake chunks or crumbs, add another third of the batter, more chunks or crumbs, and then pour the remaining batter on the top and bake it. You can add candied or fresh fruits, or, for a coffee royal souffle, add instant coffee to the white sauce before adding the eggs.

Any imitation flavors and food coloring may be added, of course, but it is important that you add these to the white sauce before adding or while adding the egg yolks.

Remember, a souffle should not be overcooked to the point of dryness. Good souffles are almost runny in the center when served. They practically finish cooking on the plate (see illustration).

Another very easy to prepare and elegant souffle is the Lemon Crepe Souffle (see below).

LEMON CREPE SOUFFLE
Serves 8

butter
1 portion basic souffle mixture
    (see page 250) with juice and
    grated zest (see appendix)
    of 1 lemon mixed with the
    egg yolks into the cream
    sauce, and with 1 or 2 drops
    lemon oil, lemon extract,
    or liquid lemon flavoring
    added to the egg whites
    while incorporating the sugar

8 crepes (see page 35)
powdered sugar for dusting

Butter two 8- or 9-inch glass pie plates. Preheat the oven to 425°.

Quickly place ⅛ of the souffle mixture in the center of each crepe. Fold the crepe almost in half, but not entirely. Fold the two corners

together, forming a triangle. Place in the pie dish. Quickly fill and fold
the remaining crepes, and place four crepes in each dish.

Bake the crepes 8 to 12 minutes. Remove, dust with powdered
sugar, and serve immediately. If you wish, decorate each with a thin slice
of peeled, seeded lemon.

PALACSINTAS (HUNGARIAN CREPES)
Serves 8 to 12

4 eggs
1 cup flour
pinch of salt
2 tablespoons sugar

1⅓ cups milk
½ cup club soda
½ cup butter
½ cup oil

Break the 4 eggs into a bowl. Add the flour, salt, and sugar and
vigorously mix with a wire whip until the mixture is smooth. Slowly
add the milk, stirring constantly. Let stand in a covered bowl at room
temperature at least 30 minutes. Add club soda and stir.

In a small pan over medium heat, heat together the butter and oil.

Place an empty 8-inch heavy aluminum frying pan (the bottom will
be 6 inches in diameter) over medium heat. When it is hot, pour in the
melted shortening and heat it about 5 minutes or more. Pour shortening
back into the small pan.

Heat the heavy aluminum pan another 2 or 3 minutes and then start
to make the palacsintas as follows: Place a scant tablespoon of shortening
in the pan and swirl pan with a circular motion. Holding the pan in the
air, pour into it a scant ¼ cup of the batter, swirling it until the batter
covers the entire bottom of the pan.

Place the pan over medium heat and cook until the batter firms up
and the edges start to look cooked. Dip the edge of a metal spatula into the
hot shortening and loosen the edges of the palacsinta all around. Ease the
spatula under the palacsinta with a wiggling motion, and turn it over.

Finish cooking. The palacsinta should be creamy yellow with very light brown areas on it. Shake the pan with a back-and-forth motion and, if the palacsinta moves, lift it out to a plate covered with absorbent paper.

Repeat until all the batter is used. This will make at least 12, but under the right conditions 13 to 14 palacsintas.

 CHEF'S SECRET   In this dish the most important ingredient is the cook's skill. In mixing the batter, don't hesitate to make necessary small adjustments in the amounts of flour or liquid used to compensate for the fact that flour is not as consistent as salt, sugar, or shortening.

For frying palacsintas, a mixture of lard and oil is, in my opinion, the very best. If you keep the shortening hot and maintain a very hot, even temperature throughout the preparation, you will need very little shortening, and the palacsintas won't be greasy.

VARIATIONS:

With apricot jam:

For each person, heat in a small saucepan 1 tablespoon apricot jam, 1 tablespoon water, and add, if you wish, for each 6 to 8 persons, 1 tablespoon apricot brandy or rum. Heat together jam and water until smooth and runny. Place the palacsintas on a dinner plate one by one, and spoon on each 2 tablespoons of the mixture. Roll them up jelly-roll fashion or fold them into triangles by first folding in half and then in a quarter with the second fold. Place in well buttered serving dish and keep warm until serving. As a rule, 2 pieces are served per person.

Ground nut filling:

Use about 1 heaping tablespoon per person of finely ground nutmeats, such as English walnuts, pecans, hazelnuts, unpeeled almonds (not unshelled, just the regular shelled almonds without being blanched), or a mixture of any of these. Add about 1 teaspoon sugar to each 2 tablespoons ground nuts, sprinkle each palacsinta generously, roll it up jelly-roll fashion, place in a well buttered ovenproof dish, and spoon on top ½ cup sour cream diluted with ½ cup milk and 1 teaspoon sugar. Heat through in a preheated 350° oven. It will take 10 to 15 minutes, depending on how cold the palacsinta was before filling.

Cheese filling:

3 cups baker's cheese
3 eggs, separated
6 tablespoons sugar
1½ tablespoons lemon zest
  (see appendix)

¾ cup seedless white raisins,
  soaked in hot water for
  1 hour
1½ tablespoons butter
1½ cups sour cream
¼ cup sugar

Prepare palacsintas from basic recipe, except omit the sugar. Preheat oven to 350°. In a large bowl, combine baker's cheese with egg yolks, 6 tablespoons sugar, lemon zest, and raisins.

Beat egg whites until stiff. Gently fold a small portion of whites into the cheese mixture, then fold in remaining whites.

Lightly butter an ovenproof dish about 9 × 6 × 2. Divide filling into even portions, and place one portion on each palacsinta. Roll up jelly-roll fashion and place rolls next to one another in the dish.

Heat the sour cream in a small saucepan, gently stirring with a wire whip until it liquefies. Pour half over the palacsintas, spread it evenly, and sprinkle with ¼ cup sugar.

Bake 20 minutes. Cover with remaining sour cream and serve at once.

Prune filling:

Very similar to the apricot, except in most cases coarsely chopped walnuts are mixed into the European-style prune butter before it is spread on the palacsinta. It is rolled and heated just like the others, either with or without sour cream.

CHEF'S SECRET   Making these light, tender, Hungarian-style crepes has only one secret: Keep making them until you master your pan, because every frying pan will give a different result. When you learn the exact heat and the exact amount of shortening you need, you will have no more trouble, but I suggest that you not use your crepe pan or palacsinta pan for anything else. We have at *The Bakery Restaurant* four pans tied together with a strong string. They hang on a special hook in a corner, and cannot be used for anything else. They are never washed, just wiped first with a wet and then with a dry cloth, and before being used they are gently heated and wiped again, first with a dry and then with a corn oil-soaked cloth. You can use the same pan for omelets, scrambled eggs, fried eggs, or French-style crepes, but that should be all.

If, for the cheese palacsintas, you cannot get baker's cheese, buy dry cottage cheese and press it through a fine sieve or food mill. If it is too moist, add about 1 tablespoon dry white breadcrumbs before mixing with the egg yolks and sugar.

DESSERT DE CLUB DE CENT
Serves 8

1 quart good quality
   raspberry sherbet
   in two 1-pint containers
1 cup heavy cream firmly whipped
   with a pinch of salt
   and 1 tablespoon sugar

1 pint fresh raspberries,
   or 10-ounce package frozen
   raspberries
1 to 2 tablespoons sugar
8 crepes or palacsintas
whipped cream for decoration

Freeze 1 pint of raspberry sherbet very firm, then remove it from its container and return it to the freezer standing upside down (the larger diameter up) and without the container.

With a knife dipped in hot water, divide the other pint of raspberry sherbet into 8 equal pieces and freeze each piece individually. The best way to do this is to cover a cookie sheet with aluminum foil and place the cut pieces on it to freeze. Whip the cream and refrigerate it.

Wash the fresh raspberries carefully so as not to bruise them, and sprinkle on them, depending on sweetness, 1 to 2 tablespoons sugar. Chill with the sugar until serving. If you use frozen raspberries defrost them, and after defrosting keep them in the refrigerator.

Transfer the whipped cream to a pastry bag fitted with a star tube.

Reheat the crepes or palacsintas at the last minute by placing them for a minute in a lightly brushed hot frying pan. After all 8 are heated, keep them warm. Now place the uncut sherbet in the middle of a large serving platter. Put in each hot crepe one of the cut pieces of sherbet, fold it over, and arrange it quickly around the sherbet. Spoon the fresh or defrosted frozen raspberries over the pancakes. Decorate the sherbet in the center and the pancakes with whipped cream and serve at once.

CHEF'S SECRET   If you prepare all the ingredients ahead of time, this is not a complicated dessert but extremely elegant. The story of it is just as divine as the dessert itself. Around the turn of the century in Paris, a group was formed that called itself the Club of the One Hundred. This was perhaps the first "gourmet dining club" in modern times. Their rules were simple: the club would meet once a month as long as they could come up with an entirely new menu, never served before— except that the grand finale of each dinner was this special dessert created for and by the club.

APPLE BERTCHY
Serves 8

4 large, tart, firm apples
1 quart water, or enough to cover
6 whole cloves
2-inch piece cinnamon stick
juice of 1 lemon
1 cup plus 3 tablespoons sugar
1 portion Basic Vanilla Cream
    (see page 267)

8 teaspoons red fruit jelly,
    such as red currant,
    red raspberry, or strawberry
2 cups heavy cream
pinch of salt
½ teaspoon vanilla
2 to 3 tablespoons toasted,
    sliced almonds

Split the apples in half crosswise. Remove the core with a melon-ball cutter, being careful not to break through the apples. Peel the cored halves.

Combine the water, cloves, cinnamon stick, lemon juice, and 1 cup sugar in a saucepan large enough to hold the apples. Bring the liquid to a boil and add the apples. Slowly bring the liquid to a boil again, then remove from heat and leave the apple halves in the syrup 5 to 10 minutes, depending on the firmness of the apples. Remove the apples with a slotted spoon and let them cool to room temperature.

Place the Basic Vanilla Cream in a round serving dish large enough to hold the eight apple halves. Imbed the halves in the cream, cut side up. Fill the holes with red fruit jelly.

Whip the heavy cream with the remaining 3 tablespoons sugar and the salt to stiff peaks, but do not overbeat. Add the vanilla. With a pastry bag fitted with a star tube, pipe the whipped cream around the jelly with a circular motion, covering the whole cut surface of each apple half. Sprinkle with almonds and chill. Serve.

CHEF'S SECRET   If you were to peel the apples first and then try to core them, you would probably damage their texture or even break the halves. They are much easier to handle if you core them first and then peel them.

It is difficult to give an exact cooking time for the apples because of the great variance even between apples of the same family.

If the Basic Vanilla Cream is too stiff, add a small amount of the cooking syrup.

FRESH BLUEBERRIES IN CANTALOUPE CROWNS
Serves 8

4 small, firm but ripe cantaloupes	2 to 3 tablespoons brown sugar
1 quart blueberries	1 tablespoon sugar
2 cups sour cream	juice of ½ a lemon
2 to 3 tablespoons milk	

Cut the cantaloupes crosswise in half or, if you are artistically inclined, cut each into two crowns by zigzagging the knife back and forth towards the center of the melons until you cut completely around the circumference. Remove the seeds and pulp and cut flat the bottom of each half.

Chill, wash, and hull the berries, shake off as much water as possible, and place them in a bowl. Mix with a rubber spatula the sour cream, milk, and brown sugar. Let it stand. Sprinkle the berries with sugar and lemon juice. Chill.

Just before serving, fold half the sour cream mixture into the berries and divide it among melon halves. Divide the rest of the sour cream mixture among the servings, spooning some on the top of each. Chill and serve. If you wish, decorate each with a couple of fresh mint leaves.

CHEF'S SECRET   The sugar sprinkled on the blueberries and the lemon juice will underline and heighten, not camouflage, the unique blueberry flavor.

If you fold the milk and brown sugar gently into the sour cream, it won't break down and will remain firm, shiny, and easy to handle. If you try to do the mixing with a wire whip or quickly with a spoon, the commercial sour cream will liquefy.

BLUEBERRIES WITH OTHER FRESH FRUITS

This is not a recipe but rather some ideas. At *The Bakery Restaurant* we serve a lot of fresh fruit salad in the summer, trying to cut the fruit into approximately 1-inch cubes or 1-inch square pieces where the thickness is less than an inch.

We use at least five or six of the following fruits, depending on quality and availability: cantaloupe, honeydew, crenshaw, watermelon, apples, pears, oranges, seedless grapes, strawberries, bananas, peaches, apricots, nectarines, papaya, and mangoes. If we mix the peeled fruits after cubing and dropping them into acidulated water (to each 3 cups of water add the juice of 1 lemon), we always keep the watermelon cubes or watermelon balls separate in an extra container and mix with the rest of the fruits just before serving.

We find that one of the easiest and best ways to keep apples and pears snow white after cubing is to cover them with oranges. Peel the oranges with a sharp paring knife, cut off at once the yellow outside rinds, the white pulp, and the membrane from the orange, then slice or cube the orange flesh over the apples and pears. Then cover the orange slices with the other fresh fruits. This prevents discoloration.

If we use fresh ripe strawberries, we also keep them separate when we prepare the fruit salad for service. Whatever mixture of fruits we use, we always use blueberries. They give a beautiful appearance and a very different and pleasant added texture and flavor to the fruit salad.

CANTALOUPE WITH BERRIES
Serves 8

1 large, ripe cantaloupe
1 pint strawberries
1 pint blueberries
1 cup sour cream

1 cup buttermilk
1 to 3 tablespoons brown sugar,
    according to taste

With a small, sharp paring knife, cut off the stem end of the melon with zigzag cuts, making a crown shape. (Before you cut the crown, mark one part of the melon with a small groove so you can easily fit the two pieces together just before serving.) Lift off the crown, cut out the flesh, and reserve for later use.

With a melon-ball cutter, cut balls from the inside of the cantaloupe, working carefully so you have even, rounded shapes. Chill the melon balls.

Carefully wash and hull the strawberries, pat dry, and chill. Pick over, wash, pat dry, and chill the blueberries. With a large tablespoon, scrape out the inside of the melon so it is evenly hollowed out. Chop these melon scraps very fine and fold them together with sour cream, buttermilk, and brown sugar. Chill.

Just before serving, take reserved melon pieces from inside of crown, cut into flower petal shapes, and stick them to the outside of the melon with a few toothpicks, to resemble an orange-colored flower. Using toothpicks broken in half, stick three or four blueberries in the middle of the flower. Place the melon in the middle of a serving platter, and pile melon balls, strawberries, and blueberries around it. Fill melon with sour cream mixture. Let guests serve themselves with fruit and top with sour cream sauce.

CHEF'S SECRET   If you wish, use blackberries, boysenberries, gooseberries, fresh currants, or any other berries you like. Or you may make watermelon balls, honeydew balls, and

cantaloupe balls, mixing only with blueberries. For a large
party, you may make this dish with a round watermelon instead
of the cantaloupe. If you wish, marinate the strawberries and
melon balls in orange liqueur or brandy. For a different sauce,
use whipped cream flavored with vanilla or a bit of cognac.

CHAMPAGNE SHERBET OR LEMON ICE IN WHOLE LEMONS OR ORANGES, OR ICE CREAM IN FRESH FRUITS

An old and admirable French custom, started at the end of the nineteenth
century, is to serve a very small amount of light fruit ice, champagne ice,
or sherbet after the fish course to clear the palate for the taste sensations of
the main course. Somehow this wonderful custom has deteriorated into a
ridiculous and sometimes ludicrous routine. First of all, in many places it
is served even if no fish course is part of the menu, but because the
management feels an obligation to serve the sherbet. So they serve it after
the salad.

The original idea was to cut off about ¼ of the top of a nice whole
lemon. With a sharp paring knife, remove the flesh of the lemon in a
conical shape to make room for the small scoop of lemon sherbet, orange
sherbet, champagne ice, or other fresh fruit gratine. This is then cupped
with the cut-off top of lemon, often decorated with a lemon leaf trimmed
to appropriate size, and served on a small doily on a dessert plate with a
teaspoon or mocha spoon.

In some instances, whole oranges or whole tangerines or even
mandarins are used for this purpose. On classic menus this course, which
was designated as an "intermezzo," was called simply "Sorbet en
surprise."

Great innovators replace the whole citrus fruit with other fruits,
such as apple and pear. They dig holes with melon-ball cutters, paring
knives, and spoons into whole fruits, discard the inside, then stuff the
hollowed out, usually green, unripe fruit with some horrible ice cream

concoction, freeze it and serve it direct from the freezer to the guest, who tries in vain to dig out some of the granite-hard ice cream from the fruit or even to chisel off a piece of the fruit itself. I have seen ladies bending their spoons and gentlemen bouncing the whole fruit off the plate high in the air as they try to dig into it, and the frozen concoction just slips away from their surprised hands. I smile on these occasions because the correct solution is so simple, or at least it would be if the innovators would use some common sense.

First of all, why would anyone freeze a perfect, beautiful pear or apple to make it inedible?

Why would someone disfigure and discolor the inside of a fruit with improper methods and improper equipment?

In most stores and supermarkets you can buy an anti-acid compound under different trade names, such as Potato Whitener, Vegetable Whitener, Fruit Fresh, etc. If you use it precisely according to directions, it won't harm the finest fresh fruit.

Now, just look at the melon-ball cutter and imagine how ideal a tool it would be if only it were the right size. When you go this far in your thinking, you have the solution. Ice cream scoops come in every size, and you can purchase for a nominal amount an ice cream scoop which is small enough to get into the pear or apple and remove the whole core with one turn of the hand. Then, dipping the fruit immediately into the whitener and rinsing it in cold water will keep the pears or apples white for several hours.

With the same ice cream scoop you can pre-measure the sherbet, fruit ice, or ice cream you want to use. Just cover a cookie sheet with aluminum foil and keep it for 30 minutes in the freezer. Let the sherbet or other ice cream product soften enough that you can handle it, then scoop as many portions as you need onto the tray and freeze them. You can keep your fruit in the refrigerator until serving time, then, just a couple of minutes before serving, place a pre-measured scoop of sherbet into each fruit, cover, and serve. This way you have complete portion control, and if someone wants a few bites of the fruit they can enjoy it.

In my opinion, pears and apples filled with ice cream are much more suitable for dessert than as "intermezzo." Nevertheless, there are menus where you can serve them advantageously.

FRESH STRAWBERRY TARTS
Serves 8

½ portion basic short paste
   (see page 287)
3 tablespoons strawberry jam
1 tablespoon water
1 tablespoon lemon juice

1 pint fresh strawberries
½ small package strawberry
   gelatin
1 to 2 cups heavy cream,
   depending on taste

Line 8 3-inch tart forms. Roll a piece of short paste to a round somewhat bigger than the form. Loosen each piece of dough with a spatula and press it into the little tart forms with your fingers. When all 8 are ready, refrigerate them.

Preheat the oven to 375°. Place an empty cookie sheet in the oven and heat it for about 10 minutes. Remove the tart pans from the refrigerator and place them on the hot cookie sheet. Bake 10 minutes. With a fork, pierce little holes in the bottom of each shell, then bake another 6 to 8 minutes, or until the edges turn brown. Remove from the oven and cool. Remove the tart shells from the pans.

Place the strawberry jam, water, and lemon juice in a small saucepan. Melt the mixture together, then cool.

Brush the bottom of the tart shells with the strawberry jam mixture. Pile the cleaned and hulled fresh strawberries into the shells and refrigerate them.

Prepare the strawberry gelatin, using one-third less water than the package directions require. Place the gelatin in an ice-water bath to cool. As it starts to get syrupy, brush some over the strawberries.

Whip the cream and pipe small stars of it between the strawberries or around the edge. Serve.

FRUITS IN VERMOUTH
About 2 quarts

1 package pitted California dates, about 10 ounces

1 package pitted California prunes, about 10 ounces

1 package California mixed dried fruits, about 10 ounces

1 package California figs, about 10 ounces

1 package dried apricots, about 10 ounces

1 package large white raisins, about 10 ounces

1 package dried apple slices, about 10 ounces

1 slice fresh orange rind (optional)

2 cups sugar

½ bottle Red Italian-style Vermouth

½ bottle Golden Bittersweet Italian-style Vermouth

Mix all the fruit together in a large bowl.

Place ¼ of the fruit in the bottom of a large container with a tight-fitting lid. Add ½ cup sugar and another layer of fruit; continue until all the fruit and sugar are used.

Fill the container with the two vermouths. Add the orange rind if desired. Store the mixture at room temperature 4 to 5 days, then refrigerate at least 1 week before using.

CHEF'S SECRET   A 2-quart jar of these Fruits in Vermouth may be stored in your refrigerator for as long as 3 to 4 years without spoiling. I am afraid, however, that you will have to keep refilling it, because it will be very popular.

It can be eaten as is or chopped and spooned over any kind of cake or ice cream. It is an excellent accompaniment for gamebirds, or you can mix 1 cup chopped Fruits in Vermouth with 2 cups whole cranberries and serve it with poultry. It is a good topping for yogurt or for broiled grapefruit. With melon balls, it makes a festive dessert, and it can turn a plain vanilla souffle into an exotic masterpiece.

PEARS HELENE
Serves 8

8 firm pears (preferably d'Anjou
   or Wilhelm)
1 quart water, or enough to cover
6 whole cloves
2-inch piece cinnamon stick
1 cup sugar
juice of 1 lemon

4 teaspoons tart jelly,
   such as red currant
8 small pieces spongecake
   or any other leftover cake
1 recipe Basic Vanilla Cream
   (see page 267)
chocolate sauce (see page 225)

Peel the pears, leaving stems on. Cut a slice from the bottom of each, so that the pears will stand on a flat surface. Remove the core from the bottom, leaving a hole large enough to turn a teaspoon in.

Combine the water, cloves, cinnamon stick, sugar, and lemon juice and bring the mixture to a boil. Add the pears to the liquid, return the mixture to a boil, then reduce the heat to low and simmer under cover until the pears are fork tender, about 1 hour. Remove the pan from the heat and let the pears cool in the liquid until lukewarm. Then remove them with a slotted spoon, place on a tray, and chill in the refrigerator.

When the pears have chilled, stuff the bottom of each with ½ teaspoon of the jelly and a piece of the cake.

Place each pear in an individual glass dish with about ½ cup of the Basic Vanilla Cream. Spoon chocolate sauce over each and serve.

CHEF'S SECRET   If you try to make this dessert from overripe, soft pears, they will fall apart before they finish cooking.

To speed the cooking of the pears, with a small paring knife gently make small incisions about ½ inch deep on the inside of the cavity, but be careful not to cut through the pears. To test for doneness, pierce the pears with a cooking needle, above the cavity. If the needle goes in easily, the pears are ready. It is most important not to cook the pears over high heat.

If the Basic Vanilla Cream is too stiff, dilute it with a few tablespoonfuls of the cooking syrup from the pears.

Do not discard the cooking syrup from the pears. Add the peelings, cores, and the pieces that were cut from the bottom, and continue to cook it over low heat until it turns into a thick, gelatin-like substance. This very pleasant pear glaze can be used to glaze fresh or cooked fruit or pastry. It can be stored in a tightly covered jar in the refrigerator for 2 to 3 months.

BASIC VANILLA CREAM
About 4 cups

8 tablespoons cornstarch
4 cups milk
3 egg yolks
½ cup sugar

½ teaspoon salt
1 teaspoon vanilla
6 tablespoons butter

Dissolve the cornstarch in 1 cup milk.

Beat the egg yolks lightly with a fork and add them to the cornstarch mixture.

Place the remaining 3 cups milk in a medium-sized saucepan. Add sugar, salt, vanilla, and butter. Heat, stirring to dissolve the sugar. Once the mixture begins to boil, stir with a wire whip and pour in the cornstarch-egg yolk mixture. You will have to beat this mixture vigorously with the wire whip as it will become very stiff. It will not be necessary to cook more than 5 minutes; the mixture will thicken almost immediately. Remove from the heat as soon as the cream is smooth and thick. Cool.

CHEF'S SECRET   Once you master this basic cream, which is not difficult, you will be able to make many variations and combinations. You can divide the amount in half and make two different flavors to be served together—chocolate and vanilla, coffee and raspberry, chocolate and strawberry, and so forth. Following are some of the variations which can be made from Basic Vanilla Cream.

Chocolate Cream:

Mix 4 tablespoons cocoa with 1 additional tablespoon sugar into 1 cup of the milk along with the cornstarch, then proceed according to the recipe.

Coffee Cream:

Mix 1 to 1½ tablespoons instant coffee with 1 additional tablespoon sugar into 1 cup of the milk along with the cornstarch, then proceed according to the recipe. (Depending on the brand and consistency of the instant coffee, you may have to add more or less.)

Strawberry Cream:

Prepare the cream according to the recipe, using only 3 cups milk altogether. Mash enough strawberries to have 1 cup fresh strawberry pulp. Add 1 to 2 tablespoons sugar to the pulp, depending on the sweetness of the berries. After the basic cream has cooled, stir in the strawberry pulp and add 1 to 2 drops strawberry essence.

All other fruit creams may be made by following the directions for the Strawberry Cream.

Chantilly Cream:

Prepare the Basic Vanilla Cream. Beat 2 cups heavy cream with 2 tablespoons sugar and a pinch of salt until very stiff. When the Basic Vanilla Cream has cooled, fold in the whipped cream.

STUFFED PINEAPPLE
(Baby's Dream)
Serves 8

1 large pineapple,
   about 12 inches long
1 quart large, firm strawberries
1 cup kirsch or orange liqueur,
   such as Cointreau or
   Triple Sec

1 quart heavy cream
5 to 6 tablespoons sugar
pinch of salt
a few drops red food coloring
8 slices poundcake, spongecake,
   or almond sponge

Split the pineapple in half from top to bottom, leaving on the leafy parts. From the outside of each half, cut a slice parallel with the cut surface so the halves will stand firmly.

With a sharp knife, remove the inside of the pineapple as follows: About ½ inch from the top, cut across the flesh, being careful to avoid cutting into the skin and to stay at least ½ inch from the sides. Make a similar cut across the bottom. Now remove the hard core by cutting first on one side and then on the other side, holding the knife so that the tip runs under the core. After removing the core, there should be a V-shaped groove inside the pineapple. Now cut parallel to the sides of the V, approximately ½ inch in from the skin and almost down to the bottom. Then cut from the bottom of the V toward the sides and remove the fleshy parts (see illustration).

Cube the flesh of the pineapple into pieces about the size of the strawberries.

Quickly wash, shake dry, and hull the strawberries. Set the eight nicest berries aside to be used for decoration. Combine the pineapple cubes and the strawberries and marinate them in the kirsch or liqueur.

Whip the cream with the sugar and salt until it is firm and holds its shape, but do not overbeat it. Remove about 2 cups of the whipped cream and fold a few drops of red food coloring into it. Coat the top of each piece of spongecake or poundcake with this pink whipped cream.

Place the two pineapple halves on a large serving platter so that the bottom ends are together and the leafy tops are at the two ends of the

platter. Secure the ends together with toothpicks or bamboo skewers. Arrange the pieces of cake on both sides of the pineapple halves.

Drain the marinade from the fruits. Divide the remaining whipped cream in half and gently fold the marinade into half the cream. Now fold the fruits into the whipped cream-marinade mixture. Heap the fruit-whipped cream mixture into the two pineapple halves.

With a pastry bag fitted with a star tube, pipe the remaining whipped cream over and around the filled pineapple halves. Decorate each half with four of the reserved strawberries. Chill about 1 hour before serving.

CHEF'S SECRET   The original of this recipe was devised by August Escoffier and called "Dream of a Baby." The main difference in our recipe is that we do not suggest that you make a pink frosting-coated spongecake base for the two pineapple halves and then discard it after the dinner. We feel the dessert is just as pretty when served as suggested here.

We always have layers of almond sponge on hand at *The Bakery Restaurant*. We bake it in "half-bun pans" and freeze the sheets 4 to 5 days, sometimes even longer. And as we have strawberries 9 to 10 months a year, it is easy to make this impressive dessert in a few minutes. A homemaker can always buy a good poundcake or spongecake in a local bakery, and the rest of the ingredients are easy to obtain, so this elegant dessert could be one of your favorites for years to come.

PRUNES FREDERICK
Serves 8

1 tablespoon butter	1 cup brown sugar
1 pound pitted prunes	¾ cup water
1 cup (3½ to 4 ounces)	1 lemon, thinly sliced
pecan halves	¼ to ⅓ cup bourbon

Preheat oven to 350°. Coat a pie dish with the butter.

Stuff the pitted prunes with the pecans and place in the dish. If you have any pecan pieces left, chop them coarsely and sprinkle over the prunes.

In a small saucepan, bring to a boil the brown sugar, water, and sliced lemon. Boil a minute or so, then strain the syrup over the prunes.

Bake the prunes about 20 minutes, then cover with the lemon slices. Bake another 10 minutes. Remove from the oven and bring to table. Warm the bourbon in a small saucepan, ignite it, and pour over the prunes. Let it burn until all flame dies.

Serve the prunes with some of the remaining thick syrup but without the lemon slices. Serve as a side dish with any poultry or game, or serve as a dessert with a scoop of vanilla ice cream on each serving.

CHEF'S SECRET   A tablespoon of butter may seem like too much for coating the pie dish, but you will need it. As soon as you pour the boiling liquid over the prunes, some of the butter will melt and cover the surface of the liquid, preventing or slowing down evaporation of the syrup.

The lemon will give the dish a pleasant, slightly tart taste. But if you don't like this taste, simply peel the lemon before slicing and add just a small piece of the rind.

BASIC BUTTER CREAM
About 6 cups

1 pound unsalted butter, slightly colder than room temperature

6 cups sifted powdered sugar
1 egg

Use an electric mixer with a wire whip or paddle. Beating at high speed, add ⅓ of the butter, bit by bit. Stop the mixer and add about 2 cups powdered sugar. Very slowly start to beat again, and beat slowly until the sugar is incorporated. Then increase the speed to high. Add another ⅓ of the butter, again bit by bit.

Add the egg and beat until smooth. Stop the mixer, add more of the powdered sugar, then slowly start to beat again, increasing the speed as the sugar is incorporated. Add the remaining butter, stop the mixer, and add the remaining powdered sugar.

Once the sugar is incorporated at low speed, increase the speed to high and beat until the butter cream is very fluffy. This basic butter cream may be flavored with bourbon, rum, brandy, or any imitation flavorings.

CHEF'S SECRET   To make a good, fluffy, smooth butter cream, you must start with a very clean, empty container. The electric mixer should run at the highest possible speed before you add the first small piece of butter. Do not add more than the size of an almond at once, and keep adding these small pieces every 15 to 20 seconds until you have about 1½ sticks or ⅓ of a pound in the mixer. All this time the beater should be at the highest possible speed. Then stop and add 2 cups powdered sugar at once and incorporate it at the lowest possible speed before you beat it again.

I judge when the mixture is ready for the next addition by the sound of the cream in the bowl. As the mixture gets closer and closer to perfection, the sound of the beater will reach a higher pitch and sound rather hollow. That's when you should make the next addition.

Be sure to scrape the sides of the bowl after stopping the machine during each step, otherwise the mixture won't be even. Be careful not to overmix, and in the summer chill the butter, the bowl, and the beater before starting.

WHIPPED CREAM FROSTING
4 cups

1 quart whipping cream
½ to ¾ cup powdered sugar,
   depending on taste

1 envelope unflavored gelatin
3 tablespoons water
½ cup water

In an electric mixer, using a wire whip, beat the cream. As soon as it begins to stiffen, slowly add the powdered sugar. Beat until stiff, but do not overbeat.

Dissolve the gelatin in 3 tablespoons water. Bring the ½ cup water to a boil, then add the softened gelatin. Cool the gelatin in an ice water bath until it becomes syrupy and is cooler than the temperature of your hand. Gently fold the gelatin, in a thin, threadlike stream, into the whipped cream. Chill before using to frost a cake.

 CHEF'S SECRET   If you use only 1 pint of whipping cream, be careful to divide the gelatin mixture only after the whole amount (1 envelope of gelatin with the 3 tablespoons plus ½ cup of water) is made according to directions. It is very difficult to make a decent gelatin mixture from half the amount given here, and it never comes out right. It costs much less to discard half an envelope of gelatin than a pint of whipping cream.

A commercial product available in large cities is called Dr. Oetker's Whip-It (Sahnesteif). If you can buy it, use it instead of gelatin.

BROWNIE BOTTOM BOURBON PIE
Serves 8

5 egg yolks
¾ cup sugar
1 envelope unflavored gelatin
¼ cup cold water
½ cup bourbon
3 cups heavy cream

pinch of salt
pinch of sugar
1 brownie baked in a 10-inch
    pie pan, from a brownie mix
    or your own recipe
    (don't overbake)

Beat the egg yolks until thick and lemon-colored. Slowly beat in the sugar.

Soften the gelatin in cold water and add ⅓ of the bourbon. Heat over boiling water until the gelatin dissolves. Add this to the yolks and stir briskly. Stir in the remaining bourbon. Whip 1 cup heavy cream and fold it into the mixture.

Pour the filling into the pie pan over the brownie and chill at least 4 hours.

Top the pie with the remaining heavy cream whipped with a few grains of salt and just a pinch of sugar. If you wish, sprinkle on top about 2 tablespoons shaved chocolate.

CHEF'S SECRET   This is one of the most American pies. Brownies as we know them are the most American cookies, and bourbon is indeed the American whiskey.

After you have made this dish once or twice, you may find you wish to use more sugar in the heavy cream or less bourbon in the filling. If you cut down on the bourbon, be sure to make up the difference in quantity with cold water, because the ½ cup of liquid is necessary.

EUROPEAN NUT SPONGE
(Chocolate Nut Roll, Chocolate Torte, and Mocha Torte)

Many of the European tortes are made from a special sponge dough also called Genoaese spongecake. If you use finely ground nutmeats (walnuts, pecans, almonds, hazelnuts, etc.) instead of flour, this basic dough is called "nut sponge," or European Nut Sponge. The following three recipes are made from different variations of this type of dough. However, you should not start to make any of these recipes if you don't have the most important item—a European-style hand grinder that grinds the nuts into a fine nut flour without pressing the oil from them. You can buy this nut grinder in Chicago at Kuhn's Delicatessen, 3053 North Lincoln Avenue, 60657, or you can order it from H. Roth & Son, 1577 First Avenue, New York, NY 10028.

It is not enough to grind the nutmeats properly. You also must fold them in by hand, with a plastic spatula. Don't "beat" the nuts into the mixture because the cake won't rise.

CHOCOLATE NUT ROLL
Serves 8 to 16

For the cake:

6 eggs
6 heaping tablespoons sugar
6 tablespoons finely ground
   walnuts

1 tablespoon fine white fresh
   breadcrumbs (see appendix)
¼ teaspoon baking powder

For the icing:

1 cup unsalted butter
1 egg
8 to 10 tablespoons powdered sugar
8 to 10 tablespoons Dutch cocoa

1 tablespoon boiling water
1 to 2 tablespoons brandy or rum
   (optional)

Preheat oven to 375°. Beat eggs with sugar on high speed in an electric mixer 15 to 20 minutes, or until they are light, fluffy, lemon-colored, resembling whipped cream just before it starts to form peaks. By hand, gently fold in the nuts (sprinkled spoonful by spoonful over the surface), then the breadcrumbs combined with the baking powder.

Grease a 10 × 15 jelly-roll pan and line it with waxed paper. Pour in batter and bake 12 to 14 minutes. Remove from oven, invert on a clean kitchen towel, and roll the dough up with the towel jelly-roll fashion. Leave it rolled up and let it cool.

For the icing, beat to a light, fluffy consistency the unsalted butter with egg. Gradually add powdered sugar sifted together with cocoa. Add boiling water and blend. Spread this icing over the surface of the unrolled cake; roll it up and frost the outside. If you wish, add 1 or 2 tablespoons brandy or rum to the icing.

For a Yule Log, cover the chocolate icing with a thin layer of whipped cream, chill, then make rows with a fork so it resembles the bark of a tree.

CHEF'S SECRET   You may bake this same batter in two 8- or 9-inch round cake pans and make a two-layer chocolate nut torte. You may also omit the cocoa in the frosting; instead add 6 tablespoons ground walnuts and 2 tablespoons rum, and decorate the slices with nut halves.

For a plain nut torte, use almonds, filberts (hazelnuts), pecans, or walnuts. The ratio remains the same.

Be sure to cover the bottom of a springform pan with waxed paper, and always bake this type of cake in a lined pan. After cooling, freeze layers for easier handling.

CHOCOLATE TORTE
Serves 8 to 16

One of our most popular desserts is the Chocolate Torte. To make it, follow the recipe for the Chocolate Nut Roll, page 276, but *don't* roll it up. Instead, cut the sheet into thirds lengthwise, assemble with the chocolate buttercream icing between the layers, then cover with the same chocolate buttercream. We find it much easier to do a nice, even covering job if we chill the assembled cake to the point where it is firm to the touch, but leave the buttercream at room temperature.

To decorate, we use a star tube and a pastry bag to press out a small rosette or star on each slice. We add one whole nut from the nuts used to make the torte itself. For instance, if we use ground hazelnuts, then a toasted hazelnut goes into the middle of the little chocolate star.

MOCHA TORTE
Serves 8 to 12

For the cake:

6 eggs
6 generous tablespoons fine
    granulated sugar
6 tablespoons finely ground
    walnuts (see page 275)

1 tablespoon fine white fresh
    breadcrumbs (see appendix)
¼ teaspoon baking powder

For the icing:

8 to 10 tablespoons powdered sugar
4 to 5 teaspoons instant coffee
2 to 3 teaspoons imported
    Dutch cocoa
1 cup unsalted butter

1 egg
1 tablespoon boiling water
1 to 2 tablespoons brandy or rum
    (optional)
2 to 3 drops yellow food coloring
    (optional)

For the syrup:

6 tablespoons boiling water
3 tablespoons apricot marmalade

brandy to taste

Prepare the cake. Preheat the oven to 375°. Beat the eggs with the sugar in an electric mixer at high speed 15 to 20 minutes, or until they are light, lemon-colored, and fluffy. By hand, gently fold in the nuts (sprinkled spoonful by spoonful over the surface), then the breadcrumbs combined with the baking powder.

Pour the batter into a well-greased and waxed-paper-lined jelly roll pan, or two 8- or 9-inch cake pans. Bake 12 to 14 minutes. Cool.

Prepare the icing. Sift together the powdered sugar, instant coffee, and cocoa.

In an electric mixer, beat to a light, fluffy consistency the butter and egg. Gradually add the sifted dry ingredients, then the boiling water. If desired, add brandy or rum to taste and a few drops of yellow food coloring.

Prepare the syrup. Bring water to a boil and then dissolve the marmalade in it. Add the brandy to taste. If you prefer a moist cake, this syrup should be used to brush each layer before covering with the icing.

Assemble the cake. Place the first cake round on a plate and brush with half the syrup. Spread ⅓ of the icing on the layer, then cover with second layer. Brush top layer with syrup, cover sides, and top with icing. Chill before serving.

 CHEF'S SECRET   To work easily with this delicate nut sponge, it is best to freeze the layers for at least 4 hours or overnight.

Cool the syrup to lukewarm before brushing, and have the buttercream icing at about room temperature.

After putting the second layer on top of the first and brushing with the syrup, freeze again before covering with the rest of the icing.

To achieve a very smooth surface, use a metal spatula to spread the icing on the cake, and keep the spatula in a large pot of very hot water.

Don't give up on this torte after one or two unsuccessful tries. It is worth mastering, and once you have made it successfully this will be your favorite cake.

LINZER TORTE
2 tortes

1 portion 1-2-3 dough,
    variation (b) (see page 284)
1 cup seedless black raspberry jam
1 cup red currant jelly
4 tablespoons powdered sugar

1 egg white
2 or 3 drops red food coloring
2 tablespoons chopped almonds
1 drop green food coloring

Line the bottom of two 8-inch cake pans with waxed paper. Preheat the oven to 375°.

Divide the dough into three equal portions. Press 1 portion of dough into the bottom of each pan.

In a small saucepan over medium heat, melt the black raspberry jam and the red currant jelly together until the mixture comes to a boil. Stir and cook 5 to 6 minutes. Remove from heat and stir until it cools to lukewarm. Chill in the refrigerator, stirring occasionally. Once the mixture has chilled, divide it in half. Reserve half, and spread the other half over the top of the dough in the two pans, dividing the mixture evenly.

Divide the third portion of dough in half. From each half, form strips ½ inch wide. Lay a diamond-shaped lace on the top of each pan with the strips of dough (see illustration).

Bake the tortes 15 minutes. Reduce heat to 325° and bake an additional 15 minutes. Cool. Cut around the edge of the tortes with a knife to loosen them from the pans, then remove.

Place the remaining jam mixture into a pastry bag fitted with a small star tube. Press some of the mixture into the diamond shapes, starting in the middle of both cakes and going in circles toward the edges, making sure you have enough jam mixture for each diamond.

In a small bowl, stir the powdered sugar and egg white with a few drops of red coloring until it turns into a smooth pink substance. Pipe this substance around the rims of the Linzer Tortes. Return them to a 200° oven for 15 minutes to dry.

With your fingertips, mix the chopped almonds with green food coloring so that all the pieces of almond become somewhat greenish.

Sprinkle the almonds over the top of each torte. Store the tortes at least 2 days before serving.

CHEF'S SECRET   If you wish, 2 to 3 tablespoons of good brandy or bourbon may be added to the dough.

Work very fast with this dough to avoid "burning" it with your fingertips. Professional pastry chefs roll the dough into rope-like pieces by hand, but this is difficult. It will be easier to roll out the dough on a pastry board dusted with a little flour, then cut the strips with a knife or with a round-bladed pastry or crinkle cutter.

If you have pistachio nuts on hand, use them instead of coloring the almonds green. To avoid green fingertips from coloring the almonds, smear some cold butter on your fingertips before starting. Or drop the food coloring into 1 teaspoon of the powdered sugar and stir it until the powdered sugar is evenly green, then rub it into the almonds.

If you like a very moist Linzer Torte, increase the baking powder in the 1-2-3 dough to 1 teaspoon and reduce the baking time 5 to 8 minutes.

MOCHA CREAM PUFFS
12 to 16 puffs

1 portion Pate a Choux
  (see page 283)
1 egg, separated
2 cups heavy cream

4 to 6 tablespoons fine
  granulated sugar
2½ to 3 tablespoons instant coffee
3 to 4 tablespoons powdered sugar

Preheat the oven to 425°. With a pastry bag, press the dough onto a cookie sheet in portions the size of a walnut or, if desired, the size of a small egg.

Beat the egg yolk lightly. With a fine pastry brush, coat the top of each puff with the egg yolk.

Bake the puffs 25 minutes. Reduce the heat to 350° and bake an additional 20 to 25 minutes, or until a tester, when inserted, comes out almost dry. Cool and split in half.

Whip the heavy cream slowly, adding all the granulated sugar except 1 tablespoon, until it forms stiff peaks. Combine the remaining 1 tablespoon sugar with 1½ to 2 tablespoons of the instant coffee. Sprinkle this sugar-coffee mixture over the top of the whipped cream, distributing as evenly as possible. Gently fold together.

With a pastry bag fitted with a star tube, divide the whipped cream among the puffs. Refrigerate.

In a small bowl or a round-bottomed coffee cup, mix the egg white, powdered sugar, and the remaining 1 tablespoon instant coffee until it turns into a light brown, shiny "royal" sugar icing. Dribble the icing over the top halves of the puffs. Let it dry at room temperature. Place the tops on the cream-filled bottoms. Serve.

 CHEF'S SECRET   This is the classic way to serve cream puffs. If you wish, you can omit the icing and sprinkle powdered sugar or a mixture of powdered sugar and instant coffee over the tops.

Sometimes, with certain brands of instant coffee, you may get dark specks in the whipped cream. I am afraid there is not too much you can do to prevent this. It is best, as a precaution, to dilute the instant coffee in a few teaspoons of brandy.

PATE A CHOUX

1 cup water
1 tablespoon sugar
7 tablespoons butter

1 cup sifted flour
4 eggs

Place the water, sugar, and butter in a medium-sized saucepan. Bring the mixture to a boil over medium heat, stirring until the butter is melted. Remove from the heat and add the flour all at once. Stir vigorously with a wooden kitchen spoon until the mixture turns into a ball.

Return to the heat and stir vigorously until the dough leaves the sides of the pan. Immediately place the dough in the bowl of an electric mixer. Beat, using a paddle or a dough hook. (If neither is available, beat by hand, but do not attempt to use a wire whip, as it will not work.)

Break each egg separately into a cup. Incorporate the eggs one by one, stirring or beating constantly after each addition until the dough turns shiny and no trace of the egg is visible before adding another egg. This is very important.

 CHEF'S SECRET   If you master this dough, you will be able to make a great number of very elegant French and continental pastries, appetizers, and main-course dishes.

Timing is very important. It is also important that you always clear the sides and bottom of the bowl while incorporating the eggs.

1-2-3 DOUGH

2½ cups flour
1 cup sugar
½ teaspoon baking powder
1 large egg

grated zest of ½ lemon
(see appendix)
1¾ cups butter

Sift the flour into the middle of a pastry board or on a clean, even-surfaced kitchen table so that the flour looks like a wide-based cone. Make a well in the middle and add the sugar, baking powder, egg, and grated lemon zest.

Dust the surface of the butter with flour and start breaking the butter into small pieces, dipping your fingers into the flour before breaking each piece. Continue until all the pieces of butter are about the size of an almond or smaller, dropping them into the well as you finish.

Quickly mix the dough together with your fingertips, incorporating the flour from the outside into the middle.

VARIATIONS:

(a) Instead of the flour, use half flour and half very finely ground almonds. Add ¼ teaspoon almond extract.

(b) Substitute ground walnuts or pecans for half the flour. Add ½ teaspoon nutmeg, ½ teaspoon cinnamon, a pinch of ground cloves, a pinch of mace, and ¼ teaspoon black walnut extract.

CHEF'S SECRET   Basically, all the Chef's Secrets of Short Paste (see page 287) pertain to this dough. This is the famous so-called Linzer dough that comes from the Austrian city of Linz. If it is rolled thin and baked into cookies, the cookies are crisp. If baked in cake form, it produces a somewhat moist dough that is between a cookie dough and a cake.

All pastries made from this dough improve with proper storage after baking.

Don't attempt to make the (b) variation unless you have a

European-type nutgrinder. (Available at H. Roth & Son, 1577 First Avenue, New York 10028, or in German-type stores in other cities.)

SAVARIN
Serves 8 to 12

For the dough:

⅓ cup milk
4 tablespoons sugar
1½ teaspoons active dry yeast
3 to 4 cups flour

pinch of salt
½ cup butter
3 eggs

For the syrup:

1 cup sugar
½ cup water

2 tablespoons brandy

For serving:

melted apricot jam

sweetened whipped cream

Scald the milk. Add the sugar and let the mixture cool to lukewarm. Dissolve the yeast in the mixture and let stand in a warm place.

Sift the flour into a warmed bowl. Add the salt.

Place the butter in a mixing bowl. Using a paddle, add one egg and one cup of the flour and beat the mixture until it is blended. Repeat until all the eggs and 3 cups of the flour are incorporated. Mix in the leavening and place the dough in a greased bowl. Cover and let rise until doubled in size.

Punch down the dough and turn it out onto a lightly floured pastry board. Knead 4 to 5 minutes, adding as much of the fourth cup of flour as necessary to prevent the dough from sticking.

Generously butter and lightly flour a Savarin ring. Place the dough in the ring and let it rise again until doubled in size.

Preheat the oven to 375°. Bake the Savarin 20 to 30 minutes, or until a testing needle comes out dry.

Meanwhile, prepare the syrup by bringing the sugar and water to a boil. Remove from heat and add the brandy. Pour the syrup over the warm Savarin and let it stand at room temperature until it cools. Turn the Savarin out onto a serving platter, brush with the melted jam, and fill the center with whipped cream. Serve.

CHEF'S SECRET   This is one of the most elegant pastries and a very versatile dough. It is also possible to buy Savarin ring sheet pans which make miniature rings, each suitable for one serving. As a rule, six or eight individual rings are on one pan; for the amount of dough this recipe makes, you would need two such pans.

After you pour the syrup over the ring, the warm liquid will be absorbed faster and easier if you pierce the dough with a testing needle. If you see that the liquid is not absorbed within an hour, gently pour the remaining liquid off into a saucepan. Reheat the syrup, adding 1 tablespoon of water, and pour it back over the Savarin. You may also remove the pan and turn the Savarin ring over after the first soaking.

If you do not have a Savarin pan, you can make and bake the same dough in loaf pans or in muffin pans. The cake will look different but will still be delicious.

SHORTCAKE
Serves 8

2 eggs
½ cup sugar
1 cup flour
1½ teaspoons baking powder

sprinkling of salt
½ cup scalded milk
1 tablespoon melted butter

Preheat the oven to 375°. Beat the eggs in an electric mixer on high speed until they turn light and fluffy. Add the sugar in a slow stream. Beat until the mixture turns lemon colored and fluffy.

Sift together the flour, baking powder, and salt. With a rubber or plastic spatula, gently fold the dry ingredients into the egg mixture. Start to beat again on low speed. Add the hot milk and the melted butter. Continue to beat until all the ingredients are incorporated.

Pour the batter into a lightly greased and floured square pan or an 8-inch cake pan. Bake about 30 minutes, or until a testing needle, when inserted, comes out dry. Cool before serving.

CHEF'S SECRET   You can use a wire whip for this dough, because it is very light.

Besides being used for the customary strawberry or peach shortcake, this shortcake may be used with many other fruits— for instance, sliced fresh banana marinated in a little sherry with sugar added; sliced oranges marinated in an orange liqueur; or any ripe yellow or green melon coarsely grated and marinated in rum, brandy, or other liqueur with a little sugar added.

SHORT PASTE

3 cups flour	1 large egg
1 teaspoon salt	½ to ¾ cup cold water
3 teaspoons sugar	1 cup butter

Sift the flour into the middle of a pastry board or onto a clean, even-surfaced kitchen table so that the flour looks like a wide-based cone. With three fingers, make a hole in the middle of the flour and sprinkle in the salt and sugar.

Break the egg into a bowl and add 2 to 3 tablespoons of the cold water, beating the mixture lightly with a fork. Pour it into the well. Pour the remaining water into the well, using only ½ cup to begin with and adding more as needed. Using all the fingertips, start to incorporate the flour with the liquid. Start on top, bringing the flour into the egg mixture. Do not wet your fingers.

With floury fingers, break the butter into small pieces, about the size of almonds. Never touch the butter with your skin; always use floured fingertips. Place the butter in the middle of the flour mixture and start kneading. Be careful to always bring the flour from the sides and incorporate it into the moist and buttery middle. Continue to knead until all the flour is incorporated, but work fast, touching the butter as little as possible. Depending on the flour and on your skill, you will probably need an additional 3 to 4 tablespoons of the cold water.

With the back of a knife, scrape off your fingers and add the scrapings to the dough. Dust your palms with a little flour and press the dough out to a square approximately 8 × 8 inches. Fold the dough into the middle, folding one-third from the left, one-third from the right, one-third from the bottom, and one-third from the top. Turn the dough upside down and quickly press it out again into a 5 × 5 square. Quickly roll this square into a ball. Wrap in a plastic bag and place in the refrigerator.

 CHEF'S SECRET   This pastry is the basic dough for lining tarts and tartlets. It is the base of petit fours and can be used for fancy butter cookies, cake bottoms, and so forth.

Before you begin, wash your hands very thoroughly, dry them, and clean your fingernails. Then rub your hands with a little cornstarch, because when you make this dough as much as a third of it will be lumping on your fingers before you are through. You would not want to scrape the dough back and use it if you were not sure that your hands were as clean as possible.

The only equipment I have found to replace your hands when making this dough is the dough hook on a heavy-duty home electric mixer. No wire whip or paddle will do, and you need a powerful motor. The result will still not be the same; the dough hook will not feel the right time to stop, and it will be harder to work with the dough.

Flouring the hands when handling the butter is very important. If the naked hand worked with the butter, it would heat the surface and the melted butter would soak into the flour. This would make the dough heavy and greasy, since the aim is to have small particles of butter surrounded with flour.

If you have never made this type of dough, or never worked with dough at all, add to the dough a 'scant ½ teaspoon baking powder. Mix it into the flour. The leavening effect will counteract the beginner's imperfect workmanship. Of course, after you master making the dough, you may omit the baking powder.

STRUDEL

Nowadays excellent commercial strudel dough is available frozen throughout the United States. In most larger cities, especially those with a Greek population, filo leaves are also available fresh, refrigerated, and frozen. If you are a homemaker, just check with the frozen food buyer of your supermarket. If he cannot get them for you, order by mail from H. Roth & Son, 1577 First Ave., New York, NY 10028.

If you are an absolute purist and must make your own strudel dough, here is the recipe. But I have to warn you: Don't try to make strudel the first time in your life for guests on the day of the party. Strudel dough is really one of the simplest doughs to make IF you master the technique and have had a chance to try the best available flours. The flour must be very dry, smooth, all-purpose flour, if possible from a Canadian Durham type of grain, such as the Four Roses flour which is available in many parts of the United States.

For the dough:

3 cups flour
pinch of salt
1½ tablespoons lard
1 medium egg

1 teaspoon plain white vinegar
1 to 1¼ cups lukewarm water
1 tablespoon farina

Sift the flour onto a pastry board into a cone shape. Make a well in the middle, and place in the well the salt, lard, egg, vinegar, and a little bit of the lukewarm water. With your fingertips, start to work all the soft ingredients into the flour, adding small amounts of water until you make the whole flour into a mass. First it will be sticky, but as you work it will turn very elastic with air bubbles inside.

Form the dough into a ball, sprinkle a corner of the pastry board with a very little flour, place the ball on it, pat it down somewhat, and with your fingertips brush the top with a very small amount of lard. Then cover the ball with a saucepan that has been warmed over medium heat.

Let it stand for 20 to 25 minutes, or even longer. Have all your fillings ready at hand before you start to work with the dough. Cover a large table with a tablecloth, dust the tablecloth with 3 to 4 tablespoons flour mixed with 1 tablespoon farina.

Now, with your fingers, brush the dough with a little bit of lard, and start to pull it first to the left and then to the right. After a little pulling, go under the dough with your fist and try to pull it over your fist from the middle towards the two edges at once. If the dough is good, it will start to get thin. Then, holding it very gently with your fingers and being very careful not to make a hole in it with your fingernails, start to lift and pull the dough all over the table, walking around the table in one direction. You have to use the kind of waving movement that you would use to straighten out a blanket over a bed. Pull the dough until it is large enough that it hangs off the table all around. Cut off the excess hanging dough and let the thin strudel dough dry for 10 minutes or so.

Now start the filling: Melt ½ cup unsalted butter and sprinkle the surface of the dough with butter. Then sprinkle the whole surface with about ½ cup of dry fine breadcrumbs mixed with ½ cup ground almonds or ground walnuts. Spread the apple, cheese, or cherry filling on about ⅓ of the strudel dough. Holding the tablecloth, start to roll the strudel dough, including the filling, by moving the tablecloth so that the strudel starts to roll up jelly-roll fashion. Keep sprinkling with melted butter as it turns, and keep rolling until the whole dough is rolled up. Now cut the strudel into the length of your cookie sheet, brush the cookie sheet and the top of the strudel with melted butter, and transfer the strudel to the cookie sheet with a long metal spatula or a long knife.

Bake in a very hot oven 25 to 45 minutes, depending on the amount and kind of strudel.

Warning: I repeat, this is not an easy technique, but it is possible to learn. In Hungary, Austria, Yugoslavia, and many other countries, hundreds of thousands of cooks do it, but first you must learn before you can excel.

FILLINGS:

Apple:

3 pounds apples, peeled and cored (winesap apples are recommended, but tart varieties like pie apples or greenings are also good)
about 1 cup sugar, depending on the sweetness of the apples

½ cup white raisins, soaked in hot water then patted dry (optional)
pinch of cinnamon
½ cup breadcrumbs
½ cup ground almonds

Grate the apples on a coarse vegetable grater. Let stand 15 to 30 minutes. Press gently but firmly through a sieve until most of the brownish apple juice has come out. Then mix with the sugar, cinnamon and raisins (if desired) and proceed as above.

Sour pitted cherries:

1 pound sour pitted cherries
about 1 cup sugar (omit sugar if
    you use frozen pitted sour
    cherries which are frozen
    with sugar)

pinch of cinnamon
½ cup breadcrumbs
½ cup ground almonds

If you wish, you may mix sour pitted cherries with pitted Bing cherries.

Cheese:

¼ cup unsalted butter
1 cup sugar
pinch of salt
4 eggs, separated
1 pound baker's cheese
2 cups sour cream

zest of ½ lemon (see appendix)
½ cup white raisins (optional)
1 to 1½ cups tiny white bread
    cubes without crust
½ cup breadcrumbs
½ cup ground almonds

In a bowl, mix the butter with the sugar, salt, egg yolks, cheese, sour cream, and lemon zest. Fold in the stiffly beaten egg whites. Fold in the raisins, previously soaked in boiling water, if you wish. Then fold in the tiny bread cubes. Sprinkle the breadcrumb and almond mixture on the strudel dough after sprinkling it with the butter, as in the previous recipes, then spread on the cheese filling, roll up, and bake at 375° for 35 to 40 minutes.

SPONGECAKE
Serves 8 to 12

5 medium eggs
5 tablespoons granulated sugar
8 tablespoons flour
½ teaspoon baking powder

1 teaspoon vanilla
    or ½ teaspoon almond,
    lemon, or orange extract
¼ cup melted butter

Preheat the oven to 375°.

Separate the eggs. In an electric mixer, beat the egg yolks and sugar at medium speed. Increase the speed to high and continue beating until the mixture becomes very light, lemon colored, and fluffy. If you stop beating, large air bubbles should come to the top and burst.

Whip the egg whites in a separate bowl until they form stiff, but not dry, peaks.

Combine the flour and baking powder and sprinkle some of the mixture through a sieve over the top of the egg yolk mixture. Fold in with a spatula. Continue sprinkling some of the flour mixture over the egg yolk mixture, and then folding it in, until all but 1 tablespoon of the flour is added. Add the flavoring.

Sprinkle the last tablespoon of flour over the beaten egg whites. Gently fold it in with a wire whip.

With a spatula, add ⅓ of the beaten whites to the egg yolk mixture and gently fold the two together. Pour the egg yolk mixture slowly over the top of the remaining whites and quickly, but gently, fold the mixtures together until the whites barely show. Do not mix completely, since overmixing must be avoided, but do not leave large pieces of the egg white either.

Brush the inside of an 8-inch cake pan with the melted butter and dust it with flour. Place a round of waxed paper in the bottom, butter the paper, and dust it with flour. Pour the batter into the cake pan and bake 20 to 25 minutes or until a needle, when inserted, comes out dry. Cool the cake in the pan on a rack. Then invert the pan and remove the cake.

 CHEF'S SECRET   The ingredients of this dough are simple, but the preparation is not easy. Don't lose your confidence if it does not work the first time. Success depends on timing, speed of movement, light-handedness, and, of course, correct temperature. The latter is probably the most important. Depending on your oven and the accuracy of its thermostat, you will probably have to make the spongecake two or three times before perfection is reached.

Possible mistakes are: underbeating the egg yolk mixture, which will result in a heavy-bottomed cake that will collapse in the middle; overbeating the egg whites, which will cause a flat, heavy cake without a good aerated texture; too hot an oven, which will cause the top to burn and the cake to rise quickly and collapse early; or too cold an oven, which will cause liquefying and hardening on the bottom and an empty, too-spongy top that will collapse.

SPONGECAKE IN FILO DOUGH
Serves 4

4 sheets filo dough or strudel
    dough, about 12 × 14 inches
4 tablespoons melted butter
2 tablespoons sugar mixed with
    2 tablespoons finely ground
    almonds or fine dry
    breadcrumbs

1 piece spongecake or poundcake,
    about 5 × 7 inches,
    2 inches high, or 2 thinner
    layers combined; or 2 thin
    layers of spongecake with
    a layer of ice cream frozen in
    between
½ cup brandy mixed with
    ½ cup orange liqueur, or
    1 cup coffee liqueur

Preheat the oven to 500°. Cover a cookie sheet with aluminum foil and spread on it one sheet of filo dough. With a pastry brush, sprinkle with about 1 tablespoon butter and about 1 tablespoon of the mixture of sugar and breadcrumbs. Cover with a second sheet of filo dough, and repeat sprinkling with butter and sugar mixture.

Continue with the third and fourth layers, then place the spongecake in the center of the dough and spoon the liqueur over the spongecake. Now fold the filo dough over the spongecake, enclosing it as you would giftwrap a package in paper. Place in the oven for a minute or so, until the filo leaves are a beautiful brown.

CHEF'S SECRET   Trying this once or twice, you will be surprised how easy it is to do this packaging. Be sure that the ends of the filo leaves are neatly tucked under the enclosed cake. After brief baking, the cake will look like it is packed in an ancient parchment or an ivory colored paper.

Sometimes we make a rope or a colored ribbon from marzipan and place it on the package after we remove it from the oven, and transfer it to a silver platter covered with a doily. Other times we use a pulled sugar ribbon that we have made previously.

This is one of the most attractive and elegant hot desserts a restaurant or a hostess can serve with very little actual skill. It is best with soft ice cream, a fresh fruit salad, or fresh raspberries or strawberries.

WOVEN PASTRY BASKET

1 package pie-dough mix, or pastry for a two-crust pie	2 to 3 tablespoons oil 1 egg, beaten

Prepare pie dough according to package directions.

Oil the outside of a stainless steel bowl. Cover the outside with aluminum foil and oil the foil.

Roll out half the dough to form a circle large enough to cover the outside of the bowl. With a pastry wheel, cut the circle (see illustration) being sure that you end up with 9 strips each about ¾ inch wide. Remove the triangles from between the strips. Fold the strips to the middle. Lift the dough and place it on the top of the bowl.

Roll out the remaining half of dough. With a pastry wheel, start to cut the circle of dough in ½-inch strips, going around in circles, working from the outer edge toward the middle (pinwheel fashion). Roll up the strips to make them easier to handle.

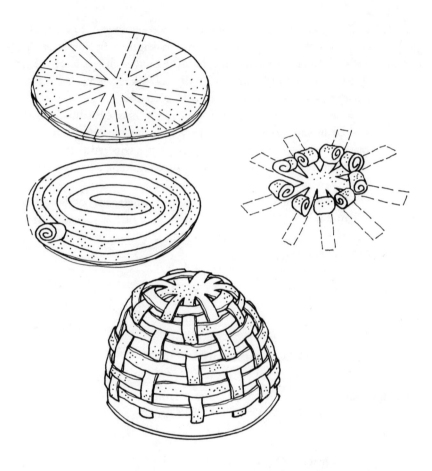

With one of the rolled strips, start to weave the basket, going around the bowl and weaving the pastry first under one strip, then over the next, continuing in a circle and covering the bowl.

Brush the edge with beaten egg. Roll the dough back to form the edge, pinching it so that the dough sticks together. Brush the entire surface of the basket with beaten egg, and chill in the freezer at least 3 hours.

Bake the basket in a preheated 425° oven for 15 to 20 minutes, or until golden brown. Cool before removing basket from bowl.

CHEF'S SECRET   At *The Bakery Restaurant,* one of our favorite special desserts for festive occasions or for honored guests is a basket made from pie dough, filled with large fresh strawberries, whipped cream, or some other fresh fruit and whipped cream, or just simply with a large assortment of fresh seasonal fruit. Sometimes, instead of filling the basket itself with fruits and whipped cream, we arrange them in a glass pie plate and cover the fruit and whipped cream with the woven basket, placing on the top a large strawberry with some green leaves, or some other fruit, or sometimes just a small bud rose with a few rose leaves. On other occasions we use two baskets, one to fill with the fruit and the second to cover it.

The most important step in making the basket is to chill it for at least an hour before baking. If the pie dough goes from room temperature into the hot oven, instead of baking it starts to melt, and as it melts it falls off the bowl.

It is important to oil the bowl before you press on the aluminum foil, and it is just as important to oil the foil.

The easiest and most successful way to remove the pastry basket from the bowl is first to let it cool completely after baking. Then carefully remove the aluminum foil from the bowl so that the basket remains on the foil. Gently hold the basket turned upside down in the palm of one hand, and remove the foil from the inside. If the foil is not well oiled, the dough will stick to it and will be difficult to remove.

If, after removing the foil, you notice that inside the basket the dough is not completely baked (which may happen if the dough is thicker in some places than in others), don't worry. Simply put the aluminum foil back on the bowl, put the basket on again, and bake in a preheated 425° oven for an additional 5 minutes.

REMARKS ON OUR WEDDING CAKES

In our 18 years of existence, we have catered more than 200 weddings at our restaurant and in other places, and we have sold and delivered about another 100 of our wedding cakes as far as Connecticut, New York, Texas, and California. Our wedding cakes usually are made from our almond torte: plain almond layers with plain, natural, butter-colored butter icing.

We don't like strong loud colors for decorations and only once had a tiny groom and bride on the top of a cake, at the request of a foreign groom's parents. (They jokingly wanted it on for a few minutes for the photographers.) Otherwise we always decorate the top of the cake with the very same fresh flowers the bride carries in her bridal bouquet and our hand-made buttercream roses made with the pastry bag. They look so natural that sometimes it is hard to see at the first moment if a flower on the cake is a fresh flower or a butter frosting decoration.

On request, we flavor our plain white buttercream with lemon zest or orange zest, or add a little liqueur or brandy instead of the plain vanilla flavor.

Practicality, economy, and the element of time at catered weddings in clubhouses and church halls, taught us to not make all three-tiers of a wedding cake edible. We make the bottom and middle tiers from styrofoam cake rounds that we cover with the very same buttercream as we use on the edible loaf cakes. The loaf cakes are cut into triangular slices to look like they are from a round cake. We pre-cut these individual portions and decorate each by hand with a tiny rosebud, so that each guest at the wedding feels that he or she received a slice from the top of the cake, instead of a pile of crumbs from the bottom or center layer, or a conglomeration of "gloop" from the frosting. This way the bride and groom can beautifully go through the cake-cutting ceremony with the top layer which is edible cake, and the servers can serve even several hundred people within a few minutes, especially if the loaf cakes are pre-plated.

APPENDIXES

APPENDIX I Basic Recipes

CHEF'S SALT

1 cup salt
1 tablespoon Spanish or
    Hungarian paprika
1 teaspoon freshly ground
    black pepper

¼ teaspoon ground
    white pepper
¼ teaspoon garlic salt

Be careful to use garlic salt, not garlic powder. If you use garlic powder, a small pinch is enough. Mix well and store in a covered jar.

MAYONNAISE
2 cups

2 large or 3 medium egg yolks
⅔ teaspoon salt
small pinch white pepper
few grains cayenne pepper
4 teaspoons sugar

2 tablespoons plus 2 teaspoons
    white vinegar
1½ cups corn oil
4 teaspoons lemon juice
1 to 2 tablespoons boiling water

Place the egg yolks in a mixing bowl and add the salt, white pepper, cayenne pepper, sugar, and vinegar. Using an electric mixer (a must for this recipe), beat the yolks and seasonings at the highest speed for 2 to 3 minutes, or until the mixture turns pale yellow and liquid. Adjust the speed to medium and add the oil, first drop by drop, then in a thin stream. When the oil is thoroughly combined, set the mixer on low speed and add the lemon juice and boiling water. Store the mayonnaise in the refrigerator in a plastic or glass container.

CHEF'S SECRET   Mayonnaise is a formula more than 100 years old, and there is very little variation in its preparation, but certain points must be stressed.

All utensils, especially the mixing bowl and beaters, must be absolutely clean and free of grease and moisture. Therefore, rinse them with a boiling mixture of 3 cups water and 1 cup vinegar. Then rinse under a large amount of cold running water and dry with a fresh, clean kitchen towel. If the bowl or the beaters is not completely dry, the mayonnaise will not be perfect.

Sometimes the mayonnaise breaks down despite the best care in preparation. To reconstitute, just use the absolutely clean and dry mixer and start to beat the mayonnaise on the lowest speed. Slowly increase the speed to medium and add ⅓ to ½ cup oil, pouring in a very thin stream. The best way to assure a thin stream is to pour the oil from a spouted container, held 15 to 18 inches from the top of the mixing bowl.

VARIATIONS:

Champagne Mayonnaise
    Add 3 tablespoons champagne for each cup of mayonnaise and omit the boiling water.

Green Mayonnaise
    Chop very fine 1 cup of green parsley and place it in a wet kitchen towel. Gather towel so that the parsley resembles a ball. Squeeze the parsley juice into a small dish. Add 2 to 3 tablespoons to 1 cup mayonnaise.

BREADCRUMBS

Commercially available breadcrumbs are sometimes stale or rancid, which is nobody's fault. It is best to make your own breadcrumbs.

Be sure to purchase a French or Italian type of bread and carefully read the list of ingredients. It should not contain any type of shortening. Flour, water, salt, and yeast are the ingredients of real Italian, French, or Vienna bread.

Air dry the loaf 2 to 3 days, perhaps in a cheesecloth bag, then slice it thick. Roll to crumbs with a rolling pin, and sift. Or, if you wish, grate the slices on a four-sided kitchen grater.

Keep the crumbs in a container, but not airtight. And don't keep them too long. It is much less expensive to throw out a quarter's worth of breadcrumbs than a dollar's worth of Wiener Schnitzel.

COURT BOUILLON

1 cup dry white wine
1 quart of water or 2 cups water
    and 2 cups clam juice
2 carrots, diced
2 medium onions, diced
2 shallots, minced

3 small sprigs parsley
1 teaspoon salt
½ teaspoon thyme
½ bay leaf
6 peppercorns, crushed

Place all the ingredients in a large saucepan. Bring to a boil, reduce heat, and simmer 1 hour. Strain through a fine sieve.

PARISIAN SPICE
(Pate Spice)

1 tablespoon crushed bay leaf
1 tablespoon dried thyme
1 tablespoon powdered mace
1 tablespoon dried rosemary
1 tablespoon dried basil
2 tablespoons cinnamon

1½ teaspoons ground cloves
½ teaspoon ground nutmeg
½ teaspoon ground allspice
1 teaspoon ground white pepper
2 teaspoons Spanish paprika
1 cup salt

Mix all ingredients well in a spice mortar, or crush them together in a deep bowl with the bottom of a cup. Sift through a fine sieve 2 or 3 times, crush again, and sift until everything goes through. Keep in a tightly covered jar.

BROWN STOCK
4 quarts

1 pound chicken necks or backs
2 to 3 pounds beef shank with
    bone in, cut into 1-inch slices
2 cups chopped carrots
1 cup chopped white or
    yellow turnip
1 large leek washed and split
    in half lengthwise, washed
    again, then sliced into ½-inch
    strips and washed again
½ cup chopped parsley root or
    parsnip

2 medium onions, skin on,
    cut crosswise at the root and
    stuck with a clove
2 pounds lean ground beef
5 quarts water
3 to 4 tablespoons salt
1 teaspoon black peppercorns,
    crushed or bruised
4 ribs celery tied with one
    bay leaf and 4 to 5
    sprigs parsley
1 clove garlic with skin on,
    halved

Preheat oven to 375°.

Place the chicken backs and necks and the beef shank in a not-too-deep roasting pan and, depending on the size of the pan, place it over one or two burners of the stove top. Add half of each of the carrots, turnip, leek, and parsley root, and one onion. Keep turning the bones and the sliced shank so that they brown. Move the vegetables around, preferably with a wooden spoon, until they start to brown, then remove from heat. Distribute the ground beef over the pan and pour 5 quarts of cold water over the mixture.

Add salt, black peppercorns, celery ribs with bay leaf and parsley, garlic, and the second onion, and bake uncovered about 3 hours. Remove and strain the liquid.

Put all bones, meat, vegetables, and remaining raw vegetables into a large (at least 3-gallon) soup pot. Add enough cold water to the cooking liquid to again have exactly 5 quarts. Pour the 5 quarts of liquid over the other ingredients, bring to a gentle boil, and then adjust heat to low and simmer for at least 4 hours, preferably longer.

Just before removing from heat, add 2 cups of cold water with 1 cup of ice cubes in it. This will help bring all the fat to the top of the liquid. Skim as much fat as possible and let the stock stand without stirring for about an hour. Then dip a kitchen towel in lukewarm water, soak it for a minute or two, squeeze it (not too dry), place it over a sieve or colander, and without disturbing the solids in the pot gently pour the liquid through the kitchen towel and colander into another container. Cook quickly and store. If you end up with less than 4 quarts, add enough water to make 4 quarts.

For twice the amount of stock, add just one half more of all ingredients, that is, 1½ pounds chicken backs and necks, 3 to 4 pounds beef shank, 3 cups carrots, etc., and proceed as for the basic recipe.

WHITE STOCK
4 quarts

2 to 3 pounds beef shank, bone in,
cut into 1-inch slices

3 to 4 pounds veal front,
neck or breast,
cut into small pieces

2 to 3 pounds chicken necks,
wing tips, or backs

1 cup chopped carrots

1 cup chopped turnip

1 leek washed, split lengthwise,
washed again, cut crosswise
into ½-inch pieces,
and washed again

½ cup chopped parsley root
or parsnip

1 medium onion, peeled and
chopped

1 clove

2 or 3 celery ribs tied with
2 or 3 sprigs parsley
and 1 bay leaf

4 tablespoons salt

12 peppercorns,
bruised or crushed

6 quarts cold water

Place all ingredients, including water, in a large stock pot. Bring to a boil; skim off the white scum from the top. Set heat very low and simmer for at least 4, preferably 6, hours.

Remove from heat and add 2 cups of cold water with a cup of ice cubes to bring the grease to the top. Skim off the grease and let the stock stand for about an hour on a wire rack.

Skim off remaining fat. Place a colander in a clean, cold, metal container. Line the colander with a moist but not wet kitchen towel and ladle the stock through it into the container. If it is less than 4 quarts, add enough water to make 4 quarts. Cool and use immediately, or store for later use.

CHEF'S SECRET   These two recipes for stocks are basic and, of course, can be improved if you add herbs or spices of your choice. If you want the brown stock to be darker, simply add a tablespoon or so of Kitchen Bouquet or Gravy Master. Or grate a 2-inch length of carrot into a small pan, add 1 tablespoon shortening and 1 tablespoon sugar, and cook over high heat until carrots and sugar start to brown. Remove, add 2 or 3 tablespoons hot water or hot stock, and strain the carrot caramel juice into the stock.

If you want the white stock to be golden yellow like chicken stock, follow the same procedure, omitting the sugar and heating only the carrots in the shortening.

Both stocks can be frozen in an ice cube tray. Pack each cube individually in aluminum foil or plastic and then put them in a plastic bag or container. Do not keep frozen longer than a month.

BEEF STOCK
4 quarts

8 ounces slab bacon
4 pounds beef bones
2 or 3 onions, depending on size,
    skin on
2 cloves garlic, unpeeled
2 cups coarsely chopped carrots
2 cups coarsely chopped
    celery tops
1 leek, or 2 or 3 scallions
1 bunch (12 to 15 sprigs)
    green parsley

1 parsley root or parsnip
about 8 ounces turnip or rutabaga
2 to 3 tablespoons salt
1 teaspoon black peppercorns
1 bay leaf
4 cloves
1 pound beef shank
2 pounds veal front or veal bones
1 tablespoon tomato paste

Cut into the top surface of the slab bacon crosswise, cutting about ⅔ of the way to the rind. Put the bacon and beef bones in a large skillet. Over medium to high heat, render the fat from the bacon. When there is a layer of hot fat in the bottom of the pan, cut each onion in half, crosswise, and place, cut surface down, in the fat. Fry until deep, dark brown.

Remove and discard bacon and place the garlic, carrots, celery tops, leek, parsley, parsley root, and turnip in the pan on top of the bones, which should be somewhat brown on the surface. Add salt, peppercorns, bay leaf, and cloves. Stir for a couple of minutes, then let the vegetables brown slightly.

Place the beef shank and veal front, cut into two or three pieces, in a large soup pot. Transfer all the contents of the skillet to the pot. Fill with enough water to cover everything and have 2 inches water above the surface. Add the tomato paste. Cover and bring to a boil. Reduce heat to low and simmer, covered, for at least 6 hours. Remove from heat and let stand 1 hour.

Skim and discard all fat from the pot. Pour liquid through a colander to another pot, pressing vegetables gently to remove liquid. Discard all bones and vegetables.

Chop the meat from the bones, beef shank, and veal front, then grind it through a meat grinder and return it to the stock pot. Again bring the stock to a boil, reduce heat, cover, and simmer about 2 hours. Let stand 1 hour, skim surface to remove fat, then strain through a wet kitchen towel. Correct seasoning by adding more salt if necessary.

CHEF'S SECRET   This is a basic stock recipe suitable for a homemaker. It may, of course, be varied by omitting certain spices or vegetables, or by adding others.

If you don't wish to use bacon, replace with a piece of suet.

The veal front contains a very large amount of natural gelatin which boils out, dissolves in the stock, and adds to its viscosity, or makes it syrupy. The bacon with the rind left on also helps in this regard, since a large amount of natural gelatin cooks out from the bacon rind.

If you want to store this stock for later use, the best and easiest way is as follows: Measure the amount of stock you have. If, for instance, it is 3 quarts, pour 1½ quarts water into an empty pot. Use a wooden spoon to measure the depth of the water in the pan, making a mark on the spoon. Discard water and pour the stock into the same pan. Simmer slowly, uncovered, until half of it evaporates, or until the liquid level in the pan is the same as it was with the 1½ quarts of water. Cool the reduced liquid, then pour into ice cube trays and freeze.

Wrap each stock cube individually in plastic wrap and store in
the freezer. When you need a little stock, take out one cube and
dilute with an equal amount of water. You can do the same thing
with any other stock or cooking liquid such as fish, chicken,
veal, or ham stock.

SAUCE ESPAGNOL
(BASIC BROWN SAUCE)
4 cups

4 tablespoons melted butter
2 tablespoons lard,
    bacon drippings,
    or rendered suet
4 tablespoons flour

1 tablespoon cornstarch
2 tablespoons tomato puree
1 teaspoon Worcestershire sauce
grinding of fresh black pepper
4 cups beef stock

Melt the butter and other shortening in a saucepan.

Stir the flour, cornstarch, tomato puree, Worcestershire sauce, and
pepper into 1 cup of the stock. Using a wire whip and stirring vigorously,
blend this mixture into the melted shortening, cooking over medium
heat. As soon as the mixture starts to thicken, immediately begin to add
the remaining 3 cups stock, pouring in a thin stream and stirring until
completely incorporated.

Cook over medium heat 3 to 4 minutes, stirring occasionally.
Reduce the heat to low and scrape the bottom and sides of the pan with a
plastic or rubber spatula so that no thick parts adhere to the pan and the
whole mixture is an even consistency.

Simmer at least 1 hour over very low heat. Correct seasoning by
adding a very little sugar if too acidic, or salt if too mild.

CHEF'S SECRET   In all older cookbooks, and even in some
of today's European cookbooks, you will find entirely different
recipes for Sauce Espagnol (Basic Brown Sauce). They will all

start by making a roux, stirring the flour into the shortening, and cooking until it turns brown, stirring continuously. This method was essential in the eighteenth and nineteenth centuries because of the lack of refrigeration and dry storage. If the two basic ingredients were not cooked together, the shortening would go rancid, and the flour would mildew. So the ingredients were cooked to keep them usable for several days or even a week.

Of course, for a twentieth-century chef or homemaker with refrigeration, freezers, and good storage, it is silly to spend hours to make a concoction designed to prevent spoilage. Thus, making a Basic Brown Sauce or Sauce Espagnol is no longer the chore it used to be.

Sauce Espagnol must be simmered for a long time over low heat so that its flavor will blend. This is essential whether the sauce is to be used alone or as a base for other sauces.

APPENDIX II Notes

CUBING

When you read about "cubing" of vegetables, it doesn't mean that you have to keep only the perfect ½ × ½ × ½-inch cubes and discard the rest. What it means is that you should try to cut the carrots, potatoes, or whatever so that most of the pieces will be cubes, but don't throw out the rest. This applies also to meat cubing.

ZEST

The zest means the outside yellow part of the skin, without the white pulpy part. The best way to remove it is to use a lemon-zester. This is a small, triangular-shaped metal tool mounted on a wooden or plastic handle. The tip of the triangle is attached to the handle; the base has a row of four or five holes, which take off the zest perfectly. If you do not have this tool or cannot obtain it in a shop, you can use a grater—very carefully so as not to grate the bitter pulp along with the skin.

APPENDIX III Conversion Scales

Weights and Liquid Measures

Weights

½ oz	=	14 grams	9	ozs	=	254 grams
¾ oz	=	21 gms	10	ozs	=	283 gms
1 oz	=	28 gms	11	ozs	=	311 gms
1½ ozs	=	43 gms	12	ozs	=	340 gms
1¾ ozs	=	50 gms	13	ozs	=	368 gms
2 ozs	=	57 gms	14	ozs	=	396 gms
2½ ozs	=	71 gms	15	ozs	=	425 gms
2¾ ozs	=	78 gms				
3 ozs	=	85 gms	1	lb	=	453 gms
3½ ozs	=	99 gms	1¼	lbs	=	566 gms
4 ozs	=	114 gms	1½	lbs	=	679 gms
5 ozs	=	142 gms	1¾	lbs	=	792 gms
6 ozs	=	170 gms	2	lbs	=	905 gms
7 ozs	=	199 gms	2¼	lbs	=	1018 gms
8 ozs	=	226 gms				

Liquid Measures

1 teaspoon	= 0.005 liters		1½ cups	= 0.36 liters	
1 tablespoon	= 0.015 l		1¾ cups	= 0.42 l	
2 tablespoons	= 0.03 l				
			1 US pint	= 0.47 l	
¼ cup	= 0.06 l		1¼ US pts	= 0.60 l	
½ cup	= 0.12 l		1½ US pts	= 0.72 l	
¾ cup	= 0.18 l		1¾ US pts	= 0.83 l	
1 cup	= 0.24 l		1 US quart	= 0.94 l	
1¼ cups	= 0.30 l				

Note: Throughout this volume, quantities quoted in pints and quarts refer to the US measures.

Fahrenheit/Celsius

−40°F = −40°C	120°F = 49°C	320°F = 160°C
−30°F = −34°C	125°F = 52°C	330°F = 166°C
−20°F = −29°C	130°F = 54°C	340°F = 171°C
−10°F = −23°C	135°F = 57°C	350°F = 177°C
− 5°F = −21°C	140°F = 60°C	360°F = 182°C
0°F = −18°C	145°F = 63°C	370°F = 188°C
5°F = −15°C	150°F = 66°C	380°F = 193°C
10°F = −12°C	155°F = 68°C	390°F = 199°C
15°F = − 9°C	160°F = 71°C	400°F = 204°C
20°F = − 6°C	165°F = 74°C	410°F = 210°C
25°F = − 4°C	170°F = 77°C	420°F = 216°C
30°F = − 1°C	175°F = 79°C	430°F = 221°C
32°F = 0°C	180°F = 82°C	440°F = 227°C
35°F = 2°C	185°F = 85°C	450°F = 232°C
40°F = 4°C	190°F = 88°C	460°F = 238°C
45°F = 7°C	195°F = 91°C	470°F = 243°C
50°F = 10°C	200°F = 93°C	480°F = 249°C
55°F = 13°C	205°F = 96°C	490°F = 254°C
60°F = 16°C	210°F = 99°C	500°F = 260°C
65°F = 18°C	212°F = 100°C	510°F = 266°C
70°F = 21°C	220°F = 104°C	520°F = 271°C
75°F = 24°C	230°F = 110°C	530°F = 277°C
80°F = 27°C	240°F = 116°C	540°F = 282°C
85°F = 29°C	250°F = 121°C	550°F = 288°C
90°F = 32°C	260°F = 127°C	560°F = 293°C
95°F = 35°C	270°F = 132°C	570°F = 299°C
100°F = 38°C	280°F = 137°C	580°F = 304°C
105°F = 41°C	290°F = 143°C	590°F = 310°C
110°F = 43°C	300°F = 149°C	600°F = 316°C
115°F = 46°C	310°F = 154°C	

INDEX

Venison, Ragout of, 90
Vermouth, (dried) Fruits in, 265

W

Walleyed Pike, Pan-fried, 135
Watermelon Ice, 245
 (illus.), 246
Watermelon hearts (in Ivory Ebony
      Salad), 196
Wax Bean Soup, 69
   variations, 70
   with Pinched Dumplings, 178
Wax Beans, Yellow with Dill, 157
Wedding Cake, 298
Weights and liquid measures, conversion
      scales, 311
Wellington Beef, 75
Whipped Cream Frosting, 273
Whipped Cream-Orange Marmalade
      Sauce, 206

White Stock, 304
Wild Onion Sauce, Bill Beecher's, 207
Wild Rice, Barley with Mushrooms,
      182
Wine Sauce, Red, 219
Wine Sauce, Red "Cumberland" for
      Beef Wellington, 221
Woven Pastry Basket, 295

Y

Yeast, how to use, 234
Yule Log. *See* Chocolate Nut Roll

Z

Zest (rind of citrus fruit), 309
Zucchini, 165
   prepared like Sugar-loaf Cabbage,
      152